"A fun must-read for leaders looking to scale their l
through continual transformational change. Grounded in a human-centered strategy, this book offers a blueprint for building a culture that creates owners, not renters—people who take initiative, drive innovation, and lead with purpose. If you're ready to grow fast without losing your soul, this is your guide."

Scott Buswell, *SVP, Professional Services*

"Finally! A strategy book that gives the reader concrete, specific ideas for improving strategy. Leaders interested in better understanding how their emotions and decisions drive strategy should read and heed."

Linda Henman, PhD, *the Decision Catalyst and author of* Healthy Decisions: Critical Thinking Skills for Healthcare Executives

Grow Your Business UP!

Packed with memorable stories, the latest neuroscience, and original frameworks and models, this blueprint for a successful "gifted" organization is a must read for any leader who is surrounded and supported by an exceptional group of people—and must keep them climbing in a market that demands hyper-growth.

A once inspired workforce is now disillusioned with the workplace, and leaders of extraordinary organizations are terrified to execute high-growth strategies because they won't survive if their precious talent leaves under the strain of such a significant change. In this pithy and pragmatic book, seasoned management consultant John Weathington helps leaders better understand the secrets of esprit de corps in a fresh way that incorporates recent discoveries in neuroscience, anthropology, and organizational behavior. John walks the reader through the technical and emotional decisions that should be made during difficult circumstances, using examples from his own 30+ years of experience working with complex and gifted organizations. This book takes on the thorny subject of collective human behavior and extracts golden nuggets for leaders to apply to their strategy, organizational design, and their own development, all while fostering a healthy, vibrant workplace where people thrive.

Distilling a vast array of science-based disciplines into immediately actionable advice, this book is a transformative resource for C-Suite leaders of mid- to large-sized companies, senior vice presidents of very large organizations, and the professionals supporting these leaders, who all face the unenviable challenge of scaling up an organization while retaining top talent.

John Weathington is a seasoned management consultant with 30+ years' experience in Fortune 100 firms and is President and CEO of Excellent Management Systems.

Grow Your Business UP!

Unlocking the Full Potential of Gifted
and Precocious Organizations

John Weathington

Routledge
Taylor & Francis Group

NEW YORK AND LONDON

Designed cover image: Garth German

First published 2026
by Routledge
605 Third Avenue, New York, NY 10158

and by Routledge
4 Park Square, Milton Park, Abingdon, Oxon, OX14 4RN

Routledge is an imprint of the Taylor & Francis Group, an informa business

© 2026 John Weathington

The right of John Weathington to be identified as author of this
work has been asserted in accordance with sections 77 and 78 of the
Copyright, Designs and Patents Act 1988.

For Product Safety Concerns and Information please contact our EU
representative GPSR@taylorandfrancis.com. Taylor & Francis Verlag
GmbH, Kaufingerstraße 24, 80331 München, Germany.

Trademark notice: Product or corporate names may be trademarks
or registered trademarks, and are used only for identification and
explanation without intent to infringe.

ISBN: 9781032854373 (hbk)
ISBN: 9781032853826 (pbk)
ISBN: 9781003518181 (ebk)

DOI: 10.4321/9781003518181

Typeset in Sabon
by codeMantra

To the love of my life always and forever, Kimberly

Contents

Foreword   *xi*
Preface   *xiii*
Acknowledgments   *xv*
About the Author   *xvi*

Introduction   1

ITERATION ZERO
Clarifying the Journey Ahead   3

1   Thereafter They Shape Us: The Precious Gift of
    Having a Precocious Team   5

2   What the Hell Am I Supposed to Do Now?
    Clarifying the Concomitant Opportunities
    of Hyper-Growth, Cultural Fissures, and the
    Post-COVID Tsunami   18

3   Are You Sure about This? Mentally Preparing to
    Lead the Journey   35

ITERATION ONE
Attempting the Adamant Triad of Strategy,
Organizational Design, and Innovation   51

4   The Heart of a General: What a Human-Centered
    Hyper-Growth Strategy Looks Like   53

5   Form Follows Culture: The Architecture of a
    People-First Organization   70

6   Edison's Boxing Cats: Leveraging Precocity
    to Weaponize Innovation and Annihilate the
    Competition   88

ITERATION TWO
Accelerating the Adamant Triad with a
High-Performing Team   101

7   Manifesting Mana: Cultivating a Healthy, Vibrant
    Workplace Where People Thrive   103

8   I Have a Dream Team: How to Lead a Gifted Team   117

ITERATION THREE
Arriving at the Final Design   133

9   The Forest Comes into Focus: Clarifying the Strategy
    and Preparing for the Transformation   135

10 Metamorphosis: Transformational Change in
    Animals and Organizations   147

DAY ZERO
Going Live and Making the Transition   163

11 The Final Approach: Going Live with the
    New Organization   165

12 Our Building Has a New Shape: Institutionalizing
    Lessons Learned from an Exciting Journey   179

REVEILLES AND BALDERDASH
Zooming In on the Luck, Skill, and Grit of the First
100 days   191

    Epilogue   205

    Index   207

Foreword

In my lifelong work on high-performance organizations (HPOs), I've met leaders who found themselves in a curious position: their organization is performing well—perhaps exceptionally so—but somehow its foundations feel uncertain, shaky. Growth has been fast. The people are talented. The energy is high. And yet, something feels precarious—fragile, even. That is the essence of what John Weathington calls a **precocious organization**.

A precocious organization is one that achieves impressive results early in its development, often thanks to a unique combination of talent, timing, and opportunity. It is the corporate equivalent of a gifted child: capable beyond its years, but not yet equipped with the structure, maturity, or resilience to sustain long-term success. These organizations tend to outpace their own systems. They grow faster than they can stabilize. And while that growth can be exhilarating, it also introduces real risk—namely, the risk of "growing kaput." The organization can no longer manage its growth, and the cracks start to appear: more mistakes are made, clients are starting to complain, talented people start to leave. And before you know it, the organization is inevitably heading for a fall.

This is where the link to the HPO framework becomes so important.

An HPO is not just a successful organization. It is one that performs consistently, intentionally, and sustainably over time. It is built on clear principles—a relentless focus on continuous improvement and renewal, high-quality leadership, a clear long-term orientation, openness and a strong action orientation, and high employee quality. Crucially, these principles are not just present on paper, but deeply embedded in daily practice. HPOs don't just do well; they are built well.

What John does in this book is offer a roadmap for helping precocious organizations become high-performance ones—not by stifling their energy or slowing their growth, but by helping leaders develop the capabilities—strategic, structural, and especially human—that allow performance to scale without imploding the organization. In that sense, this book is not only timely, it is necessary.

John speaks directly to the dilemma that many leaders face today: how to grow quickly without losing your people, your culture, or your edge. And he does so without clichés, false promises, or management jargon. Instead, his book offers honest reflections, practical models, and a clear invitation to lead with both ambition and responsibility.

This book will resonate with any leader who feels the tension between success and sustainability—between the excitement of now and the sustainability demands of the future. It is a welcome contribution to the conversation about what it truly means to grow up as an organization.

I am pleased to see how John's insights complement the HPO philosophy. And I'm even more pleased to recommend this book to anyone committed to building an organization that not only performs at a high level—but continues to do so, even when the pressure is on.

Dr. André A. de Waal, MSc MBA
Author of *What Makes A High Performance Organization: Five Validated Factors of Competitive Advantage That Apply Worldwide* (Wardy Press) and *The High Performance Managerial Leader* (Praeger)

Preface

If I had written this book in 2019, it would have been a completely different book; it would have been a good book, but it wouldn't be this book. I feel like the global pandemic fundamentally altered the relationship between leaders and the people who follow them in ways that are irretractable. We have encountered the first generation in our history where dissatisfied young people are willing to leave a job before having another one lined up. Essentially, they would rather have no paycheck than collect one from a firm that is not meeting their personal needs. That's not a good state of affairs.

It seems organizations, especially for-profit companies, are not on the same team as their employees anymore. They do not share the same goals, and they are using different success measures that often conflict with each other. Companies are out for profits, and unfortunately, employees are often viewed as an expense that destroys profitability. I know this firsthand as a specialist in organizational design (OD). As much as I really hate this part of the profession, we are often called in to help a firm reduce expenses by designing an organization with less *headcount*. And the dehumanization process has already started—they are not people anymore, they are *headcount*. We need to bring humanity back into the core strategy of an organization.

I could have easily written a book on strategy (which is badly needed) or organizational design, or innovation, or any one of the many models that I have developed over the past few decades while helping leaders solve difficult leadership and management problems. Or, I could have reflected on my illustrious history of working with iconic Silicon Valley companies, to write a book on creating a workplace where people love to work—we have had plenty of those out here over the last few decades. But, if I went down any of these routes, I would probably only exacerbate the core issue of companies and employees being on opposite sides.

So, I wrote this book to solve everybody's problems with the same solution and hopefully in a fun and interesting way. There is a scenario where top leaders get what they want (revenues, profits, competitive positioning, etc.) and the people who work for them get what they want (a nice salary, benefits, a great place to do their best work, etc.), but there's a catch. It only works under the right leadership, with the right *type* of people: people with above-average talent who can get in front of an innovation curve before its tipping point—in other words, a *precocious* organization.

There are a lot of different ingredients that must come together in the right combination for this dish to come out right: precocity, leadership, strategy, organizational design, innovation, decision-making, complex adaptive systems, iterative emergent solutions, transformational change management, neuroscience, anthropology, humanity, and the culture of ancient ninja clans (I'm only half-way kidding on this last one). We could explore any one of these topics singularly, but that would make the book more academic than practical and pragmatic.

This may sound like a very specific challenge for a very specific type of leader. Well, if you feel that way, there is a wealth of leadership information to garner from this book, and I hope you pick up at least one or two things that make your leadership life a little bit better. Here is the way I see it: the next few generations of leaders will see the third tidal wave of Northern California magic. In 1849, we had gold in the hills, and about 100 years later, we had silicon. We are just about due for this cycle to repeat, and when it does, our leaders will need to know how to survive a hyper-growth transformation with a precocious organization without tearing apart at the seams.

So, whether this book is valuable to you in 2025 or 2049 or any time in between, good luck and godspeed.

Acknowledgments

This book would not be possible without all the great leaders who have partnered with me over the past 33 years to achieve amazing organizational feats of strategy, organizational design, innovation, and transformational change. I am also deeply grateful to all my family, friends, and colleagues who unconditionally provided sage counsel and emotional support when I needed it the most.

Many thanks to Ken Lizotte and Elena Petricone from Emerson Consulting Group for helping me find a great publisher and for working with me month after month to develop a great product. You have been terrific to partner with. And I'm appreciative of Taylor & Francis Group and Bethany Nelson for their trust and support in publishing my first book.

And a very special thanks to Garth German for somehow translating all the crazy ideas in my head into the amazing illustrations that bring this book to life. You are a great artist, colleague, and friend.

About the Author

John Weathington is a seasoned management consultant, strategic advisor, and executive coach who specializes in navigating transformational change. For 30 years, he has helped clients of all sizes, including an impressive list of Fortune 100 firms such as Chevron, Salesforce (MuleSoft), Cargill, Wells Fargo, Adobe, Cisco, Dell, Visa, eBay (PayPal), Hewlett Packard, Pacific Gas and Electric, Sun Microsystems, Hitachi Data Systems, and Silicon Graphics. His unique blend of leadership, behavior science, and analytic skills is a rare find in the consulting arena. In a recent effort, he helped the leaders of a precocious, high-tech firm develop a strategy to accelerate their growth from $1B to $5B in revenue within four years.

Over his long and illustrious career, he has worked with hundreds of leaders of all levels, in dozens of companies, across a diverse set of industries, including High-Tech, Oil & Gas, Financial Services, Manufacturing, Public Utilities, Consumer Electronics, Government, Health & Medical, and Commercial Shipping. He helps leaders overcome a wide spectrum of challenges that typically involve strategy, organizational design (OD), governance, cultural realignment, organizational change management (OCM), and/or talent management.

He is a Summa Cum Laude graduate in Organizational Leadership, Certified Management Consultant (CMC), Executive Coach certified by the International Coaching Federation (ICF) and the NeuroLeadership Institute (NLI), Six Sigma Black Belt, Project Management Professional (PMP), and SAFe (Scaled Agile Framework) Program Consultant. He is formally trained as a leader, manager, software engineer, data scientist, and combat soldier (United States Army, Cavalry Scout). And he holds a special passion for cooking, games of chance, and equine athletes—and of course, his lovely wife of over 20 years.

Introduction

Some leaders suspect their organization is special, or "gifted"—and some leaders just **know** it. They recognize that their organization has accomplished something extraordinary—like reaching $1 billion in annual sales or achieving a breakthrough that nobody else in their industry could accomplish. And they realize they wouldn't be in this envied position if it weren't for some magic that happened when all their talented people came together to serve the mission, vision, and purpose of their organization.

However, they now face an existential crisis.

The market is forcing them into a hyper-growth strategy that they are terrified to execute, because they won't survive if their precious talent leaves under the strain of such a significant change. So, the $64 million question for today is: How might we rapidly scale the organization to meet market demands without losing the very talent that made us the success we are today? It appears the answer isn't so obvious.

Despite a full century of solid thought leadership on the human side of leadership, employees today are infuriated with the way they are treated by their employers. Regardless of decibel level, people—even those with high potential—are quitting (some are doing it "quietly"). Once inspired and eager to apply their talents to further an organization's strategic goals, they are now disillusioned and at best explicit and proactive about it, but in the most insidious cases, they are accepting a paycheck for nothing more than a barely plausible, zero-calorie performance. And this is in companies where the strategy is relatively stable (e.g., low to moderate growth). Now imagine a situation where a leader is charged with taking this workforce through a radical hyper-growth gauntlet! A leader in this position is well-justified in their anxiety that their best people will walk out the door before the transformation is completed. It doesn't have to be this way.

In this book, I help leaders better understand the secrets of *esprit de corps* in a way that could not be explored before. I leverage recent discoveries in

DOI: 10.4324/9781003518181-1

neuroscience, anthropology, and organizational behavior to buttress decades of lessons learned in the trenches, helping leaders overcome very difficult organizational challenges. It is specifically directed at C-Suite leaders of mid- to large-sized companies (i.e., approximately $1 billion in annual sales with 1,500–2,000 employees), Senior Vice Presidents of very large organizations (with similar financial and talent management responsibilities), and the millions of employees and management consultants in a position to support these leaders; all of whom face the unenviable challenge of scaling up an organization while retaining top talent.

For instance, in a recent effort, I was called in to help a precocious high-tech firm develop a strategy to grow from $1 billion to $5 billion in four years. Before that, I helped a large, multi-national oil and gas company survive an enterprise-level Digital Transformation. These kinds of significant challenges require a sophisticated management approach that only a seasoned practitioner like me can share. Using stories and examples from my past and original models and frameworks that I have developed over the years, I will help you get "unstuck" and walk you through the technical and emotional decisions that should be made during these difficult circumstances.

This book distills a vast array of science-based disciplines into practical advice that you can apply today, without boring you with theory or regurgitating the same empty advice that has been given to leaders and managers over the last century. Most books for leaders today are either too myopic to be useful, too conceptual to be practical, or just a bunch of hyped-up, bad advice (typically written by someone who hasn't actually tried their ideas in the real world). This book takes on the very difficult subject of collective human behavior and extricates golden nuggets that are practical and relevant for you to apply to your strategy, organizational design, and your own development as a leader, all while fostering a healthy, vibrant workplace where people thrive.

It is my honor and pleasure to help you rapidly scale your organization to meet market demands (which might be four or five times current annual revenues) while developing an environment where everyone in the organization thrives and loves to do their best work. Regardless of mission or purpose, there is no strategic imperative greater than unlocking the full potential of the precocious group of individuals that undergirds your competitive advantage. And within the red seas of talented but disillusioned starlings lies one of the greatest opportunities in history for leaders to inspire a following of loyal, passionate, and brilliant individuals. Join me on this journey, and together we will identify this potential and translate it into strategic success.

Iteration Zero

Clarifying the Journey Ahead

Go slow to go fast.

You may have heard that phrase before. For some, the phrase conjures up an anxiety and for some comfort. This is the difference between Drivers and Analytics; the Drivers always want to go fast and the Analytics always want to stop and think.[1] It is dangerous to use psychological types like this as dogma, but there is some utility when used properly.[2] If you are uneasy going slow because you need to take some kind of action right now, I understand—I really do. However, if you are anticipating a seismic shift in your firm's near-term future, I exhort you to take a little bit of time to clarify your thoughts, before ringing a bell that you cannot unring.

I see companies trip over their own untied shoelaces all the time. One of the first things I do when a company hires me to help them with a program or project that has gone awry is to ask for any documentation on how it started. About eight times out of ten, the documentation is either scant, perfunctory, or non-existent, because some impatient Driver with enough influence decided to go when they were neither ready nor set.

Iteration Zero is about getting ready and getting set, before we go. It is a practical adjustment to nascent Agile philosophy that espouses jumping straight in to write code with nothing more than a brief planning session. That works in some situations, like building simple software applications. But it was not long before we figured out that in some situations, you must take some time to lay down a foundation before construction starts.[3] This is one of those situations.

We are about to embark on a fantastic journey that will change your organization forever in a significant way. We will build a new strategy, a new organizational design, and grow our capability for innovation so large that competitors won't even have a chance against your products and services in the marketplace. And as fun as it would be to jump right in and start building our new strategy, we cannot do that just yet. We need to embrace

DOI: 10.4324/9781003518181-2

a brief lacuna—a purposeful pause—to think about where we might be going, and more importantly, why.

To be clear, Iteration Zero is not just an excuse for Analytics to wallow in analysis. I have seen this extreme too many times in my life as well; a program never gets off the ground because everyone is paralyzed in analysis and nobody can make the decision to get going. This is a Driver's worst nightmare, which is exactly why they would rather just get going now and figure it out as they go. Again, I understand—I really do. Just give me *one* iteration to get set up—a Zero Iteration. I will even "time box" it to three chapters—that's it. Then we will get going, I promise. Is that a deal?

If so, then let's get going.

Thank you.

Notes

1 These labels come from a psychological typing approach called Social Styles (Bolton & Bolton, 1996). This is one of my favorite typing tools because it is based on observed behavior and not just psychoanalysis.
2 Never try to presume someone is going to think or behave a certain way because of their declared psychological type. Instead, use psychological typing to communicate more effectively with someone. For instance, Drivers like to get to the point quickly; whereas Analytics appreciate a lot of data and detail.
3 I happen to be an Agile maven and philosopher; a soldier during the Agile Wars of the 1990s with battle scars to prove it. So, I am allowed to call out Agile when it just is not fit for a situation.

Chapter 1

Thereafter They Shape Us

The Precious Gift of Having a Precocious Team

Precious Gifts

Life is full of surprises, some of which are disappointing, and some of which are quite pleasant; however, if you are lucky enough, something absolutely extraordinary happens to you that radically alters the trajectory of your life and those around you.

A three-year-old little girl playfully danced out to her backyard, skipping breakfast, to set up for a fun game of marbles. Dad had already left to work in the lumber yard about a block away, and Mom was inside taking care of her little brother and sister, Stan and Rita. It was a gorgeous morning in Honolulu, Hawai'i, on the morning of December 7, 1941; not a cloud in the sky, allowing the brilliant sun to partner with a light breeze that gently warmed the blessed inhabitants of this magical island.

Koloke (pronounced koh LOH kay) carefully sketched a circle in the ground and neatly arranged all of her marbles within the circle. She then snatched up her big shooter marble and positioned herself outside of the ring to take her first shot. Cradling the shooter in the crook of her index finger, she lined up her sights on the big group of marbles within the ring. Just before flicking her thumb, she noticed a faint, high-pitched whining noise that she had never heard before.

She paused in wonderment, breaking her concentration for a moment, then resumed with her critical first shot, successfully breaking a few marbles out of the ring. She celebrated in silence, but the whining didn't go away. In fact, it grew louder and louder and louder, to the point where Koloke put her tiny hands over her ears to shut out the noise. Then quite unexpectedly, she heard and felt a thunderous crash in the front yard. Startled, she rushed into the kitchen, through the parlor, and out the main door to see what had happened.

It was the oddest thing. There was a huge metal propeller, larger than her, sticking up out of the ground! She had never seen anything like it! Curious, she slowly walked up to the unexpected visitor and carefully placed

DOI: 10.4324/9781003518181-3

her hand on the cold, grayish metal. You could hear a pin drop as she lightly caressed her newfound play-toy with inquisitive amazement.

The suspenseful silence was shattered by the frantic screams of Mom at the front door, "Koloke, get away from that thing and get inside this house. That's a bomb!"

Koloke didn't know what she was touching, but she knew what a bomb was! So, in a terrified sprint, she made her way back into the house. As part of the infamous Attack on Pearl Harbor, the Japanese had dropped a 550-pound bomb in Koloke's front yard—and it did not explode. If it had, Koloke, my mother, would have been instantly killed along with her entire family. And I would not be around to tell this story.

I have lived my whole life with extreme gratitude, knowing it's a great gift to even be here. I strongly believe that life is not predestined. It is full of uncertainties, the likes of which can be conceptualized as an Uncertainty Matrix (see Figure 1.1). What's fascinating about Koloke is that,

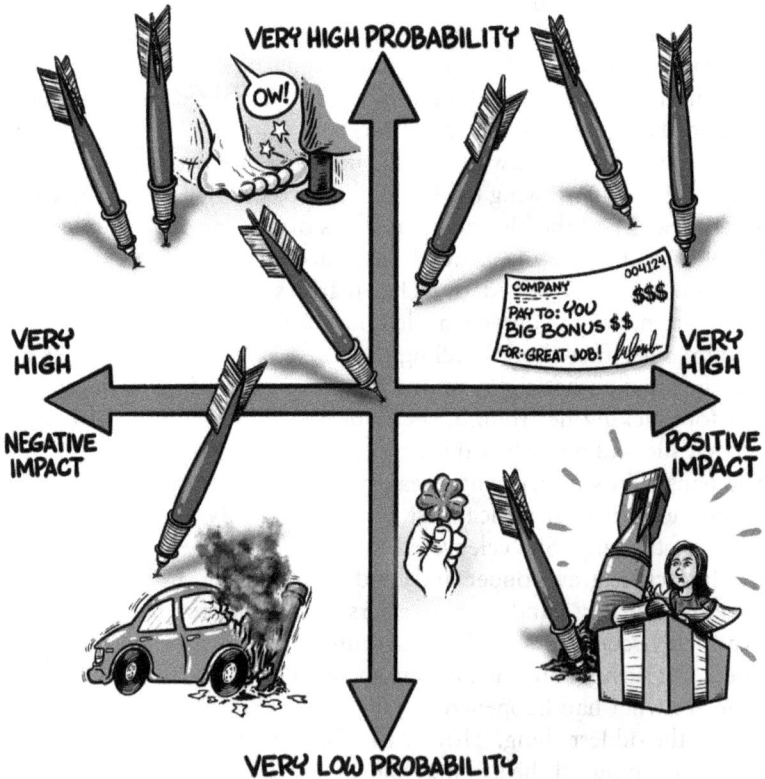

Figure 1.1 The Uncertainty Matrix.

as a very little girl, she had an event in her life show up that is in the bottom-right corner of the lower-right quadrant—an exclusive area called life's precious gifts. What are the chances that a 550-pound bomb lands in someone's front yard—and doesn't explode? Imagine the far-reaching consequences and impact of such an extremely low probability event. In that moment, Koloke was gifted a full and enriching life of 85 years (and counting!), not to mention the hundreds, if not thousands, of lives she touched along the way. This is extraordinary, and although it doesn't happen often—it does happen.

Take, for instance, a leader who runs an organization that has recently experienced an unusual, maybe even unprecedented, level of success. And as much as they would love to ascribe their brilliant strategy and maneuverability to the base warrant for such amazing success, in their heart, they know that is not true. Sure, the right moves were made at the right time, and perhaps some risky gambles paid off, but there's more to it than that. They have been handed one of life's precious gifts. And upon reflection, they realize their gift is packaged as a precocious team of talented people; an amazing group who seem to routinely outperform their competitive peers.

Ah, but what a simultaneously envious and unenvious situation to find oneself in. As thrilling as it feels to be in the top quartile in all the categories that matter—where does one go from here? That's the existential question that keeps our illustrious leader up at night—every night.

Although there's no easy way out of this situation, there is comfort in knowing that it has been done before. In fact, there's a special place nestled between the Santa Cruz Mountains and the Diablo Range in Northern California where a disproportionate amount of life's precious gifts has been doled out to leaders of precocious organizations, and these leaders and companies are now iconic: Apple, Meta (Facebook), and Alphabet (Google), to name a few. And although past performance does not guarantee future results, we can certainly learn valuable lessons from those who have already been through the gauntlet we are about to traverse.

When Koloke was 30, she met a nice gentleman at church who was serving in the Armed Forces at Schofield Barracks near Wahiawa, Hawai'i. They would soon marry and leave Hawai'i to settle down in Milpitas, California, which is located at the heart of what would eventually be called Silicon Valley.

Silicon, a Gift for the Valley That's Greater than Gold

As of January 6, 2025, Silicon Valley has produced five out of the ten wealthiest companies in the world (The Motley Fool, 2025), amassing a staggering combined market capitalization of over $10 trillion (see Table 1.1).

Table 1.1 Ten Wealthiest Companies in the World (Based on Market Capitalization), as of January 6, 2025

Rank	Company	Market Cap (Approximate)	Year Founded	Headquarters	Silicon Valley?
1	Apple	$3.6 trillion	1976	Cupertino, CA	Yes
2	Nvidia	$3.3 trillion	1993	Santa Clara, CA	Yes
3	Microsoft	$3.1 trillion	1975	Redmond, WA	
4	Alphabet (Google)	$2.3 trillion	1998	Mountain View, CA	Yes
5	Amazon	$2.3 trillion	1994	Seattle, WA	
6	Saudi Aramco	$2.0 trillion	1933	Dhahran, Saudi Arabia	
7	Tesla	$1.2 trillion	2003	Palo Alto, CA	Yes
8	Meta Platforms (Facebook)	$1.1 trillion	2004	Menlo Park, CA	Yes
9	Berkshire Hathaway	$1.0 trillion	1839	Omaha, NE	
10	Johnson & Johnson	$0.9 trillion	1886	New Brunswick, NJ	

It also carries a distinct brand for incubating companies that experience explosive growth; Meta Platforms (formerly Facebook) amassed a trillion-dollar fortune in only seven years! And that's just one of many Silicon Valley companies that catapulted from a garage-headquartered dream to a market-dominating powerhouse at a breakneck speed. There are definitely lessons we can learn by studying these companies, especially if our objective is surviving a hyper-growth strategy.

There's definitely gold in them thar hills. During the 1849 Gold Rush, prospectors from all reaches of the United States fled to Northern California in hopes of striking it rich. And just about 100 years later, auspicious lightning struck the area again, this time in the form of silicon.

I loved growing up in Silicon Valley. I actually spent my years "growing up" in two places: Hawai'i and Northern California. Mom and I would go back to Hawai'i once in a while for extended periods of time; however, Northern California is where I've spent most of my life. It is where I found my first best friend, graduated high school, met my wife, and started my consulting career. I consider Hawai'i as my *mana* (Hawaiian for "spiritual energy"), but Silicon Valley as my *hale* (Hawaiian for "home"). I know I am biased, but I've been all around the world and I still have not found a place on earth where I would rather live.

It was fun to witness the rise of Silicon Valley, especially as a consultant in the area. I always had a proclivity toward computers and technology, but I did not realize how significant the valley was from an innovation and technology standpoint until consulting found me in the early 1990s.

I never sought to be a consultant. One of my college professors caught the Silicon Valley bug and decided to start his own software business. He approached me to help him build his business, and thus, my consulting career was launched. I never looked back since then; I've been an independent consultant for almost all my adult life. And Silicon Valley, back in the day, wasn't a bad place to be a consultant!

My first big gig was with SGI (Silicon Graphics, Inc.). I started there in 1992 and had a terrific run, switching from one great client to the next, until 2001, when they just weren't viable enough to keep me around anymore. That's not how things started though. Working in Silicon Valley in the 1990s was a blast. SGI at the time owned the visual simulation and animation markets, which required its patented graphics technology. They were untouchable. When I started there, I consulted for the Silicon Studio—the engine that drove fantastic animation blockbusters such as Jurassic Park and Toy Story. The experience was unforgettable and served as a terrific launching pad for my career. As a bonus, I met some friends for life.

I'm extremely grateful to have had the opportunity of being a trusted advisor to a myriad of Silicon Valley leaders as the world moves through the largest technological revolution of its time. I guess one of the biggest gold nuggets I have pocketed from Silicon Valley over the years is that people who are smart, happy, and a little bit lucky (or a lot) achieve unimaginable results. I understand "smart" can take a lot of different forms, but I believe the kind of smart we have out here is unique: super-intelligent, creative, loyal, tenacious, fun-loving, and risk-seeking. That is a bundle you do not see very often. A lot of "smart" people that I have encountered outside of the area are very serious and risk-averse. To each his or her own—I'm not trying to judge. That's not the life for me though. What's more important is that it is hard to be creative if you are too serious, and it's hard to innovate if you are not creative, and it's hard to grow if you don't innovate. That is the secret to Silicon Valley. Well that and the fact that we are pretty darn lucky out here!

I'm not suggesting that to be successful, you should move your company to Northern California (although it wouldn't be the worst idea). But, you would be remiss to ignore the tremendous success that companies here have experienced over the last half-century. If your prime imperative right now is to strike gold with your next big idea, why not pan for it in the hills of Silicon Valley?

The Unexpected Power of a Precocious Team

The opportunity to work with smart people is a blessing, but when the right combination of people comes together to form a precocious team, that's a gift. To be clear, there is a difference between a team of high-performers and a high-performing team. It is quite common to bring a group of high-performing individuals together as a team, only to find out that they do not really function well as a team. Furthermore, not everyone on a high-performing team needs to be a high-performer.

Precocity takes the bar even higher. The implication with a **precocious** team is that not only are they high performing but also advanced for their (presumed) early stage of maturity. You hear this term quite often when referring to equine athletes (i.e., horses that compete in racing events) who show exceptional talent at only two years old. These are the types of horses you find racing in the Kentucky Derby, a prestigious race in which only three-year-olds are allowed to run. Precocious teams are often characterized as being "ahead of their time," for better or worse.

Your job is not to build a precocious team—that is a fool's errand. Instead, recognize and appreciate the great gift you have been given when you have a precocious team under your leadership, and then nurture it as best you can, for their sake and yours. Everyone wins in this scenario. Your team appreciates the focus and respect, and you benefit greatly by having a key capability at your disposal that your competitors do not have.

I spent some time working with a precocious high-tech firm whose aspiration was to grow from $1 billion to $5 billion over the span of four years. My good friend and colleague had been working with members of their top leadership (she does more executive coaching than I do), so she was aware of their aspiration and their desire to think more strategically. Up until that point, they had just done annual planning, and they knew they needed to anchor on a longer-term horizon to be successful in the future. Recognizing the need, I was called in to help develop their strategy, organizational design, and high-level management system.

The culture and climate of the company were amazing to experience in person. They were extremely proud of who they were and what they had accomplished over the last decade or so. Precocity oozed out of this organization, reminiscent of the glory days of Silicon Valley before the bubble burst. A highly talented and intelligent group of people who had a "magic touch" when it came to client-facing Professional Services. Any time they were involved in a sale, customer satisfaction went through the roof. They had a great product, but it wasn't their product that accelerated them to $1 billion; it was their people.

Although I cannot share the details of the strategy with you, or the specifics of the organizational design that we landed on, let's just say it was neither conventional nor straightforward. What I can share with you is that it had a lot to do with people. They were sharp enough to figure out that, at some point in their history, a lot of very smart people came together in the right combination, and sparks flew. The whole was orders of magnitude greater than the sum of its parts. That's the power of precocity.

With all its tremendous benefits, precocious organizations do come with risks and tradeoffs. Perhaps the most unsettling consequence of leading a precocious team is the degree of uncertainty and ambiguity that must be embraced. In the same way you cannot codify its formation, it is very hard to understand the rationale for why it works and how it was able to bring the organization to such amazing levels of success. Furthermore, it is difficult to project what sort of condition a precocious team of people will leave your organization in. Let me explain.

A precocious group of people will eventually define the way an organization works. The bombing of Pearl Harbor that Mom witnessed as a young girl brought America into World War II. The Axis powers (Germany, Italy, and Japan) were fierce opponents who, during a successful blitz just months earlier, destroyed the United Kingdom's House of Commons Chamber. Several years later, the Commons was faced with a decision on whether to restore it to its original form or rebuild it with a different design that some legislators preferred. Winston Churchill, the United Kingdom's Prime Minister at the time, made the decision to restore it to its original form under the reasoning that it better reflected the original spirit of their democratic system: "We shape our buildings; thereafter they shape us."[1] If handled the right way, a precocious organization will bring great success, but it will also shape the way the organization functions.

Choosing Humanity

There are some important decisions to make along your journey of becoming a leader, usually made as a consequence of some event that triggered an emotional insight. For instance, if you encounter a pattern of unruliness and insubordination early in your career as a leader, you might adopt a more autocratic style of leadership to ensure you always have control of the situation. Or, if your ego lands you in enough embarrassing situations, you might adopt a more inclusive style of leadership to either keep you out of those embarrassing situations (more heads are better than one) or have an out to spread the blame around (it was a group decision). It is a journey, and you will keep adjusting along the way until you reach an equilibrium between your outcomes and your expectations.

But wherever you land with your style of leadership (and we all land in different places), there is one thing that fundamentally underpins your style: your perception of people, specifically as they contribute to your organization's success and your success as a leader. To be blunt, either you perceive them as real human people, or you do not. It may sound outlandish to accuse a leader of thinking the people around them are just parts of a larger machine, but it is true. The reason why it sounds outlandish, is that in organizational society, calling out the inhumanity of leaders and those that support them is taboo—undiscussable. And the fact that it is undiscussable is also undiscussable—a self-sealing organizational defense (Argyris, 1990).

Over the years of helping leaders design and redesign organizations, I have met my share of professionals in OD (organizational design). The ugly truth of OD is that we often get called into situations where there will be an employee reduction (also known as downsizing, or more euphemistically right-sizing), usually with the aim of cutting costs. If an OD professional spends too much time focusing on this area, there is a tendency to harden, often viewing people as just numbers that aggregate to percentages. That is why I choose to focus more on growth; it is just more fun and rewarding. Plus, it gives me more opportunities to take a human-centered approach to strategy and organizational design.

Taking a human-centered approach to leading an organization is not a novel concept; it is over 100 years old. It was one of a few prevalent theories and approaches to management during the 1920s as companies grappled with booming economic times, innovative advancements in technology, and stark changes in the social fabric of the Western World, especially in the United States. Mary Parker Follett emerged as our heroine for humanity during those times, espousing humanistic organizational theories that emphasized the power of community, collaboration, and inclusion. This was a direct assault on the scientific management theories of Fredrick Winslow Taylor and the bureaucratic management theories of Max Weber, whose perspective of people was more of just another variable to control for a profitable outcome.

Oh, Mary, where did we go wrong? Have we learned nothing in the last 100 years? In 2021, the first year of the Great Resignation, an average of 4 million people quit their jobs every month. That is almost 50 million people in one year! And although the Great Resignation doesn't look so "great" when you look at the trend (see Figure 1.2), in my not-so-humble opinion, the trend line on quit rates should be flat or negative, not heading north! If we, as a collective society of leaders, had better embraced Mother Mary's advice, the Great Resignation would be neither a news story nor a soundbite for clever pundits to get airtime.

But choosing humanity is not easy for a leader. It seems deciding what to eat for breakfast is difficult for some leaders, let alone something of such monumental consequence. It requires making fiscal decisions in the face of uncertainty, investing in assets that are unpredictable at best. When I studied Six Sigma at Motorola (the place where Six Sigma was born), my Master Black Belt mentioned they were trying to figure out how best to remove the human element from Six Sigma, because that is always the biggest source of variation. That's nice.

Figure 1.2 Quit Rates over the Great Resignation Period.

Wasabi Moment

Top leaders can and should delegate a lot; however, they cannot delegate the responsibility of making strategic decisions. Being decisive, especially when it comes to choosing a human-centered strategy, takes courage—the type of courage most leaders do not have

Look, there is nothing wrong with taking a process-led approach if that is your philosophy; however, know that this perspective will likely result in suboptimal use of your humans. If quality control of your products and services is your primary goal, then any activities that fall into the category of well-being, community, or human relationships will likely look like waste that should be "leaned out." As a proud Lean Sigma Black Belt, believe me, I get it. But that is exactly why choosing humanity is difficult. Be that as it may, it is very important if your strategy fundamentally depends on maximizing human potential.

The Scaling Dilemma

In the mid-1990s, Sun Microsystems had a simple and memorable strategy that centered around a series of one or two words, one of which was "grow." I remember asking my client at the time, "Why 'grow'?"

His response was concise and acute, "If you don't grow, you die." An eerie adumbration of times to come.

Sometimes growth is a choice, sometimes it is involuntary, and sometimes it is imperative. Intentionally growing your company is nice because you are largely in control of the pace; however, with no pull from the market, you must do all the work yourself. Involuntary growth is really nice, sort of like "hands-free" growth. This is when there is so much demand for your products and services that your only job is to stay out of your own way. And then there is what I call *The Hyper-Growth Imperative*, and suddenly things aren't so much fun anymore.

When market demands swell to the point where you no longer have the internal capabilities to service those demands, then growth is not on your terms anymore. You are riding a horse that has just been spooked by a rattlesnake, and survival eclipses every other thought in your mind. When the Java rage swept through Silicon Valley, Sun Microsystems could not even process all the service orders it received. My friends told me the backlog was so enormous that they had warehouses packed with service contracts that needed processing. It seems like a great problem to have, but it's not.

This can happen with a precocious organization. If the precocity of the organization successfully attaches to a market, they will respond. And sometimes this response is so large and fast that it starts tearing the organization apart from the inside out. Top leadership can do any number of things at this point, but if they actually care about the bright group of individuals that got them here in the first place, they have a Scaling Dilemma: they must grow fast, but they must also bring their whole organization along with them—and keep it intact.

In neuroscience, a dilemma happens when the brain tries to hold two conflicting patterns in the same space. The Hyper-Growth Imperative is the first pattern of the Scaling Dilemma. The conflicting pattern comes from the love, care, and respect for the people in the organization and the impending threat to its fabric caused by the first pattern. To add, there is a more strategic anxiety that is bundled into the mix. Their people are their strategy. So, what happens to their strategy if something happens to their people? Biologically, your brain does not function well with dilemmas, so it will work overtime to try to resolve them, whether you like it or not. Ergo, sleepless nights.

Our precocious high-tech firm was in that spot when I showed up. They had recently experienced explosive success to reach $1 billion in sales, but warp speed was starting to rattle the starship. The organization had grown to the point where it was difficult for everyone to be on the same page, and that was causing a lot of anxiety in the upper ranks. In the past, it was effortless to coordinate activity because there were only a few moving parts, and everybody knew what play to run at any given time. When I showed up, that was not the case! They needed help just to sustain current performance, let alone **quintuple** sales to $5 billion!

The Scaling Dilemma kicks into this scenario because the high-tech firm was all but forced into a human-centered strategy. If buying five more machines to crank out 5× more widgets would suffice, that would be an easier problem for them to solve. In this case, the firm needed to somehow extend the magic touch of its Professional Services team into more of its customer base. And all while the market was pulling hard on the organization for more products and services.

Know and Grow

A Scaling Dilemma Statement is a statement that succinctly describes a leader's Scaling Dilemma in a structured way. It greatly helps in clarifying the issue, especially when working with an Executive Coach who can help generate insights from the dilemma

The Scaling Dilemma[2] is a tough one to get through. Once you receive and accept the precious gift of a precocious organization, it is difficult to throw that all away and start over whole cloth with a different approach. And why would you? Isn't it better to double down on your competitive advantage? Sure, but easier said than done. If you think making it to $1 billion in sales was hard, try surviving to see the $5 billion mark. That would put you in sub-1% territory (Kutcher, Nottenbohm, & Sprague, 2014). And somehow, you are supposed to keep your whole organization happy along the journey or risk resignations, poaching, and all other calamities that befall an organization with disgruntled employees?

Yes.

That's what we will do.

That's what we must do.

Putting It into Practice

Here is a brief exercise to help make the concepts in this chapter more concrete. The Scaling Dilemma, like all other dilemmas, is best resolved with insights. Ideally, you want a good Executive Coach to help generate insights; however, if you do not have a coach, this is a good exercise to help rationalize the conflicting patterns and maybe get a decent night's sleep.

1 Start with a 10-minute guided meditation. Find a quiet place where you can be alone and centered. Make sure the room is at a comfortable temperature and there are no distractions. The type of meditation (body scan, etc.) does not really matter; what matters is that you clear your mind and focus on the present. If you are new to mindful meditation, don't overthink it. The only way to do it wrong is not to take it seriously. There are plenty of places, online and otherwise, where you can find a 10-minute guided meditation

2 Maintain your post-meditation mental state while you complete your Scaling Dilemma Statement. Complete the sentence, "I would like to grow my company by [blank], but I am worried that my people will [blank]." Fill in the first blank with specifics regarding your growth aspiration. Fill in the second blank with the one biggest concern you have regarding your people

3 Once you are happy with your Scaling Dilemma Statement, start asking yourself some questions about the first part of the statement. How long have you been thinking about your firm's growth? On a scale from 1 to 10, how important is it to grow your company? Compared to other issues in your life, how does this issue rank? What would it mean to achieve your growth goal? How would that impact you personally and professionally? What advice would your grandmother give you about this situation?

4 Continue having an internal dialogue with yourself, spending far more time on the answers than the questions. Stay positive, don't let yourself go down a negative road at all. Let your mind wander in different directions while you playfully explore your current situation. Remember, this is just about the growth part; don't worry about your people just yet, unless they are part of a positive narrative or vision

5 If you have a bright idea (i.e., insight), follow that path. What sort of options do you have for pursuing that path? Come up with at least three. Of all the options, which one seems like the best option? What would be your next one or two steps to move in that direction?

6 Capture your insights and actions as they are happening! These things tend to be fleeting like butterflies, so make sure you have your catcher ready!

7 If you draw a blank on insights, that is okay. Just having your Scaling Dilemma Statement articulated is a good takeaway from this exercise. If this happens though, I strongly suggest you seek the counsel of a good Executive Coach. They are specifically trained to bring out insights when you get stuck like this

Executive Debrief

- A precocious organization is not something that is built; it is something that is handed down from the heavens to leaders who take risks and get lucky
- Silicon Valley is a rich repository of lessons to learn from the wealthiest organizations on the planet
- When the right group of talented people comes together to form a precocious team, division, or entire organization, the whole is greater than the sum of its parts. Not only is this a fun place to work, but it can also be a force in the marketplace that is tough to compete with
- To maximize the potential of a precocious organization, its leaders must embrace a humanistic approach to management. This is a tough decision to make, as it requires them to make investments in human capital that may seem unorthodox and fiscally irresponsible
- The Hyper-Growth Imperative coupled with a human-centered strategy presents a Scaling Dilemma: a confluence of goals that ostensibly conflict, creating tension in the management environment
- A precocious organization needs a lot of tender loving care to sustain performance, let alone accelerate. Too many mistakes in the execution of a Hyper-Growth strategy may cause irreversible damage

Notes

1 Sir Winston Churchill when he addressed the House of Lords on October 28, 1943.
2 A Scaling Dilemma Statement for the leader of our precocious high-tech firm might be: "I would like to grow my company from $1 billion to $5 billion in the next four years, but I am worried that key people in my organization will resign due to the turbulence before my strategy is fully implemented."

Bibliography

Argyris, C. (1990). *Overcoming organizational defenses: Facilitating organizational learnings*. Allyn & Bacon.
Bolton, R., & Bolton, D. G. (1996). *Social style/management style: Developing productive work relationships*. AMACOM.
Kutcher, E., Nottenbohm, O., & Sprague, K. (2014). *Grow fast or die slow*. McKinsey & Company. Retrieved from https://www.mckinsey.com/industries/technology-media-and-telecommunications/our-insights/grow-fast-or-die-slow
The Motley Fool. (2025, January 6). *Largest companies by market cap*. The Motley Fool. Retrieved January 22, 2025, from https://www.fool.com/research/largest-companies-by-market-cap/

Chapter 2

What the Hell Am I Supposed to Do Now?

Clarifying the Concomitant Opportunities of Hyper-Growth, Cultural Fissures, and the Post-COVID Tsunami

An Opportunity for Hyper-Growth

The opportunity for hyper-growth is an exquisite, aromatic rose covered by huge, razor-sharp thorns. You can spend your days and nights thanking the market gods for such a rare opportunity to propel your company at warp speed to a whole new, higher-stakes playing field, or you can remain paralyzed in worry and fear, convinced that you don't have enough time to find the exit to a very complex escape room. If you are lucky enough to find yourself in this situation, you are much better off being grateful than stressed—I know, easier said than done. But perspective helps.

The worst kind of growth problem for a business to have is no growth opportunity at all. As a business leader, I would much rather solve an under-supply issue than an under-demand issue. In all my years of consulting, I have never seen a business challenge greater than having no market demand. Once Silicon Graphics, Inc. decided to go after the low-end consumer market, where there was no demand for its computers, it was only a matter of time before it faced insurmountable financial doom.

Of course, the goldilocks spot is to have an opportunity to grow *without the imperative to grow*. This is a business where the market has demonstrated higher levels of interest in its products and services and the leaders feel like they have options as to whether or not to pursue these market opportunities. The top leader is in the driver's seat and has a firm grip on the steering wheel. It is a nice place to be, but it is not without issues. The most insidious issue for a leader in this situation is that they have options, and that often breeds either poor or nonexistent decision-making.

Then there is the Hyper-Growth Imperative. If your products, services, or some combination thereof make an overwhelming impression in the marketplace, then you will experience a commensurate demand on your business—overwhelming. At first glance, this seems like a wonderful problem to have; however, if you know your business cannot meet that demand, you are left with a mix of emotions that create a very uncomfortable cocktail of empowering and limiting beliefs.

DOI: 10.4324/9781003518181-4

Many leaders use the word "opportunity" euphemistically, as a more palatable substitution for "problem" or "pain point." This is not a productive mental frame for the opportunities we are discussing here. If you view the hyper-growth opportunity as a "problem," you are certainly setting yourself up to fail. Hyper-growth is not a problem that needs to be solved, even though it feels that way sometimes. Hyper-growth is more like a high-stakes game show. You could walk away with a ton of money, or a box of macaroni and cheese. It all depends on how accurately you perceive the situation, how well you perform, and how much luck falls your way.

Although each organization has its own journey, all hyper-growth opportunities have similar characteristics. There is an exceptionally strong pull from the market for the organization's products and services. In fact, the pull is so strong that if the business succeeds in fulfilling the demand without blowing up, it will land in a completely new realm of strategic metrics, often orders of magnitude from where it started. Revenues will triple, quadruple, or even quintuple like the high-tech firm we introduced in the last chapter. Operating costs will explode as well, and the organization will likely take on new levels of short- and long-term liabilities (e.g., debt).

Using a process that I call *Cinematic Visionography* (Weathington, 2023) is a good way to clarify your opportunity. It starts with strategic measures like revenue, costs, number of employees, etc.; however, it is not complete until all the details of the future organization are fleshed out in accurate detail. It is challenging to complete due to the uncertainties of the future, but it is not impossible. The key is to make sure it is as thorough and as accurate as possible. Remember, this is your non-fiction of the future, not some fantastic science fiction that is more entertaining than believable.

Know and Grow

Cinematic Visionography is the art and science of creating the non-fiction of the future. When applied to an organizational strategy it represents a very robust process of producing a detailed and accurate movie (virtual or literal) of the organization's future state. After selecting a strategic horizon, the organization undergoes successive cycles of closely examining:

1) the macro-environment, and then

2) the competitive environment, and finally

3) the organization's internal environment

Every opportunity comes with problems or pain, despite the fact that most leaders actively avoid processing anything that doesn't sound positive. The biggest pain point with a hyper-growth opportunity is the organization's inability to supply what the market is demanding. Its key capabilities are just not there—yet. Furthermore, retaining customers, investors, and especially employees, while building key capabilities, requires a delicate dance.

Finally, the type of change the organization will navigate with any hyper-growth opportunity is always *transformational*. The market pull on the organization will force it into metamorphosis. So, you never want to extrapolate from the present; that would be like a caterpillar projecting that they will be a bigger caterpillar. Instead, spend an uncomfortable amount of time, energy, and resources on your vision of success—your butterfly— and then work back from there.

An Opportunity for a Thriving Culture

Let us set the hyper-growth opportunity aside for a moment to focus on another type of opportunity that is relevant to precocious organizations—the opportunity to create a working environment (physical, virtual, or both) where people thrive. There are many reasons to invest in the well-being of your people, not least of which is simply to retain good talent. After all, organizations are fundamentally collections of people, so it stands to reason that creating a culture where people love to do their best work is not that far-fetched an idea. And yet, we have still managed to create working conditions so seemingly abhorrent for some that they would rather leave a company *without another job lined up* than continue dealing with the current perceived hell they are in now.

Despite the fact that the Great Resignation wasn't so "great" when you step back and look at the actual trend data (see Figure 1.2), it was still an event that holds remarkable records for employee disgust that will likely never be broken. Four million people every month walked out of their jobs in search of something better. And things didn't get better in 2022; they got worse! At the height of the Great Resignation in 2022, an astonishing 4.5 million workers quit their jobs each month—an exodus that sent shockwaves through industries and boardrooms alike. That year, over 50 million people quit their jobs. That's like the entire country of South Korea emptying out with a mass exodus over one year, 4.5 million people at a time!

And yet, it seems like so many companies these days do not care enough about their employees to make sure they do not leave. Of course, every leader wants to retain talent, but how *badly* do they want their best employees to stay? What are they willing to sacrifice to keep them happy?

As a leader, that's a tough corner to be wedged in. This is where you will often find a corporate cognitive dissonance; a disconnect between espoused beliefs and observed behavior. The annual report will extoll the virtues of their talented workforce, and then a top leader will call me or one of my colleagues to help them design a "leaner" organization—maybe one that's about 40% leaner, if you know what I mean.

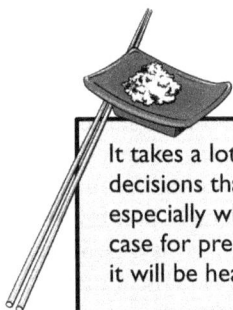

Wasabi Moment

It takes a lot of courage and conviction to make financial decisions that favor people over other areas of the business, especially when money is tight. Be prepared to justify your case for precocity and defend your position on people because it will be heavily scrutinized for as long as you hold it

So, the opportunity to create a harmonious culture (i.e., where espoused beliefs align with observed behavior) where people thrive is inherently quite compelling. When people are thriving en masse, there's a contagious energy in the organization that is not like anything else. People love to come to work. People love to work at work. And because of it, people do their best work—effortlessly. Retention becomes a non-issue at that point. There is no need to focus on retention, because nobody wants to leave! Furthermore, burnout is not an issue, because it is pretty hard to burn out when you are doing something you love to do.

When Silicon Graphics Inc. (SGI) was flying high in the 1990s, it absolutely pampered its workers, employees, and consultants alike. When I arrived in 1992, I was warmly welcomed into a hard-working, fun-loving family of extremely talented people who would eventually go on to help build Google, Facebook, and other iconic tech giants. We had private offices, catered food, snacks, and soda everywhere, ping-pong tables readily waiting for a quick pick-up game with colleagues, and of course, all the fancy tools and technology needed to do our jobs. On any given day, there was a huge party somewhere. And all of our buildings were in the same general area, which was conveniently close to a huge concert venue called Shoreline Amphitheater, where we would throw the most outlandish of our parties. It was a marvelous time and place that really brought out the best in all of us.

And that was very intentional—Silicon Valley companies figured out that the key to their success was unlocking the human creativity that was harnessed within their corporate walls. Let's face it, we are neither known for our operational discipline nor our product reliability. How often have you wanted to chuck your laptop across the room because something wasn't working properly?

Where we do excel though—unequivocally—is innovation; it is bundled with our brand of taking extraordinary measures to make our corporate citizens happy. The strategic bet was—and still is—on human ingenuity, because the payoff is enormous when innovation is commercialized properly. Google, Facebook, Apple, and many others made a king's ransom on cleverly packaged human insights translated into bits and bytes and then delivered by ether.

Where the biggest upside of this opportunity is the humans, the biggest downside is—well, the humans. Keeping humans happy is very difficult, especially if you start running out of money. Once you place your bet on human ingenuity, you cannot back out without extremely painful and irreparable consequences. The key is to clarify exactly who is a good fit for your organization and, more importantly, who is not. And then, make sure you do everything in your power to ensure that your best people flourish, personally and professionally.

New Opportunities for 2020 and Beyond, Including the Great Resignation, Quiet Quitting, and Hybrid Work

SARS-CoV-2, or more commonly known as COVID-19, has taken a lot of lives since it broke out in 2019, and it has also taken away an age of blissful ignorance. I was working with a large international shipping company in March of 2020. My client was going through a transformational change and needed a new organizational design to fit its new strategy. We had just completed an in-person workshop to optimize workflows in California, and we were all set to run a similar workshop in Texas. We were well aware of the COVID-19 threat; however, we were willing to take the risk. There were no company-wide travel restrictions—until the weekend we were supposed to fly out. We never made it to Texas, but the project continued, and we developed a fantastic design and operating model together. But from that point on, all our work was virtual. I could not even imagine at the time that it would be 2024 until I saw my client face-to-face again.[1]

COVID-19 disrupted the business ecosystem so profoundly that, despite the burning desire of many companies to return to those ways of working, the pre-COVID days are gone forever. We have entered a new era of leadership, management, and the challenges that accompany the leadership and management of any organization. The intrinsic, perilous threat of

COVID has since waned, but the mental scars it left behind are indelible. We know that life and health are important and should not be taken for granted. We know how important it is to be around family, friends, and loved ones, and how much we miss them when we cannot be around them. We now know that we can be just as productive (if not more) working from home than commuting every day to an office. And we know we are social creatures that need social interactions for our spirit to survive.

We have a few post-COVID opportunities worth exploring, some born from the onset of the pandemic and some exacerbated by it, but all novel as we enter this new era of leadership and management. We have already discussed the Great Resignation for what it is worth, but what does it mean for a leader in this post-COVID era? It is an opportunity to compete and win on the basis of talent retention like never before. We now know it's *possible* for more than 50 million people to quit their jobs within the span of a year, given the right climate. Will there be another Great Resignation? Only time will tell. But one thing that is for certain is that those of us who have been through the experience, whether we quit our jobs or not, won't soon forget it. This forever alters the macro-propensity for resignation and bolsters worker loyalty in organizations that demonstrably value their people.

A more insidious phenomenon that garnered headlines during this period was Quiet Quitting, resignation's passive-aggressive cousin. As its name implies, Quiet Quitters have also left the company; however, they have decided not to inform anyone. Happily collecting a paycheck for doing nothing more than staying quietly out of sight, they bide their time until they are either exposed or find a better place to work. In truth, this has always been a condition that has existed in the workplace. What the pandemic did was amplify its visibility and intensity. Now it has a name, a signature, and probably its own social media profile.

Quitters quit quietly because: (1) they don't care about doing their job, (2) they don't care that they don't care about doing their job, and (3) nobody else cares that they don't care about doing their job. The opportunity is to build a culture of engagement where people can express their thoughts and feelings without fear of any negative consequences, including normative sanctions from their peers. This concept, known as *psychological safety* (Schein & Bennis, 1965), has experienced a renaissance in recent years (Edmondson, 2018), no doubt in part due to the trauma people experienced through the dark days of the pandemic.

Quiet Quitting is yet another reason to build accurate personas of those who fit well within the company's culture. It also opens an opportunity to identify those who really should not be with the company, despite their great technical talent. When coupled with psychological safety and an authentic concern for humanity, the company can then help those in the out-group find their own in-group where they will thrive, even if it is with a different organization.

The pandemic forced most of us to figure out how to be productive on the job while working at home. It was the first time in my life that I designed an entire organization without one face-to-face interaction. During that period, I partnered with a large, multi-national client to successfully develop a transformative business strategy, without ever setting foot on the steps of their corporate headquarters. And I helped operationalize a massive digital transformation for another client without having one physical face-to-face meeting with the Chief Digital Officer, even though I virtually sat right by his side throughout the entire two-year journey. Every one of these large-scale programs was massively successful and entirely virtual.

Of course, once the frigid conditions of the pandemic began to thaw into a more controlled endemic, companies were eager (or maybe anxious?) to see their workers back in the office, so we ushered in the post-pandemic wave of hybrid work environments—a few days back in the office, but not all five. In most cases, that meant people were *allowed* to work from home on Mondays and Fridays; however, they were required to be in the office on Tuesdays, Wednesdays, and Thursdays.

With all its merits, hybrid work is more of a compromise between companies and employees than anything else, and it is a bad one at that. Both sides feel like they lose a little—a sort of middle ground that is less terrible than any one extreme. The opportunity is to find a solution that works fantastically for all involved.

Clarity through Convergence

Let's summarize the opportunities we have explored thus far:

1 The opportunity to grow exponentially, catapulting the organization into a new level of strategic measures (revenues, costs, profits, etc.) and build much-needed capabilities to ease relentless market demands
2 The opportunity to build and continually nurture a thriving community of skilled workers who love coming to work to do their best work, while simultaneously unlocking precious human creativity and commercializing it for an unassailable competitive advantage
3 The opportunity to effortlessly attract and retain the best people in the talent pool that match clearly defined best-fit personas
4 The opportunity to build a psychologically safe environment where people express their thoughts and feelings without fear of any negative consequences, including normative sanctions from their peers

5 The opportunity to master hybrid working environments that transcend
   the limitations of physical boundaries and maximize organizational performance through deliberate application of collocated teaming

Each one of these opportunities is a standalone opportunity worth pursuing. There are many ways to survive a hyper-growth scenario; a human-centered approach is not required. You can certainly architect a
people-first organizational design without the market demands that force a
hyper-growth strategy. And you would be remiss if you ignored the opportunity to learn and grow from the significant post-pandemic lessons that
have been handed to us. The following chapters in this book are designed
to help anyone pursuing any one of these opportunities; however, there is
synergistic value at stake when some or all of these opportunities converge.

Precocity is a critical factor in how compelling it is to converge opportunities when given the option. If you sense that your organization is
precocious, but you do not yet have an overwhelming pull from the marketplace for your products and services, you are in a very interesting spot.
Unfortunately, the streets of Silicon Valley are littered with worthless stock
certificates of companies that had a great idea, great people, way too much
funding, and no profits. So, proceed with caution here. Before launching
into a full-blown transformation, it is important to validate the precocity
of your team and, more importantly, the potential demand for your products and/or services.

If you happen to be in that Goldilocks growth spot with a bona fide precocious organization—great! You are still in the driving seat for now, but
I would still plan and brace for a hyper-growth strategy. You don't know
where the tipping point is until you cross it, and as soon as you do, you
are in trouble. It happens too quickly to prepare, so you are best off con-
verging your human-centered strategy with an anticipated hyper-growth
strategy (opportunities 2 and 1, respectively). Worst-case scenario is that
you overbuild capabilities that aren't needed (yet), but that's better than
getting caught in level five rapids with no oars.

Once you have decided to compete based on the commercialization
of human innovation (opportunity 2), talent retention and psychological
safety (opportunities 3 and 4) are natural complements, but not required.
Nurturing a thriving community of skilled workers should organically
ward off resignation, Quiet Quitting, and all those other nasty bugs that in-
fest our organizations today. However, going the extra mile to pursue these
opportunities provides worthwhile buttresses to protect your competitive
advantage. This is particularly important when dealing with a precocious
organization, as they tend to be a little more volatile and temperamental
than other organizations. We can't upset the talent!

Hybrid work environments present an interesting and compelling opportunity for precocious organizations, mainly because this is a post-pandemic opportunity. Although we had plenty of high-performing, precocious organizations in Silicon Valley back in the good ol' days, we never really saw too many remote workers, let alone high-performing teams that included remote workers. We had a lot of great technology, but videoconferencing was still in its infancy, and web-based collaboration wasn't really mainstream. People were expected to come to an office, but that was never a problem, because the office was a great place to be!

There's an interesting intersection between building and nurturing a thriving community of skilled workers (opportunity 2), effortlessly attracting and retaining top talent (opportunity 3), and mastering hybrid work environments (opportunity 5). If you master the hybrid work environment in a way that workers feel a legitimate win (instead of a compromise), you *will* effortlessly attract and retain top talent. The real challenge is finding the right way to manifest an environment that nurtures a thriving community while embracing a location-agnostic way of working.

Of course, there is a scenario where all these opportunities converge, and that is the focus of this book. This is no easy task. The pain that is attached to any one of these opportunities is usually enough for a leader to digest; however, the pain multiplies as opportunities converge. We must build key capabilities under overwhelming pressure from market demands while keeping our precocious organization happy enough to stick with us through a major growth transformation! We must make hard strategic decisions that support hyper-growth while making sure they align with the hard people decisions that support an investment in the happiness and well-being of our humans. And we must ensure diversity, inclusion, and a frictionless work experience for those who are not physically in the office.

Hold on tight, this is going to be a fun ride.

Understanding Your Deeper Purpose

If your organization vanished from the earth tomorrow, how would the world be impacted? What exactly is your organization's *raison d'etre* (reason for being)? These are big questions—questions not taken seriously enough by many organizations. Questions you cannot ignore when contemplating a seismic shift in your organization's strategy, especially one that converges hyper-growth, human-centered design, and bleeding-edge ways of working. The important answer to these questions is your company's *purpose*, an often underdeveloped but critical element in your company's overall strategic philosophy.

Figure 2.1 Strategic Philosophy.

A strategic philosophy has four main elements: vision, mission, purpose, and values (See Figure 2.1). It is so unfortunate that these terms are often confusing and ambiguous, because they don't have to be. Simply put, *vision* is where you are going, *mission* is what you do for whom and how, purpose is why you exist, and values are what you care about. Each has its own place and function in your strategic philosophy, but they often overlap (as they should), and this can cause confusion if you feel they should be mutually exclusive with clean lines.

The other misconception about all these elements is that the only final product is a set of concise statements and bullet points. If leaders ever go down the journey of creating a strategic philosophy (or something like it), they often feel like a good outcome is something that would fit on a simple webpage: vision statement, mission statement, purpose, and values. And that's usually where it lands, to be comfortably forgotten by all, including the leaders who created them. We have already discussed the folly of treating your vision like this, and the same applies to your purpose.

The reason why an organization's purpose is so important is that it is the fundamental axiom for inspiring the people who really need to be inspired by the organization. When reading your purpose, customers should be inspired to buy your products and services, investors should be inspired to invest in your organization (or donate in the case of a non-profit), and employees should be inspired to do their best work at your organization—does that sound familiar?

So now, given the clarity of thought around this incredible opportunity to embark on a hyper-growth journey at warp speeds to an unprecedented competitive level while creating a magical Nirvana where unbridled brilliance flows freely and effortlessly, affording you game-changing products and services that cannot be challenged in the marketplace—I ask again—why does your organization exist? What is the overall impact on the world that your organization does not exist in this state today?

How can the answer to this question be anything but absolutely compelling? It must resonate with the people who wake up every workday to forward your organization's mission. Your purpose must be inspiring and compelling to *them*, in a way that pulls them toward your vision of success. When they wake up in the morning, you want them to be excited to start working and not just clock in to quietly quit. There is no way to build this work environment (physical or virtual) without an absolutely compelling purpose. Your purpose forms the foundation of the foundation of your human-centered strategy; it is the bedrock upon which your foundation sits.

Consider Intel's purpose statement: We create world-changing technology that improves the life of every person on the planet (Intel Corporation, n.d.). I don't know about you, but when I read this, I get a little excited. I'm not going to leave 30 years of consulting behind to apply at Intel just yet, but this purpose is no doubt inspiring. I would be proud to be part of a solution that enriches the lives of every person on earth. It's no surprise that Intel is another one of Silicon Valley's icons that has completely dominated the CPU space.

A small note for consideration before we move on: the elements of your strategic philosophy are tightly interwoven, so if, after reflection, your purpose changes, it makes sense to revisit your mission, vision, and values. Your vision might shift without affecting the other elements, but a change in purpose will almost always have a domino effect on the others.

Navigating Uncharted Terrain

The last thing to clarify about the journey ahead is exactly when it will be done and precisely what it will look like when we get there—and wouldn't that be nice if that were even remotely possible? As uncomfortable as it feels, it is impossible to predict with any degree of accuracy what your firm will look like once it emerges onto the other side: or even *when* the

Table 2.1 Types of Organizational Change

Type of Change	Vision of Destination	Path to Destination	Level of Difficulty
Transactional	Clear	Clear	Low
Transitional	Clear	Unclear	Medium
Transformational	Unclear	Unclear	High

journey will end. The type of change that you are about to embark on, given the comprehensive opportunity that we have discussed in this chapter, is categorized as *transformational* change, and it is very important that you treat it as such.

There are three types of changes that differ based on how accurately we can articulate the destination and how accurately we can articulate the path to get there (see Table 2.1)

Transactional changes are the easiest types of changes and typically do not require help from experts (inside or outside). *Transitional* changes are a little bit harder; you know what good looks like, but you are not sure how to get there. This is playing a par six hole in golf, something not too many golfers have ever encountered. You know the ball must eventually go into the hole, but how you go about it may be a head-scratcher. A good caddy who knows the course would be a great help in this situation. *Transformational* changes are a whole different beast to deal with; you honestly don't know where you are going, let alone how to get there.

In fact, you *cannot* know where you are going; the destination is unascertainable. An expert is definitely required here, not because they somehow know where to go, but because they are more comfortable and confident operating in unfamiliar territory. The label of *transformational* fits, because the journey truly transforms the organization into something that intrinsically resembles the former organization (because of its DNA, which does not change), but its design is radically different. A metamorphosis takes place, like a caterpillar transforming into a butterfly.

Unfortunately, there is no way to predict exactly what this new butterfly will look like, so more traditional and comfortable means of managing change must be thrown out the window—they are no good. In fact, it will do more damage than good if you try to force-fit transactional or transitional change management over a complex system, which is where transformational change lives.

The Cynefin Framework (see Figure 2.2) helps us make sense of complex systems and situations (Snowden & Boone, 2020); thereby, helping us understand the difficult, uncharted terrain that is characteristic of transformational change. The key difference between a complex system and an ordered (i.e., simple or complicated) system is the degree of predictability between actions and results. In an ordered system, results

Figure 2.2 The Cynefin Framework.

are largely predictable; however, in a complex system, they are not. In a complex system, you can perform the exact same actions twice and get two completely different results. What's tricky, though, is that the results in a complex system are not completely random—that would be a chaotic system. So, complex systems sit in a very confusing space that is neither orderly nor random. Unfortunately, this is also the space where transformational changes live.

Surviving transformational change requires an iterative mindset that is filled more with curiosity than control. An overabundance of control in a complex environment will lead to nothing but frustration and ultimate failure. If you force a sailboat into a strong headwind because that's the direction you need to go, you will just end up sailing backward.

As the Cynefin Framework suggests, the best decision-making approach when dealing with a complex system is *probe–sense–respond*. That means our transformational change journey will be iterative, filled with experiments that fail intelligently (Edmondson, 2023). After each experiment, regardless of the outcome, we learn and grow and progressively emerge into the organization we were destined to become. That is how transformational change works.

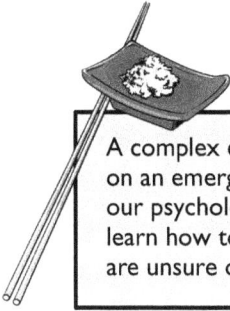

Wasabi Moment

A complex environment, where the vision shifts around based on an emergent solution, is very unsettling for humans due to our psychological need for certainty. As a leader, you must learn how to keep people motivated and inspired when they are unsure of their final destination

Complex environments also force us to reframe our mental model of visions. How can you create a clear vision of success knowing that the future cannot be predicted? That is a great question. While your purpose, mission, and values should remain constant, expect that your vision of success *will change* as the organization organically emerges through intentionally progressive and adaptive development. Be prepared to improve your vision after every iteration of probe–sense–respond.

We have briefly visited organizational change management, a topic that we will cover in much more detail later when we cross that bridge of our journey. It is important to set your expectations upfront, while framing the opportunity, as transformational change is very difficult and very unsettling. It requires us to enter a space that our brains are not physiologically equipped to handle. So, it is important that we respect the emotional side of being a leader through this transformation as much as we respect the logical side of framing up the opportunity, as we have done here. This is a topic we will discuss in the next chapter.

Putting It into Practice

Now that you have a better idea of the opportunity in front of you, it's time to clarify your own opportunity, in terms that are specific and meaningful to you, into a solid frame. This is probably the most important strategic piece of work that you will be directly involved in, so take it very seriously. Most leaders either try to rush through this process because they are eager to get started with the "real work," or they get stuck in analysis paralysis because of the enormity of the challenge ahead. Get started with a viable first pass, and then continually iterate as the solution emerges. Start a document in Microsoft Word, Google Docs, or something similar, and complete the following sections:

1 **Opportunity:** Restate the opportunities discussed in this chapter in your own words, using the specific details of your situation, building on the Scaling Dilemma that you crafted in the last chapter. Express a sense of urgency when describing the opportunity. Be explicit about the pain or problems in the organization, but do it in a way that is honest, accurate, and inspiring

2 **Background and Context:** Provide supporting details not covered in the Opportunity that are relevant. This helps people who are less familiar with your situation (like outside experts) quickly come up to speed

3 **Strategic Realignment:** Explain how your strategic philosophy (e.g., purpose) has shifted, considering the opportunity ahead and the insights that compelled you to make these shifts

4 **Leadership Approach:** Describe in your own words the complex nature of the environment that you are in right now and your decision-making approach (i.e., probe–sense–respond). Acknowledge that you cannot predict the future, but that you will continually guide the organization based on the best information known at the time

5 **Leadership Team:** Explain who will lead the effort with you and why. Select your best resources and top influencers, regardless of position or rank

6 **Vision of Success:** Use the techniques in this chapter to develop your initial vision of success. Acknowledge that your vision will change along your journey of discovery; however, there will always be a North Star to keep everyone aligned on where we are currently heading

7 **Measures of Success:** How will you know if the organization is moving in the right direction? How will you know when you are done? What are the factors that ultimately drive value for the organization, regardless of how much control you have over them?

8 **Boundaries:** What is clearly in scope and, more importantly, what is clearly off limits? Are there any other previously made strategic decisions that will absolutely not be revisited?

9 **Stakeholders:** Who are the people, inside or outside of the organization, that are critical to your success (e.g., key customers)? How will you engage with them to create a win–win situation?

Make sure to keep this a "living document," especially in its nascent stages of development. When the mood strikes you or anyone on your leadership team, jump in and capture those insights.

Executive Debrief

- Clarifying or *framing* the opportunity that lies ahead is a critical first step that a leader cannot delegate. It helps the leader clearly think

through the problem that needs to be solved in a comprehensive, accurate, and honest way
- Framing an opportunity has nothing to do with *solving* the problem. That comes later, once we understand exactly what the problem or challenge is
- Precocious organizations today that are lucky enough to strike gold with their market typically find themselves at the convergence of numerous opportunities:

  - The opportunity to grow exponentially, catapulting the organization into a new level of strategic measures (revenues, costs, profits, etc.), and build much-needed capabilities to ease relentless market demands
  - The opportunity to build and continually nurture a thriving community of skilled workers who love coming to work to do their best work, while simultaneously unlocking precious human creativity and commercializing it for an unbeatable competitive advantage
  - The opportunity to effortlessly attract and retain the best people in the talent pool who match clearly defined best-fit personas
  - The opportunity to build a psychologically safe environment where people express their thoughts and feelings without fear of any negative consequences, including normative sanctions from their peers
  - The opportunity to master hybrid working environments that transcend the limitations of physical boundaries and maximize organizational performance through deliberate application of collocated teaming

- A comprehensive opportunity of this magnitude often forces leaders to re-evaluate their vision, mission, purpose, and values (collectively their strategic philosophy); especially their purpose or *raison d'etre*
- Surviving a strategic shift of this significance requires navigating a complex environment where the future is unknown, and the players interact with each other in related but unpredictable ways. As such, a leadership approach that embraces low-consequence experiments and iterative decision-making provides the best chances for making it out alive
- Transformational change management—which is very different from transactional or transitional change management—is required in a complex environment, where the future state cannot be accurately defined in advance

Note

1 Eerily, it was March of 2024, almost exactly four years after we started, that I accidentally bumped into my client in Texas, where we were supposed to run our workshop.

Bibliography

Edmondson, A. C. (2018). *The fearless organization: Creating psychological safety in the workplace for learning, innovation, and growth*. Wiley.

Edmondson, A. C. (2023). *Right kind of wrong: The science of failing well*. Atria Books.

Intel Corporation. (n.d.). *Company overview*. Intel. Retrieved February 7, 2025, from https://www.intel.com/content/www/us/en/company-overview/company-overview.html

Schein, E. H., & Bennis, W. G. (1965). *Personal and organizational change through group methods: The laboratory approach*. Wiley.

Snowden, D., & Boone, M. E. (2020). *Cynefin: Weaving sense-making into the fabric of our world*. Cognitive Edge.

Weathington, J. C. (2023, July 15). Cinematic visionography: The three cycles of creating a strategic vision. Excellent Management Systems, Inc. Retrieved from https://xmsystems.com/cinematic-visionography/

Chapter 3

Are You Sure about This?

Mentally Preparing to Lead the Journey

Why Emotions Matter So Much

If you were to place a racehorse on one plate of a huge balancing scale, you would need to put about ten jockeys on the other plate before the horse begins to lift. It is a fallacy to believe that a jockey controls a racehorse like a driver controls a car. Horses are sentient beings; they are aware of stimuli in the environment and process threats just like we do. So, regardless of their training and connection with the jockey, at ten times the weight of its rider, the horse will win any sort of difference of opinion.

It is hilarious watching horses load into the gate for a race when one decides they just don't feel like going in. About a half-dozen assistant starters rush over to the horse to coax this huge animal into doing something it doesn't want to do. They tug and pull, but the horse goes nowhere. Most of the time, the horse eventually loads—when she's ready. These are trained equine athletes, so they are in no way threatened by the gate. I think they just like to mess with the crew for kicks. Every human's cognition (higher-order thinking) and emotions have a similar relationship. Emotions have much more power over your behavior than your rational brain.[1] That's why, if your strategy fails, emotions are at the root of the failure about 95% of the time.

About 80% of strategy failures are due to implementation. And, most implementations fail because of emotions (pathos), not logic (logos) or leader credibility (ethos). Aristotle's Rhetorical Triangle of ethos, pathos, and logos has been used for centuries as a fundamental concept in communication and persuasion. It is often depicted as an equilateral triangle, but this is not accurate. Not all sides of the triangle carry the same weight. Pathos carries the lion's share when it comes to winning over hearts and minds. Logos and ethos must be there; however, they play a significantly lesser role.

When Adolf Hitler started his political career in the early 1920s, the Nazi Party had only a very small minority following. By the mid-1920s,

DOI: 10.4324/9781003518181-5

the party was starting to gain traction, but still insignificant compared to some of the other more popular parties like the Social Democratic Party of Germany (SDP) or the German National People's Party (DNVP). Hitler, with relatively low credibility (ethos) and very few constructive platform points (logos), rode a campaign of emotions (pathos) to one of the most powerful dictatorships the world has ever seen—in less than ten years. Although this is a dark period in the history of humanity, it illustrates the enormous effect a leader has when they can build a strong emotional connection with their followers.

Consider now the difficult road ahead for a workforce that is about to embark on a transformational journey into an unknown future. The stress of hyper-growth will invariably test the intestinal fortitude of the organization. If you have the type of firm that encourages open and honest communication, trust me, you will get some when things start getting difficult. If you do not, then you have a bigger problem; good people will just start leaving, and you won't have a hint of why.

One of the most challenging aspects of a hyper-growth strategy in a precocious organization is the risk of cannibalizing the human ingenuity that fuels its competitive advantage. If you lose too many of your best people, you won't have a competitive advantage anymore. And if they go, they will probably go for emotional reasons. Sure, they will form logical reasons to support their feelings, so they sound intelligent when asked about it. We humans are very good at that; the mind has an infinite capacity to form rational responses to emotional drivers. To mitigate this risk, the leader must understand emotions in a way that most leaders don't care to understand and then lead by appealing to the true desires of the racehorse and not just the jockey who thinks he is in control.

How People Emotionally Process Change

The notion that change is hard is rooted in our psychological need for certainty, which, by nature of the way we survive, is usually found in the status quo. Our psychological need for certainty drives us to build and systematically maintain an environment that is fundamentally comfortable and predictable. We all have different thresholds, but our brains are not physiologically equipped to deal with too much uncertainty, and a primal panic signal wails when our sensors detect something that is too far out of alignment with our expectations. So, unless the status quo is inherently threatening, the idea of separating from the status quo into an uncertain future *is* very threatening. This loss of the status quo forms the basis of the change curve, an emotional journey that all humans go through when they face losing their comfortable and familiar circumstances.

I call the change curve the Emotional Journey, as that language more accurately describes the human process that we all go through when facing difficult situations. It is modeled against the great work that Elizabeth Kübler-Ross did in the 1970s to understand how humans grieve during the loss of a loved one. According to Kübler-Ross (1969), there are five stages of grief: denial, anger, bargaining, depression, and acceptance. The change curve, which is OCM's (organizational change management) adaptation of the Kübler-Ross model, contains a very similar set of stages[2]: denial, resistance, exploration, and commitment. To help solidify the concepts, my Emotional Journey brings the change curve to life with vivid metaphors (see Figure 3.1).

At first awareness of a significant change, we completely ignore it as we blissfully stroll across the Bridge of Denial. This is a learned response based on preternatural agents called emanations. Thoughts are things. Many times, our emanations change the course of our experience. So, when we banish an undesirable outcome with our convicted will, like a scary change

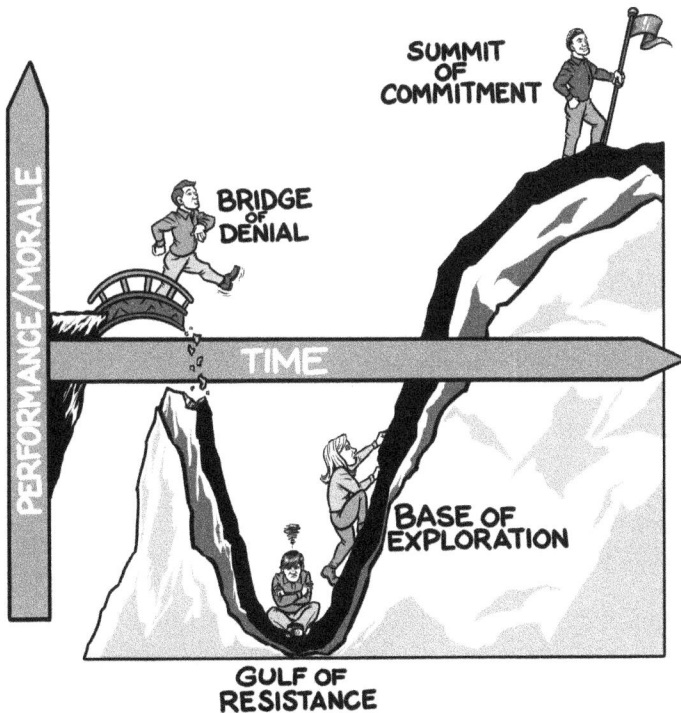

Figure 3.1 The Emotional Journey.

that will disrupt our cozy status quo, sometimes it works! But when it doesn't, it takes a while for us to come around to that reality. While we are in denial, our performance and morale are quite normal because there is nothing to be worried about; the change is not real—until it is.

Once we realize the change is unavoidable, we descend into the Gulf of Resistance. This is a dark place, full of negative emotions, low morale, and petulant behavior. The Gulf of Resistance can turn otherwise polite and rational people into angry trolls and warlike ogres. Of course, this is just a spell that lasts while they are mired in the gulf. Most people are inherently good people, but the stress of a difficult transformation can affect even the best of us. The Gulf of Resistance brings us down, physically and emotionally. It doesn't matter how much you tell the workforce to focus on operations and maintain high performance—it just won't happen, and you have to be okay with that until they get through it (if they get through it).

Wasabi Moment

Actively resisting change is a very normal behavior that is part of a human process associated with difficult circumstances. Do not use your power to punish or control people who are explicitly opposed to your vision or direction at this point. They have not had as much time to process the change as you have

If the Emotional Journey is managed properly, people will emerge from the Gulf of Resistance into the Base of Exploration. This is a very vulnerable state for people, having just overcome the trauma of the gulf, but at least they are trying to look forward instead of clinging on to the past. Performance is still low as they experiment with new ways of working, like a six-year-old learning to ride a bike without training wheels. But, with the right encouragement, small successes build confidence, and this reinforcing loop elevates people to the Summit of Commitment, where morale and performance are higher than ever before.

It is important to note that the Emotional Journey is a human process that is neither avoidable nor predictable in progression. We cannot choose not to go through the emotional journey when faced with a significant change, and there is no chance that anyone will go smoothly from one stage to another, especially without the help of skilled leaders and change managers.

How to Manage Emotions through Transformational Change

The late, great Dr. Maya Angelou once said, "people will forget what you said, people will forget what you did, but people will never forget how you made them feel." When managing the Emotional Journey attached to any transformational change, it is very important to adopt a performer-centric philosophy and approach. In layman's terms: it's not about what you do, it's about how they feel. I have been on too many programs where leaders insist that I plot the Emotional Journey on a Gantt chart, as if I somehow know that most of the workforce will clear the Gulf of Resistance before their Winter Celebration Party. Managing emotions requires a structured event-based approach, not the typical time-based approach that you see in most project plans. You are not done until your organization empirically arrives at the Summit of Commitment, an event that you cannot force-fit into a timeline.

The structure of managing emotions starts with interviews and/or focus groups and continues with surveys (i.e., qualitative followed by quantitative). When I helped a strategic business unit of a large, multi-national oil and gas company manage through a large-scale transformation, I wasn't there more than a few weeks before we ran structured focus groups with individual contributors and front-line supervisors. I facilitated the focus groups with the deputy program manager who was a talented employee of the company and a terrific manager in her own right. As part of the icebreaker, we went around the room at the beginning of each focus group, asking each individual how they felt—in one word—about what was happening in the business unit. This is how we collected "feelings" data to build qualitative themes that we would later use in pulse surveys.

The focus groups and first pulse survey gave us valuable feedback to analyze. To help analyze the feedback, I enlisted the help of a brilliant colleague who has a Ph.D. in Psychology. She helped me map the emotional themes from the initial wave of feedback into likely stages of the Emotional Journey. For instance, people who expressed frustration or anger were clearly in the Gulf of Resistance; whereas people who felt unconcerned or unaffected at this stage were probably on the Bridge of Denial. This gave us a nice snapshot of where cohorts of people in the organization were on their Emotional Journey through the transformation. Although this might sound a bit over-engineered, you cannot exactly ask people on a survey if they are in the Gulf of Resistance!

When analyzing emotional themes related to any transformational change, we must prepend one stage to the beginning of the Emotional Journey: Pre-Denial. You cannot approach the Bridge of Denial if you do not even know that it exists! In many cases, when leaders embark on a transformational change, the general workforce has no idea what's going on until long after the planning is done. And even if there is a town hall where the leader hints that change might be on the horizon, chances are most people will remain clueless until the messaging starts to be more focused and relevant. This is the stage of Pre-Denial, and to be honest, it's a wonderful place for employees to be!

Emotional thematic analysis illuminates the events that help you manage people to the next stage of the Emotional Journey. Different groups or cohorts are managed based on where they show up on your analysis. Reference Table 3.1 for some tips on how to manage people through each stage of the Emotional Journey. After you execute your management plan to move people emotionally forward, the cycle starts all over again with interviews, focus groups, and or/surveys to see how well it worked.

This cycle must happen on a pretty frequent basis (at least quarterly). Do not make the mistake of assuming you understand the system (i.e., causation) or expecting that the organization will always progress. It's not uncommon for teams that were previously at the Base of Commitment to slip back into the Gulf of Resistance. Or, for a team to somehow hydroplane

Table 3.1 Managing the Emotional Journey

Stage	Sample Feelings	Management Tips
Pre-Denial	Uncertain, skeptical	Ramp up the change management effort. Start running focused campaigns with clear messaging. Make it impossible for anyone in the organization to not know what's coming
Bridge of Denial	Unconcerned, happy[3]	Hold large- and small-group engagements to review data and evidence that the status quo is not sustainable. In an odd way, you must push them into the Gulf of Resistance
Gulf of Resistance	Exhausted, frustrated, angry	Hold small-group engagements to listen, understand, and uncover barriers and roadblocks that you can clear for them. Meet them where they are, but work with them on solutions instead of commiserating with them for extended periods of time
Base of Exploration	Concerned, optimistic, relieved, curious	Hold productive working group sessions to progress solutions and capture small wins. Be more encouraging than critical. Assure them that low performance is okay for now and that things will get better very soon
Summit of Commitment	Excited	Celebrate new levels of performance and reward the team for a job well done

over the Gulf of Resistance straight to the Base of Exploration. It's an unpredictable process, so maintain a healthy level of curiosity and do your analysis before you assume your way into a mess that shouldn't happen.

The Five Non-Delegable Responsibilities of Top Management

Nothing irritates me more than a leader who cannot make a decision. One of my favorite clients was a senior director at a well-known high-tech company named Linda. Technically, my client was Linda's boss, a vice president, but I have always considered Linda as my client because she was the only one around who could make a decision. I loved witnessing Linda go to work in a room of vice presidents and other senior directors. She would tell them what was going to happen, and nobody would oppose her. It was great. There are many things a leader can and should delegate; making important decisions is not one of them. In fact, there are five important areas of organizational leadership that top management *must* take full responsibility for:

- Strategic decision-making
- Strategy development
- Organizational design
- Innovation
- Employee inspiration and motivation

At your firm, what role does top management perform in each of these areas? Use this quick self-assessment to understand whether any adjustments should be made in this area (Table 3.2). Assign a score of 1 for every area/role combination (top management can play multiple roles in any given area). Use my MEDAL™ model (Figure 3.2) as a reference when completing this self-assessment.

Table 3.2 Non-Delegable Responsibilities Assessment

Focus Area	Manager	Expert	Doer	Approver	Leader
Strategic decision-making					
Strategy development					
Organizational design					
Innovation					
Inspiration and motivation					
Totals:					

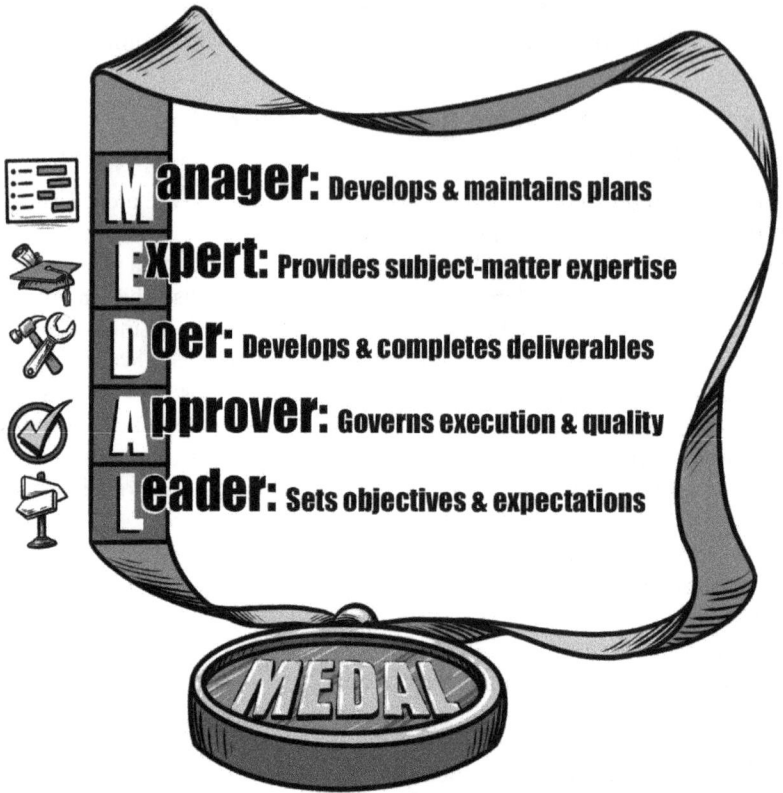

Figure 3.2 The MEDAL™ Model.

Scoring:

- If you scored anything but 5 in the Leader column, stop here and re-evaluate your governance
- If you scored 5 in the **Doer** column, congratulations! Your firm has all of its priorities in the right place
- If you scored 3–4 in the **Doer** column and at least 4 in the **Manager** column, your firm is pretty good at managing the priorities of top management. However, you should re-evaluate the areas where you are not Doers
- If you scored less than 3 in the **Doer** column and less than 4 in the **Manager** column, you should rebalance your priorities as a top management team; you are probably delegating more than you should

Using the MEDAL™ Model to clarify roles and responsibilities:

- **Manager:** Develops and maintains plans for achieving objectives and deliverables. Provides work direction for Doers and holds them accountable for execution. Adjusts plans, resources, schedules, etc. to ensure deliverables are completed on time and within budget
- **Expert:** Provides advice as needed to the team, based on subject matter expertise. Does not directly progress deliverables, but may assist Doers by way of templates, facilitation, instruction, etc. Experts cannot constrain execution; however, they may advise Approvers who can
- **Doer:** Works with other Doers to develop and complete deliverables. Takes work direction from the Manager, receives help and advice from Experts, and meets conditions specified by Approvers. May make tactical decisions regarding deliverables when under an autonomous philosophy
- **Approver:** Controls/governs the execution of the deliverables to ensure quality and fitness of purpose. Clarifies the conditions that must or should be met for objectives and deliverables to be considered successful. Protects the interests of the invested stakeholders
- **Leader:** Clarifies direction, objectives, expectations, and guidelines. Monitors the environment and adjusts course when necessary. Makes key decisions that affect the outcome. Motivates and inspires team members with incentives and rewards

The development of your organization's strategy cannot be delegated! Your strategy provides the fundamental chassis that supports every significant decision your firm makes regarding its place, position, and role on the competitive playing field. This is not to be left in the hands of anyone but top management. Leaders sometimes feel like they can delegate the heavy lifting to another function (e.g., Corporate Strategy and Planning) and reserve their energy for Leader and maybe Approver responsibilities. This is a huge mistake. Top management must be hands-on in the development of the strategy to fully understand and appreciate the nuances of their strategic decisions.

Similarly, the organization's design cannot be delegated to HR (Human Resources) or any other function. Proper organizational design takes craftsmanship and very intentional placement and balance of interlocking elements that are incredibly difficult to steady, like a baby's mobile.

It's more than just drawing boxes on an org chart; it is designing a complex system of formal and informal reporting lines, workflows, governance, communities, talent, etc. that all fits perfectly together to support the firm's strategy. Top management will definitely need help, but they need to get their hands dirty as well.

Innovation is a key focus area that, if ignored, will certainly be the demise of any organization. If you don't grow, you die, and you cannot grow without innovating at some point. Of course, in a precocious organization, innovation is its oxygen. Delegating innovation in a precocious firm is like trusting someone else to provide the air you breathe. It's absurd! I was helping a high-tech firm redesign its organization some years ago, and its current-state design had innovation bundled with a basket of other random capabilities and shoved into a group that had too many initials to remember (a telltale sign of an "other" group). Bad move; this was one of the first things we fixed.

Finally, the buck stops with top management when it comes to keeping the workforce inspired and motivated. Motivational speakers are fun to listen to, but they won't keep your workforce motivated all year long. I have been in several situations where the employees manage to succeed *despite* top leaders, especially when they know their leader(s) will be moving on in a few years. Leaders tend to delegate inspiration, motivation, and all this other "touchy-feely" stuff to HR, because that's apparently their job. Not really. HR should help facilitate the process, but top management must own the overall morale of the firm.

Facing Your Fears and Making the Commitment

Understanding the convergent opportunity discussed in Chapter 2 is one thing, but as you review the full depth of the opportunity, how do you feel? As we discussed earlier, the logical brain and the emotional brain need to be in sync before you can lead anyone through a transformational change. If you feel nervous, anxious, or doubtful about the opportunity, it will emanate out to your team and ultimately the workforce when you address them.

A leader must move themselves emotionally to the Summit of Commitment before asking their followers to join them on the transformational journey and then maintain their composure throughout the entire metamorphosis. It is not easy to keep cool under pressure, but here are 12 techniques to help regulate your emotions through this difficult personal and professional experience:

- Learn the language of emotions. Study the emotion wheel and practice pinpointing exact emotions within yourself and others

- Talk with yourself about your emotions when you are feeling them (out loud if it's safe). What is the exact label for this emotion and why am I feeling this way?
- Avoid situations that you know will trigger you
- Practice reframing or re-interpreting a situation when you feel triggered
- Get at least 7 hours of sleep every night
- Meditate daily for 10 minutes
- Exercise at least three times per week
- Routinely talk with people you trust about your thoughts and feelings
- Take time every day to get some fresh air and connect with nature
- Do what you absolutely love to do at least two to three times a week
- Spend time with your kids and/or pet(s)
- Be kind to your spouse or significant other

Know and Grow

Logic and emotions are more physiologically connected than most people realize. There are three areas of the brain that involve emotion regulation: The PFC (pre-frontal cortex), Amygdala, and Insula.

When a threat is sensed, the Amygdala fires a signal to the Insula, which monitors your organs and their physical response to the threat. All of this is regulated by your PFC, which is (hopefully) deciding how to respond.

Your ability to regulate emotions depends on the strength and health of your PFC, so take care of that thing!

It is difficult to manage the emotional side of leadership alone, and I do not advise it. You and your Guiding Coalition will steer the organization to its next destination, but who is going to steer you? There are three types of counselors that I recommend adding to your inner circle to help you be the best leader for your people: Coach, Advisor, and Therapist. Collectively, they are what I call your **Executive Mental Team** (EMT).

An **Executive Coach** can help you generate insights to resolve troubling or difficult issues. They are quite skilled at facilitating "aha" moments, but strictly speaking, they will not offer advice or opinions based on their own education or life experiences. That is why you need an Advisor.

Your **Trusted Advisor** should be next to your side at all times, seeing what you see and hearing what you hear. This is someone you trust for advice, who has skills, education, and life experiences that are valuable to your circumstances. They are typically seasoned leaders and/or management consultants like me who have already encountered similar circumstances in their past. They are great to collaborate with as they often contribute new insights and perspectives that you would not otherwise have access to.[4]

Finally, a **Licensed Psychotherapist** should be on call to help you with deeper psychological issues. They are good for helping you understand who you are and why you behave the way you behave.[5]

Your EMT will help you in many areas, the most important of which, at this stage, is an emotional commitment to the culture of your organization. As Table 3.3 illustrates, your commitment to culture affects every opportunity discussed in Chapter 2 and has a direct line of sight to your competitive advantage (see Figure 3.3)

Leadership is not as easy as it seems. There are highs and lows, but it's important to navigate the ups and downs of life and leadership with grace and resilience. Once you can look at yourself in the mirror and honestly say that you are *committed* to your culture, your people, and the journey ahead, then it is time to get started on the strategy.

Table 3.3 How Each Opportunity Involves a Commitment to Culture

Opportunity	Cultural Commitment	Top Management's Roles (MEDAL)
The opportunity to grow exponentially, catapulting the organization into a new level of strategic measures (revenues, costs, profits, etc.) and build much-needed capabilities to ease relentless market demands	A commitment to building capabilities that support a culture of innovation	Leader, Doer
The opportunity to build and continually nurture a thriving community of skilled workers who love coming to work to do their best work, while simultaneously unlocking precious human creativity and commercializing it for an unbeatable competitive advantage	A commitment to put people first when deciding where to allocate valuable resources	Leader, Approver
The opportunity to effortlessly attract and retain the best people in the talent pool that match clearly defined best-fit personas	A commitment to excel at attracting and retaining the people best suited for your organization	Leader, Approver

(Continued)

Table 3.3 (Continued)

Opportunity	Cultural Commitment	Top Management's Roles (MEDAL)
The opportunity to build a psychologically safe environment where people express their thoughts and feelings without fear of any negative consequences, including normative sanctions from their peers	A commitment to defend open and honest communication and eradicate any fear of negative consequences of any sort	Leader, Approver, Doer
The opportunity to master hybrid working environments that transcend the limitations of physical boundaries and maximize organizational performance through deliberate application of collocated teaming	A commitment to crack the code on hybrid work in a way that creates an authentic win–win for everybody	Leader, Approver

Figure 3.3 Line of Sight from Commitment to Culture to Unassailable Competitive Advantage.

Putting It into Practice

The journey of overcoming your own emotional roadblocks unveils a valuable treasure that will help you connect with your leaders, your workforce, and everyone invested in your success. It is time to express your ideals and personal convictions in a way that will viscerally resonate with everyone involved. Use the following guidelines to create your *Clarion Call*, a compelling message to inspire and motivate the masses when the time arrives:

1 Leverage the opportunity frame from the last chapter to communicate your purpose and (current) vision of the future in simple, clear terms
2 Develop a vivid story or metaphor that gives your vision context and credibility
3 Explain why it is so important to achieve your vision. Explain why it is important to you, your customers, your suppliers, your investors, and most importantly your workforce
4 Communicate your personal convictions about the purpose, vision, and transformation. Leverage insights from the work you did in this chapter to explain your initial fears and anxieties and how you overcame them
5 Describe two or three actions people (e.g., your employees) can take as they embark on the transformational journey
6 Describe all the personal commitments that you have made (including the ones in this chapter) and the specific actions you will take to personally support your people. Make one or two promises that you will unwaveringly fulfill
7 Articulate all of these elements into a well-crafted, stately letter: suitable for a State of the Union address
8 Read it out loud to yourself. How does it make you feel? Do you believe it? Are you committed? If not, you still have some work to do on yourself before you engage with anyone else. The worst thing to do at this stage is to come across inauthentically
9 Work with everyone on your Leadership Team or Guiding Coalition to complete their own personal Clarion Call that specifically addresses the people they will influence the most

Executive Debrief

- If a strategy fails, 80% of the time it is due to implementation, and most implementations fail for emotional reasons (not logical)
- When emotions get the best of people during a difficult transformation, they typically look for another job

- A hyper-growth strategy in a precocious organization carries a high risk of cannibalizing the human ingenuity that fuels its competitive advantage
- The Emotional Journey (often referred to as the Change Curve) that most people traverse during times of difficult change resembles the grieving process. It generally involves four stages: denial, resistance, exploration, and commitment
- The Emotional Journey is a human process that is neither avoidable nor predictable in progression
- The five non-delegable responsibilities of top management are: strategic decision-making, strategy development, organizational design, innovation, and inspiration/motivation
- A leader must move themselves emotionally to commitment before asking their followers to join them on a transformational journey
- To help you with the mental and emotional side of leadership, it is best to assemble an Executive Mental Team (EMT) consisting of: an Executive Coach, a Trusted Advisor, and a Licensed Psychotherapist
- Every element of the hyper-growth opportunity for a precocious organization has a cultural commitment that must translate to personal convictions before engaging the workforce on a transformational journey

Notes

1 For another great metaphorical treatment of change management, read "Switch," by Chip Heath and Dan Heath (2010). In it, they use an elephant and a driver to represent emotions and logic, respectively. It is similar to my racehorse/jockey metaphor; however, there are subtle nuances that make equine athletes a bit more appropriate for our purposes.
2 You will often see the change curve depicted with an overlay of the original stages from the Kübler-Ross model.
3 A feeling of happiness during very early stages of the transformation will likely indicate denial; however, during later stages of the transformation, happiness might signal exploration. Unfortunately, this is not the only feeling that is very contextual and prone to misinterpretation.
4 It is not uncommon to find one person who fills the role of both Executive Coach and Advisor. I have clients who have hired me to play this dual role, and it is quite effective.
5 The exciting and emerging field of Positive Psychology is producing licensed specialists that can help you be the best leader you can possibly be, regardless of your current mental health.

Bibliography

Heath, C., & Heath, D. (2010). *Switch: How to change things when change is hard*. Crown Publishing Group.
Kübler-Ross, E. (1969). *On death and dying*. Macmillan.

Prosci. (2024, November 1). *Applying the Kubler-Ross change curve to change management*. Prosci. Retrieved from https://www.prosci.com/blog/kubler-ross-model-change-management

Rock, D., & Ringleb, A. H. (2013). *Handbook of neuro leadership*. CreateSpace Independent Publishing Platform.

Seligman, M. E. P. (2002). *Authentic happiness: Using the new positive psychology to realize your potential for lasting fulfillment*. Free Press.

Attempting the Adamant Triad of Strategy, Organizational Design, and Innovation

The first "real" iteration of any iterative effort is always fun, exciting, and a little bit nerve-wracking due to the inherent newness and uncertainty of it all; the next three chapters will have the same effect. There are a lot of novelties to process: concepts, models, and approaches; many of which you will see for the first time.[1] To add, true to Agile philosophy, we cannot keep this iteration purely conceptual. We will actually develop your first *viable* alternative to realize the riches attached to the fantastic opportunity explored in Iteration Zero—what an Agilist calls a Minimum Viable Product (MVP). If that doesn't generate a bit of nervous energy, I would check your pulse.

More specifically, we are going to evolve the exploration of our opportunity into three areas that I collectively call the *Adamant Triad*: Strategy, Organizational Design, and Innovation. Each of these elements has been explored in detail for decades; however, the fusion of the three, forged from adamant by none other than Hephaestus himself, has never been considered the way it is presented here. Like the shield of Aegis, wielded first by Zeus and then by his daughter Athena, the Adamant Triad is divine, indestructible, and symbolic of strategic strength and prowess. It forms the basis for addressing the strategic opportunity, once framed. We will iterate three times over the Adamant Triad before we call it ready; this part of the book is our first attempt.

Using the language of *attempt* is very intentional. One of those "new" things you will learn in the next chapter, worth bringing forward to introduce now, is the principle of setting low expectations when producing an MVP out of your first iteration. Our MVP, by definition, will be *viable*, but it will also be the bare *minimum*. Even with the luxury of having an Iteration Zero to get situated, your first *product* must be basic, barely meeting the minimum requirements for being viable. This is a very uncomfortable place for smart, precocious people who shudder at the thought of submitting anything less than exceptional. Bear this in mind as you internally wrestle with this concept, as your leadership will be important when this

DOI: 10.4324/9781003518181-6

situation inevitably lands on your team. The three-iteration progression discussed a little later is attempt, accelerate, *and then* arrive. If your goal is to arrive on your first shot, you defeat the whole purpose of iteration.

So, in this part of the book, just like every first iteration I have been through (there have been a lot), you will do more learning than doing— however, we must do a non-zero amount of *doing* to stay true to the philosophy. We will cover four out of your five non-delegable responsibilities (see Chapter 3), saving the best (motivation and inspiration) for later after we take a first pass at the fundamentals. Furthermore, we will extend the great work that we have done so far in framing the opportunity into an adamant-clad compass for navigating the treacherous, uncharted waters ahead.

I love the smell of fresh strategy in the morning, so let's get this iteration started!

Note

1 Most of what is presented in this chapter is original, based on my experiences in the trenches. So, unless you know me personally or have otherwise come across my work somewhere, prepare your brain to receive a lot of brand-new information.

Chapter 4

The Heart of a General

What a Human-Centered Hyper-Growth Strategy Looks Like

What a Strategy Is, and What It Is Not

If you just picked up this book, scanned the contents, and then jumped straight to this chapter because you simply want a straight definition of what a strategy is, I don't blame you. Strategy is—bar none—the most ambiguous concept in leadership and management circles. Unfortunately, there is little agreement among leaders, and all the gurus they listen to, as to what exactly a strategy is. To make matters worse, any dictionary you pick up will have a horrible definition of the word, implying that it has something to do with planning, which it definitely does not.

So, let's get straight to the point: An organization's *strategy* is the framework that guides decisions about what it is and where it is going (Tregoe & Zimmerman, 1980). This is how I learned it from Alan Weiss, one of the most brilliant strategists and management consultants that I have ever personally met, and how he learned it from Ben Tregoe, co-founder of Kepner-Tregoe, when Alan was cutting his teeth as a consultant (Weiss, 2023). I come from a long lineage of strategists who believe strategy is all about the *what* and nothing about the *how;* I exhort you to do the same.

How I manifest a strategic framework is based on my own experience in developing organizational strategies for clients; however, I am grateful for having met Alan and learning from him, before making the mistakes that so many others have (and still do), because their paradigm is ineffective. If you start bringing the *how* into strategy development, not only are you wasting your energy on something that should be delegated to lower levels of the organization, but you also run the great risk of tactics influencing your strategy; that's the cart leading the horse.

A strategy is not needed for how to get from here to where you want to be; that's what planning is for. Instead, a strategy is critically important for guiding the decisions that fundamentally affect what the organization is and where the organization should be going at any point in time. If an organization does long-term planning without the framework of a strategy

DOI: 10.4324/9781003518181-7

to guide decision-making,[1] it will likely end up with a good plan for going to the wrong place. And if top leadership is involved in that process, it is a gross waste of their time and energy. Remember from Chapter 3 that top leaders are responsible for developing the organization's strategy and making strategic decisions to keep the organization on its intended course. There is nothing mentioned in that list about planning—even long-term planning.

Think about your natural process[2] for "planning" a vacation. You do not just book tickets for the first destination that comes to mind. Even if you are spontaneous, there is a quick process before you book tickets that engages your prefrontal cortex (PFC)—your executive brain—for a bit of insight generation, decision-making, and problem solving. Given a field of seemingly infinite places to go on vacation, you must have some mental framework in place that rules out Antarctica and puts Hawai'i in as a contender. Now, you haven't decided on Hawai'i, but there is some internal rule that tells you that the frigid conditions of Antarctica do not fit within your parameters for a nice vacation, and the warm trade winds of Hawai'i do. This is what a strategy does. Whether you are developing a plan or executing a plan that has already been developed, your strategy helps you make decisions that keep you consistent with your organization's intended state of being and/or its current understanding of where it wants to go.

As such, the central theme of the strategic framework that I submit for your consideration in this chapter is *guidance*. Your objective in strategic development is to build a frame that guides the most important decisions that impact the organization. And, if you read Chapter 2, that should sound familiar; this is no accident. Framing is one of the most valuable and useful skills a leader can learn. It clarifies intent while leaving adequate space for autonomy and progressive elaboration of emergent solutions. When complete, your organization's strategy is the critical coupling between your opportunity and your plan for seizing its treasure.

Building Your Strategic Framework

Your organization's strategy is essentially a framework. On occasion, I doff my red tie, don my go-to jeans and favorite T, and switch gears into serious data scientist mode. When that happens, it is nice to have frameworks like PyTorch, TensorFlow, or even something as fundamental as Pandas to help me quickly build a deep learning machine. Sure, I could build one from scratch,[3] but why would I? Using PyTorch, I can build a fully functional neural network with just a few lines of code. Building the same functionality from scratch would take several thousand lines of code, and as good as I am, I am humble enough to know my code would not be as stable or reliable as a simple program built using PyTorch. This is what a strategy,

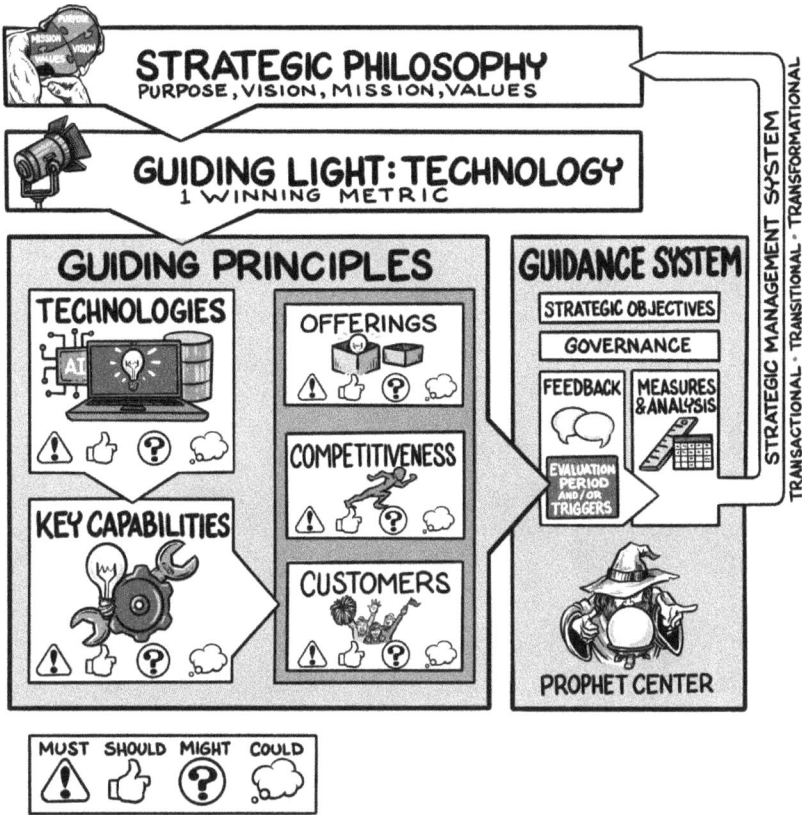

Figure 4.1 The Strategic Framework.

or strategic framework, does for your organization. Once in place, it geo-metrically accelerates decision-making at all levels of the organization, thereby having a profound effect on the pace of emergence and overall quality of your future organization.

Once completed, all the elements of your strategy will have a logical re-lationship (see Figure 4.1). Up until this point we have primarily focused on systems that are *complex (unordered)* like the business environment that our opportunity is cradled in. However, our strategic system, if designed properly, is not. It is an *ordered* system that vacillates between *complicated* and *simple* (see Figure 4.2). When your Strategic Philosophy changes, your strategic system is *complicated.* A reliable cause-and-effect relationship ex-ists between the elements; however, you don't know what it is—yet. As you actively work within your strategic system and intentionally move your system from *complicated* to *simple*, these relationships will surface.

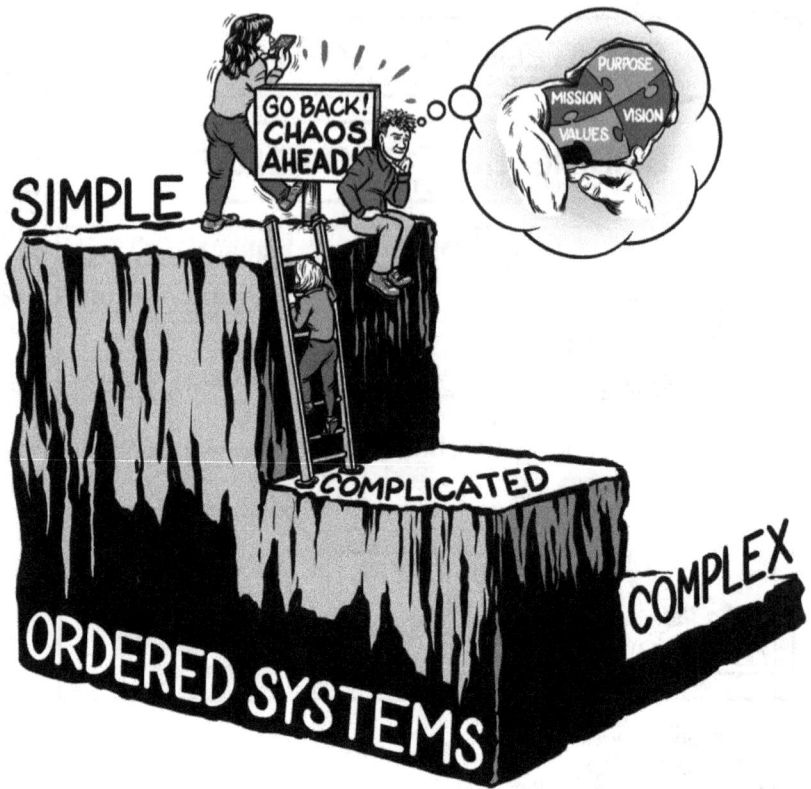

Figure 4.2 The Cynefin Framework with a Focus on Ordered Systems.

Once you tune your system to the point where you can reliably predict the effects of moving one or more strategic elements, you are operating squarely within a *simple* system. When your Strategic Philosophy changes again, the cycle starts over.

Illuminating the path to your vision is your Guiding Light.[4] Your organization's Guiding Light provides the most fundamental and foundational guidance for what your organization is and where your organization is going—what the Preamble does for the U.S. Constitution. In strategy, there are several pre-defined Guiding Lights to choose from, the most common of which are *Products Offered* and *Market Needs*. A *Products Offered* company will find customers to buy its chosen products, and a *Market Needs* company will build products to fulfill its chosen markets' needs. In almost all cases, a precocious organization has a different variety of Guiding Light, called *Technology*. Technology, in this context, refers to a confidential body of knowledge (i.e., intellectual property) and the organizational capability required to capitalize on it. For this book, it is not worth cataloging and evaluating the appropriateness of each Guiding Light; it has been handed to you by dint of your situation—your Guiding Light is *Technology*.

Your Guiding Light shapes Guiding Principles in five distinct areas: Customers, Offerings, Competitiveness, Org Capabilities, and Technologies (e.g., IT systems). Your strategy defines neither your customers nor your market offerings; that comes later when you build your go-to-market plan.[5] In the same way your Guiding Light shapes your Guiding Principles, your Guiding Principles shape the development of downstream efforts where customers, offerings, offering-specific competitiveness, etc. are identified and decided upon.

A simple tool that I have developed and use frequently to help structure any type of guidance is MSmc.[6]

How to use MSmc (must, should, might, could) to provide guidance

Agree with those receiving guidance that the following words will be used to clarify intent:

- What **must** be true (do not violate this principle)
- What **should** be true (there better be a really good reason for violating this principle)
- What **might** be true, (use your best judgment, apply the principle if it makes sense)
- What **could** be true (not expecting this to be true, but if it is, that's terrific)

Simply articulate three to eight Guiding Principles for each of the five areas (Customers, Offerings, Competitiveness, Org Capabilities, and Technologies), using MSmc language (e.g., "we *must* develop our people to within an inch of their lives"). We will dig deeper into this process later in the chapter when we build our Minimum Viable Product (MVP) strategy.

Your Guiding Principles also shape the development of your Guidance System. This is where development is more concrete. Unlike Guiding Principles, which are abstract, the elements of your Guidance System serve as a tangible support system for decision-making. Once clear Strategic Objectives are established, a Feedback Mechanism must be built for probing and calibrating targets (e.g., external and internal benchmarking), a Measurement and Analysis System must be built for sensing, analyzing, and monitoring performance (e.g., Balanced Scorecard), and an omniscient Prophet Center[7] (e.g., Organizational GPT) must be established to serve as a source of truth and insight for all who seek it. Finally, Governance must be clearly documented to serve as the policy of record for who makes decisions and under what circumstances.

The last component of your strategy is your Strategic Management System, which is influenced by your Guidance System. Your Strategic Management System is principally the high-level processes by which you continually evaluate and manage different degrees of change to your strategy: transitional, transactional, and transformational. This process architecture is cleanly and intentionally aligned with the three types of organizational change discussed in Chapter 2.

We covered a lot here; if you sense some gaps in understanding, that is normal. Remember, we are making our first *attempt* at building a brand-new strategic framework—keep your expectations low for now, it will make more sense as we progress through this book.

Understanding the Leader's Role in Strategy

Developing your organization's strategy is one of your five non-delegable responsibilities, so it behooves us to delve into your role, responsibilities, and pathos in this space. Over the historical landscape of strategies, *organizational* strategy is a relative newcomer, pulling many insights from military strategy, which has been around for thousands of years. So, when discussing the more technical aspects of strategy, like the Strategic Framework, it is useful to draw on more contemporary concepts, resources, and experiences. However, the heart of strategy is more primitive and traceable to its earlier evolutionary forms.

Organizational strategy and military strategy are two different species of the same genus. They are different in obvious ways; however, leadership is one area where we see very strong similarities—a gene more characteristic of the genus than any given species. Regardless of the type of strategy, strong leadership and decisiveness are crucial to the success of the mission. This takes heart. And whether you are leading a precocious high-tech firm into a hyper-growth transformation or the U.S. Third Army into the Battle of the Bulge, to succeed, you must have the heart of a military general.

On December 16, 1944 (during World War II), the Germans successfully created a "bulge" in Allied lines with a successful surprise attack that grounded our air forces and pinned down our 101st Airborne Division in the town of Bastogne, Belgium. We were able to hold our position, but we were surrounded, and it was not looking good. Three days later, General George S. Patton, leader of the U.S. Third Army, met with General Dwight D. Eisenhower, Supreme Commander of the Allied Expeditionary Force, to propose a swift and aggressive counterassault on Bastogne to relieve our troops. It would require a rapid pivot from the Third Army's current position under the same terrible weather conditions that gave the Germans their initial advantage of a surprise attack. The pace was fierce, and the conditions were grueling. Nonetheless, on December 26, just ten days after the Battle of the Bulge started, our Third Army penetrated the German encirclement and saved our troops from what would have been an almost certain demise. This was an inflection point in the German advance; they never recovered from it.

The bravery and courage that it took for every soldier in the Third Army to execute this move is awe inspiring—this is the heart of a soldier. However, the leadership that General Patton displayed under these conditions is profound—this is the heart of a general. Fortunately for you, the stakes are much lower, but that does not mean your heart should be any different. Leadership is a characteristic of the genus, not the species. All great leaders are cut from the same cloth, regardless of the type of strategy they are responsible for.

I have been around the world and worked with hundreds of leaders, and yet some of the best leaders I have ever met in my life, I met while serving in the U.S. Army. I was just a kid back then, barely 17, and intentionally way out of my element. I was stationed in Erlangen, Germany, from 1987 to 1989 as a Cavalry Scout in the 1st of the 35th Armored Division. That was back when "the wall" was a real thing and East Germany was a real threat. Even though we were in peace time, our job had very serious implications. The folklore was, if war actually broke out between East and West Germany, our estimated lifespan was about six seconds. We trusted our leaders with our lives, and they were very good leaders.

Like most aspects of leadership, once you get the pathos right, the rest easily falls into place. Your role in strategy development is chief strategist (a hands-on role), and your responsibility is to lead your people to fulfill the organization's purpose, uphold its values, and activate its mission to arrive at a better place. It is very difficult to lead an organization through a transformation, especially a hyper-growth transformation. As you build your strategy, never lose sight of what you are asking your troops to do and the bravery and courage you must muster to lead them to victory.

A Simple Three-Iteration Methodology

Before we attempt the MVP for our strategy, let's revisit our overall approach to developing our Adamant Triad of strategy, organizational design, and innovation. Over the years, I have found iteration to be a valuable alternative to the more rigid "phase-gate" approaches that were emphasized prior to the arrival of the Agile methodologies and philosophies of the 1990s. When Agile showed up, it needed a useful metaphor to compare itself to, so it started propagating the idea of the traditional approach as a "waterfall." Truth be told, the early pundits of Agile methodologies went a little extreme in their characterization of how we developed software prior to Agile; we always did some form of iteration, even within the strictest of Software Development Lifecycle Management (SDLC) methods, and in some areas, people were doing fairly aggressive iterative development.[8]

Iteration is not a panacea, though. Contrary to what many Agilists would have you believe, iterative development is not categorically better than phase-gate development. It works well in software development because the cost of change is minimal, given the right mindset. However, in the physical world, the cost of change can be very significant, regardless of your mindset. If you are three-quarters of the way done building a house and you decide you want a completely different floor plan, that will cost hard dollars, no two ways about it. I have been at many companies that have tried to "Go Agile" with disastrous results.

Iteration should be used when there is very little material cost in changing or even completely revamping a potential solution. We talked earlier about creating an MVP solution, which comes with the assumption that once completed, we will evaluate whether it is good enough or whether we will spend another iteration trying to come up with something better. In reality, most MVPs are improved upon—the product is acceptable, but with a little more functionality, it would be better. That is not always the case, though. In some circumstances, you actually throw everything out and start over, carrying forward whatever lessons you can into the next iteration. So, if you are working with the type of solution that has unavoidable and unpleasant consequences (other than emotional) for changing direction, then you should not use iterative development. Fortunately for us, the Adamant Triad is meaningful, but at the end of the day, the hard cost of rework is negligible.

After a few decades of doing iterative development under a variety of circumstances for a variety of clients, a pattern emerged that inspired me to create a simple three-iteration methodology called AAA: Attempt, Accelerate, Arrive (see Figure 4.3).

My insight was that in most *legitimate*[9] iterative development projects, you can reach 80% of the value of a solution in only three iterations. And thanks to the wisdom of an Italian named Vilfredo Pareto, who gave us the 80/20 rule, it all made sense. It is not uncommon to see an iterative development project last for 12–15 iterations or more. And yet, most of the value of a solution is usually available after the third iteration.

The AAA Methodology also helps in setting expectations, especially for the first iteration which is usually where things unfortunately go off track. In the Attempt iteration, you should only expect to deliver an MVP that is 10%–20% of what the perfect solution would be. It's *viable*, but not very

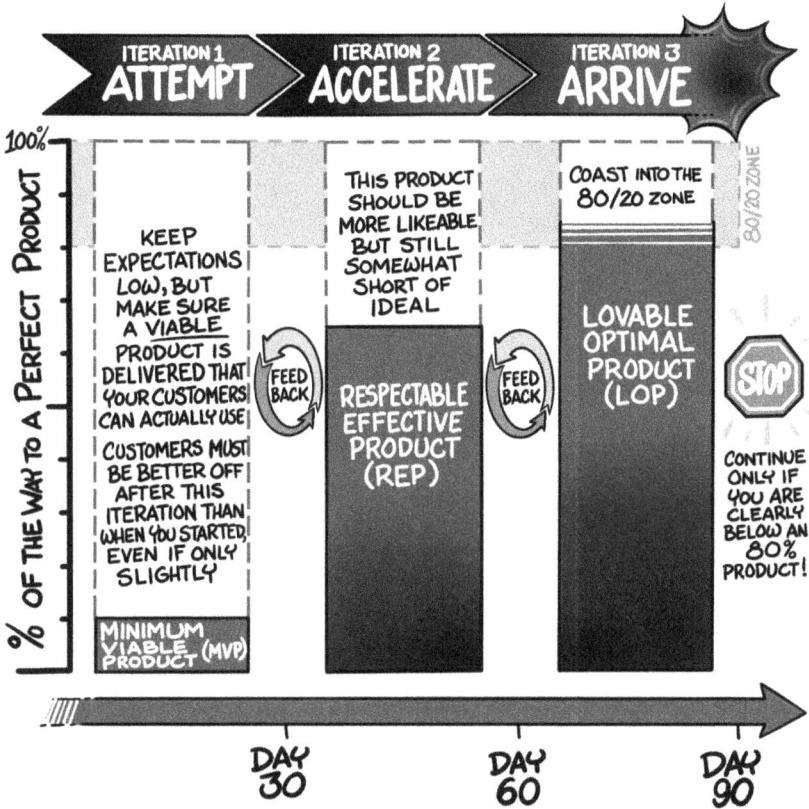

Figure 4.3 The AAA Methodology.

desirable. Desirability is not the goal for the first iteration! Viability *and desirability* are too much to handle for one iteration.

If done properly, the solution usually takes off in the Accelerate iteration. That is usually when the biggest gaps in learning are closed because it is the first time the team gets valuable feedback about a tangible solution (i.e., the MVP). It usually takes three shots for a soldier to calibrate their M-16 rifle. For the first shot, they do the best they can, but it won't hit the bullseye; there are too many variables. However, that first shot tells them a lot about how to adjust their sight. Provided they have good breath and body control, the second shot will be very close to the bullseye, if not dead-on. The third shot is either very fine-tuning or, in most cases, confirmation that their sight is good.

The third and last iteration should be a coast into 80/20 territory: however, not perfunctory. It is needed to take you over the edge, well into the desired solution. But this should be an easy walk, adding just enough value for you to feel confident and proud about your solution. Bear in mind that we must avoid the path to perfection; this is a very costly path with very little value. That's why, once we comfortably arrive in Pareto land, it is time to fold up our tents and call it a success.

Know and Grow

The **Pareto Principle** (80/20 rule) states that 80% of the effects (outputs) of a systemic relationship come from 20% of the causes (inputs). Remember that, although related, inputs and outputs are two different things. Unfortunately, the two sides of the ratio (20 and 80) deceptively add up to 100, which often leads to a conceptual misunderstanding. The Pareto Principle is not about dividing the whole of anything into an 80% part and a 20% part. It is about leveraging the few (20%) inputs that produce the lion's share (80%) of the overall value

Using Key Decisions to Drive Strategy Development

Decisions, Decisions; Decisions!

I have never seen more chaos created than in situations where top leadership does not make strategic decisions. It is the one area where I still find it difficult to regulate my own emotions, usually ending in more martinis than meditations. Strategic decision-making is a critical and non-delegable responsibility of top management because the impact of not making these decisions creates chaos, stagnation, and malaise, and the high consequences of making the wrong decisions make them inappropriate for lower levels of management. I have seen three types of mistakes top leaders make when it comes to strategic decision-making: (1) not clearly understanding the strategic decisions that need to be made; (2) not making them when they must be made; (3) delegating them to lower levels of management only to overturn them when they do not like the decision. Let's tackle the first one here; the others are principally emotional.

I espouse the idea of not only identifying strategic decisions upfront but also subsequently using them to pull your strategic implementation forward. All implementation activity must be in support of the next set of strategic decision(s) to be made. This is what I call DDM (Decision-Driven Management). In the same way a steam engine pulls the cars behind it along the railroad tracks, your strategic decisions should pull your objectives and deliverables through the transformational journey to your ultimate destination. Unfortunately, since we are working within a complex business environment, we must lay tracks ahead of us while the train is moving.

The *complex* business environment that we are in forces us to take a *probe–sense–respond* approach to management (see Figure 2.2). So, instead of contemplating the more intuitive phase-gate decisions that we would make in an ordered system, we must think about the strategic decisions required for each iteration of this complex decision-making cycle.[10] Here is a list of ten strategic decisions I recommend for starters (note the intentional use of MSmc to succinctly clarify some of the decisions):

- *Should* our Feedback System be more effective in probing our business environment?
- *Should* our Measurement and Analysis System be more effective in sensing and analyzing our business environment?
- Have we developed MSmc guidance based on the analysis from our Measurement and Analysis system (i.e., how we will respond)?
- Are we ready to execute plans, based on the analysis from our Measurement and Analysis System?
- Do our people fully understand our Strategic Philosophy?
- Are our people progressing through their Emotional Journey?
- Are we doing everything we can to retain our best people?
- Do we have enough small wins? Are we leveraging them into larger wins?
- Have we arrived at our ultimate destination, or *must* we keep going?
- Does our strategic system feel too simple and comfortable? *Should* we revisit our vision and the other elements of our Strategic Philosophy?

Hopefully, that last bullet jumps out as particularly interesting. Although our business environment is unordered (i.e., complex), your strategic system is ordered (see Figure 4.2). You should actively manage your strategic system from *complicated* (*sense–analyze–respond*) to *simple* (*sense–categorize–respond*) until it feels *too simple*. This is a warning sign that you may be floating too close to the falls that will hurl you into a *chaotic* system. Complacency is a strong signal to re-evaluate your vision and the other elements of your Strategic Philosophy that are connected to it, before your strategy crashes on the rocks of chaos.

DDM works well on a smaller scale to develop your Adamant Triad before we launch into the gauntlet. As we work through the first ten chapters of this book to arrive at a lovable, optimal Adamant Triad, consider the following key decisions:

At the end of Iteration Zero:

- Am I personally committed and emotionally prepared to make this change?
- Do we have the Opportunity Frame that we *should* move forward with?
- Do we have the leaders and influencers that we *must* have on our Strategic Leadership Team?
- *Should* we move forward with the first iteration?

At the end of Attempt, when we deliver an MVP:

- Have we developed an Adamant Triad that we *could* use (regardless of how much we like it), without another iteration of development?
- Have we captured valuable feedback that we *should* apply to the next iteration?
- *Should* we move forward with another iteration?

At the end of Accelerate, when we deliver a Respectable Effective Product (REP):

- Have we applied feedback from the last iteration to develop a significantly better Adamant Triad?
- Do we feel like we are about 60%–70% of the way to a perfect Adamant Triad?
- Have we developed an Adamant Triad that we *might* use, without another iteration of development?
- Have we captured additional feedback that we *should* apply to the next iteration?
- *Should* we move forward with another iteration?

At the end of Arrive, when we deliver a Lovable Optimal Product (LOP):

- Have we applied feedback from the last iteration to develop a really lovable Adamant Triad?
- Do we feel like we are at least 80% of the way to a perfect Adamant Triad?
- Have we developed the Adamant Triad that we *should* use?
- Is everyone on our Strategic Leadership Team aligned and committed to making this change?
- *Must* we move forward with another iteration?

This is not a complete list, but it's enough to get us started on the first draft of our strategy. Remember—low expectations for now. We have six more chapters to go before we land on an LOP.

Our First Attempt at Building a Strategy

We are going to assemble the strategy portion of our MVP rather quickly for three reasons. First and foremost, it is philosophical; M stands for *minimal*. Don't lose sight of that; it is an important concept that sometimes takes a while to sink in, especially for people conditioned to submitting only high-quality work. Second, if you have gone through the exercises in Iteration Zero, you already have a frame around your opportunity and a Strategic Philosophy, so you have a great head start. And finally, we are following DDM, so we are *only* doing the work necessary to support our end-of-iteration decisions.

I cannot overemphasize the importance of taking the shortest route to a viable solution during the Attempt iteration. I was called in to help the federal-facing division of a large high-tech company respond to a GSA (General Services Administration) request for all similar sales made to their commercial customers. The GSA is a way to centralize and simplify sales and contracting for many federal-facing organizations; however, they want to make sure you are offering the government the best deals, and if you do offer a commercial customer a better deal than the government, then you'd better have a good explanation as to why. Because some of these deals spanned across multiple divisions (products, services, training, etc.), each with its own sales database, the scope of the project was huge—we needed to connect all the relevant databases together, then sit a reporting engine on everything so that we could generate meaningful reports for the GSA.

Under my management, we took an Iteration Zero (three weeks) to get everything set up: databases, tools, etc. Then, we could have gone down the traditional route of building out connectors for the databases and setting up mock reports in the reporting engine; however, we only had three weeks for our first iteration, and there was zero chance we could get anything the federal division could actually use in that short amount of time if we went down the traditional path. So, I instructed our team members to hack their way through all the existing data in all the different databases, in a very focused and deliberate way, to pull out only the data that we needed. We then manually stitched it together in Excel using simple rules and hands-on guidance from someone in the federal division who was assigned to our team. In just three weeks, we had something valuable to provide to our customers in the federal division, and we were well-positioned to receive valuable feedback from them. They were blown away at how fast we delivered something useful and provided incredibly valuable insights (that first shot tells you a lot).

Wasabi Moment

A leader needs courage and bravery (the heart of a general) to iterate over a strategy three times (as opposed to big bang) and accept an undesirable (but viable) outcome for the **Attempt** iteration. Speed and feedback are far more important than quality at this point of development

Quickly run through the Strategic Framework (Figure 4.1) and write some bullet points under each section to clarify your own thinking; maybe even write a few paragraphs if the mood strikes you. You know your Guiding Light is Technology, so explain in your own words what that means to your organization: you will build products and services (offerings) and find markets that leverage the unique and proprietary technology that your organization creates. You already have at least one offering and a market that loves it, how else might you apply your technology to new offerings? Offerings are not just products and services, they include data, insights, and customer experiences. What kinds of data and insights will you provide with your technology? What about unique customer experiences? Remember, we are not trying to list out every customer, offering, etc. in our strategy, we are only trying to provide *guidance* (using the language of MSmc).

Clarify guidelines regarding competitive positioning (i.e., for your offerings) in the Competitiveness section. Not all offerings need to be Game-Changing, for some you might just want to be a *Leader*, or maybe even just *Competitive* (second quartile? third!?). Sometimes, non-competitive offerings are retained for various reasons (regulatory, legacy/brand, etc.); these are known as *Obligatory* offerings.

What are your guidelines around Org Capabilities? Which capabilities *must* be grown to succeed? What about Technologies? What *systems* must be bought or built to succeed?

Flesh out your Guidance System, but don't overanalyze it. You must establish some key Strategic Objectives for the organization; they will be the launching pad for your long- and short-term planning. And think about your requirements for a Measurement and Analysis System. This is one of those technologies (systems) that must be built. One important metric that you must determine is the One Winning Metric (OWM) that attaches to your Guiding Light. What is the **one** lagging indicator that will mean success for you? Does your Governance structure need to be revisited? What about your Prophet Center (i.e., Knowledge Base)? Will this be humans, artificial intelligence, or a combination of both[11]?

Finally, what are the high-level processes that drive your Strategic Management System? How often will you evaluate your strategy, and/or what will trigger an evaluation of your strategy? What are the processes for handling transitional, transactional, and transformational changes in your strategy (see Table 2.1)?

Put some meaningful thought into completing your first strategy; however, don't spend more than a few days—a week max. When done, you should have a document that you are eager to get feedback on!

Putting It into Practice

If you completed the last exercise, then you have already put a lot of theory into practice! Well done. If you did this in isolation, that is okay, but before you move forward, you will need to send it through a round of reviews with your Strategic Leadership Team (SLT)—but please do it quickly. If you and your SLT are anything like *every other* SLT that I have worked with, you will have over-engineered the design for your Guidance System. Don't feel bad, it happens to everyone. However, you cannot go for six months (or more) without a Guidance System for your strategy. So, once you and your SLT have the first draft of your strategy developed, conduct this **Bare Bones Workshop** on your Guidance System:

1. Assemble your SLT and a special Strategic Technology Team (STT) for a full-day workshop (or two half-day workshops), with the focus of designing a Guidance System for your Strategic Framework *that will be operational in three weeks*[12]
2. Divide into three teams to brainstorm the designs of a *simple* Feedback System, Measurement and Analysis System, and Prophet Center. Your SLT members are accountable for viability, and your STT members are accountable for feasibility (i.e., it can be built in three weeks or less)
3. Come back as a whole group to review and challenge each other. Is this a *bare bones* design, or is there *anything* we can pull out while still maintaining viability?
4. Do not stop stripping down the design until you are left with the bare bones *minimum* Guidance System that can be built in three weeks
5. Commit to working with your STT on future iterations of your Guidance System, until it is a Lovable Optimal Product (LOP)

This is a very challenging workshop that requires creativity and grit. Do not give up and resist all attempts at defeatism—yes, it can be done, and you will figure out a solution before the workshop is over.

Executive Debrief

- An organization's strategy is the framework which guides decisions about what it is and where it is going. It is all about the what and *nothing* about the how
- The Strategic Framework consists of: Strategic Philosophy, Guiding Light, Guiding Principles, Guidance System, and Strategic Management System
- Guiding Principles are best clarified using the language of *must, should, might, and could* (MSmc)
- Since Organizational Strategy has its roots in Military Strategy, lessons involving the heart of great leaders can be learned from great military generals, specifically the ones who physically led their troops into battle
- A useful three-iteration approach to management involves Attempt, Accelerate, and then Arrive (AAA). Hold very low expectations for the output of the Attempt iteration (albeit it must be *viable*)
- Decision-Driven Management (DDM) is an approach to management in which all work is driven by key decisions that are established upfront
- A Bare Bones Workshop may be necessary to build your first Strategic Guidance System

Notes

1 This happens more often than you might suspect, even in large companies. In fact, it is very common for a precocious organization to have nonexistent or very immature strategy development capabilities because they have not fully appreciated the need to build them.
2 David Allen (2001) does a nice job at explaining our "natural" or intrinsic planning process for achieving objectives, which is a bit different from how we are typically taught to build a plan. I find it's always better to work with your natural abilities than invent ways to intentionally circumvent them.
3 I actually have built a neural network from scratch. For the capstone course of my Software Engineering degree, I convinced my team to build a grass-roots graphical neural network using Windows C of all languages. It was pretty cool, but a lot of work to code and train a network that can only add two digits together. We received an A, so it was worth it.
4 Similar to what Tregoe (1980) calls a Driving Force and Weiss (2023) calls a Propelling Force.
5 Often referred to as a go-to-market *strategy* (the author sighs in exasperation). And you wonder why there is so much confusion in this area. For the love of Persephone, please help the cause and refrain from this terminology—it is a go-to-market *plan*.

6 I originally developed MSmc a long time ago as a priority-setting tool. Over time, I realized that it also serves well as a tool for helping leaders delegate authority and responsibilities.

7 Indeed, this is a play on the words "Profit Center." In Greek mythology, prophets like Tiresias were often consulted for their insights and foresight, as they were granted the gift of prophecy by the gods.

8 Rapid Application Development (RAD) showcased iterative development long before Agile became popular.

9 On many, many occasions I have seen waterfall projects packaged up into "iterations," so that they don't look like waterfall projects. This usually happens when a company is "Going Agile," so everything needs to look iterative, even when it is not. This is what we call "Faux Agile."

10 Unless you have a compelling reason to differ, I recommend a decision-making cycle of three months, or one quarter.

11 This is what I call a *Cybernetic Organization*, or CybOrg for short. You will read more about these in later chapters.

12 Hey, if my team could produce a GSA report in three weeks, you can produce a Guidance System in three weeks!

Bibliography

Allen, D. (2001). *Getting things done: The art of stress-free productivity*. Viking.

Tregoe, B. B., & Zimmerman, J. W. (1980). *Top management strategy: What it is and how to make it work*. Simon and Schuster.

Weiss, A. (2023). *Sentient strategy: How to create market-dominating strategies in turbulent economies*. Routledge.

Chapter 5

Form Follows Culture

The Architecture of a People-First Organization

Organizational Design: The Good, the Bad, and the Ugly

Org charts are the bane of my existence. Despite what many leaders believe, org charts are the *least* significant aspect of organizational design (OD) and should not enter your neural pathways until the very end of the design process. You can achieve 80% of the value of any organization's design without ever considering formal authority, let alone the org charts that represent it. For the accomplished OD professional, org charts are distractions that never fail to interfere with the most important work of OD, which is actually designing an organization that works effectively. I can walk into your organization today, rip out all its structure (i.e., formal reporting relationships), and develop a highly effective OD that has nothing to do with org charts—regardless of your strategy. And yet, *every single time* I engage with an organization that wants OD assistance, I encounter leaders who have a condition that I call Obsessive Restructuring Disorder (ORD)—a compulsive need to build new org charts. It's a widespread dysfunction that is truly out of control.

So, if OD is not building org charts, then what exactly is it? For our purposes, *Organizational Design* is a comprehensive set of plans, visuals, and specifications that guide the development and realignment of an organization. When I recently helped a global shipping and marine services company redesign its organization, they found far more value in understanding their fundamental operating model than building any org chart. Once we clarified their operating model, the org chart easily fell into place.

An organizational designer sets out with a comprehensive set of focus areas when approaching the design or realignment of an organization:

- Functionality (i.e., how well it supports the organization's strategy)
- Aesthetics and visual appeal (i.e., brand and image)

DOI: 10.4324/9781003518181-8

- Survivability (i.e., resilience, adaptability, flexibility, solvency)
- People's experience and well-being
- Competitive awareness and sensitivity
- Non-competitive stakeholder (e.g., Investors, Regulators) experience
- Sustainable development responsibilities (i.e., corporate and social responsibility)
- Application of industry (OD) best and emerging practices

The collection of these focus areas will manifest into various assessments, diagrams, detailed specifications, and implementation plans. Technically, OD stops at the design and planning phase; however, it is not uncommon to utilize the OD team in the deployment of the design and subsequent *implementation* of the design. This scope of work that extends the OD work to include *implementation and realization of the design's intent* is sometimes referred to as Organizational Design and Development (OD&D).

The organizational designer will adopt one of three different perspectives: egocentric, allocentric, or ambicentric. An egocentric design focuses inwardly on the internal efficiency of the organization. An allocentric design focuses outwardly on the perceived value recognized by a target market. And an ambicentric design achieves both egocentricity and allocentricity coextensively, resulting in an *ambidextrous organization*.

Allocentric designs are particularly well suited for firms comprised of precocious teams and individuals. Leaders of these firms adopt a strategy of effectively delivering results to highly satisfied customers. They are constantly innovating with the customer in mind, often anticipating needs and wants before its customers even realize them. They are less concerned about internal costs and other efficiencies; they grow margins and profits by increasing revenues, not cutting costs. They are constantly scanning their environment and very adept at processing large amounts of new and varied information to quickly make strategic adjustments.

The best allocentric designs cater to an environment that has very few significant *value drivers* (factors that influence the success of an organization) that are unrelated and typically hard to accurately forecast. They principally comprise several strategic business units, each of which is responsible for a particular offering, market segment, and/or geography. They favor parallel processes over sequential processes to better accommodate the creative, tacit, and variable nature of their work activities. Decisions are made at the lowest levels of the organization, and there is a lot of unstructured information exchanged through people, not data systems. People in the firm are generally positive with a willingness and desire to share information, experiment with new ideas, and change directions if needed. People are rewarded based on individual performance that delivers strategic results.

Egocentric design is the diametric opposite of allocentric design. At the time of this writing, I am helping an environmental management firm realign its strategy and redesign its organization; I have chosen an egocentric perspective. They have a well-defined process, a very stable customer base, and very low variability in the way value is delivered to their customers. Their strategy is inwardly focused: to be as efficient and reliable in the execution of its process, which is fundamentally their operating model. The recommended structure is functional, aligned with each stage of the process. This will allow specialization to drive efficiencies in each stage of the process, which is coordinated and governed at the highest levels of the organization. In the ideal state, the firm will operate like a well-oiled machine. Remember, this is their strategy, not yours! Adopting any elements of an egocentric design into your firm will just diffuse an otherwise solid allocentric design.

Design dilution will also happen if you are lured into attempting an ambicentric design. Most leaders are uncomfortable with the idea that operational efficiency is unimportant, or that work activities should not follow a structured, repeatable, and sequential process, or that their organization should not take on some sort of matrixed structure to accommodate separate and sometimes competing strategic objectives. If your perspective is allocentric—which it really must be—all these very enticing design elements will just introduce massive complexity for no valuable reason. Do ambidextrous organizations exist? Yes. However, they are extremely complicated, unstable, expensive, and often germinate a culture of confusion, frustration, and malaise. That is not really the organization we want, right? Let's just stick with an unadulterated allocentric design.

Embracing an Architect's Mindset

My approach to designing an organization resembles the approach an architectural design team takes in designing a building. Organizational design is a craft that requires craftsmanship, attention to detail, creative expression, and a keen appreciation for the specific circumstances that surround the project. The project could be an entire compound (organization), a standalone building in the compound (strategic sub-unit of the organization), or even a self-sufficient section of a building (an autonomous group within a sub-unit of the organization). Upon completion of the design, the design team will deliver a comprehensive set of illustrations, models, and plans that reflect a holistic and rigorous study of the environment, culture, and stakeholder intent—most importantly, the purpose and aspirations of the client.

The structural engineers on a design team have an intimate understanding of how to arrange the different structural elements of a building (foundation, columns, beams, walls, slabs, roof, joints, etc.) in a way, such that its load is properly supported and distributed into the ground, and the building is able to reasonably withstand anticipated forces from the environment (e.g., blaring sunlight, heavy winds, tropical storms, earthquakes, etc.). Meeting stability requirements is table stakes; the design team's responsibility extends far beyond that. The architects on the design team are responsible for understanding how the building will be used (function) and how visually interesting and appealing the building will be (form).

In the late 1800s, an American architect by the name of Louis Sullivan made a profound impact on the architectural industry by introducing and championing the design philosophy of *Form Follows Function*. He espoused the idea that a building's purpose and *function* should be the primary consideration when designing a building, with form (visual interest, visual continuity, visibility, hierarchy, etc.) being an important but subservient concern. Conversely, Frank Gehry, a modern-day architect, exemplifies *form* with his magnificent accomplishments, including the Bilbao Guggenheim, the Louis Vuitton Foundation in Paris, and the Walt Disney Concert Hall in Southern California.[1]

With all due respect to Gehry, I find Sullivan to be my source of inspiration for OD. When designing an organization, it is far more important to understand why the organization exists (purpose), what it aims to do and for whom (mission), and what the organization believes in (values); than how the organization looks (brand and image). It is very common to see an organization go Agile or bossless or four-dimensionally matrixed; when they have no reason to do it other than it sounds like a cool thing that everyone else is doing. The prime imperative for your design is to support your strategy, but, since culture eats strategy for breakfast,[2] the design philosophy for your organization should be *Form Follows Culture*; and you should treat it as seriously as an accomplished and respected architect designing the Schlesinger & Mayer Building.[3]

Understanding the OD Model

The model that we will use to design our organization has foundational roots (e.g., five-star model), includes contemporary theories (e.g., multi-contingency theory), and draws from hard lessons learned from my time in the trenches. It also carries heavy influences from structural architecture, cultural anthropology, and data science. I call it DHARMA (Design Harmony, Alignment, and Reinforcement Modeling Approach), and I use the Dharmachakra (the Dharma Wheel) to help represent the eight critical elements of OD. DHARMA is a general-purpose OD model that I use for all types of organizations; however, we will tailor our discussion to take on an allocentric hue, given your circumstances with an organization that comprises precocious teams and individuals.

Figure 5.1 DHARMA: Design Harmony, Alignment, and Reinforcement Modeling Approach.

DHARMA has eight OD elements: strategy, value, image, information, defense, culture, contribution, and power (see Figure 5.1). The elements are highly interconnected with each other in a delicate balance, like a baby's mobile. Even the slightest adjustment in one element will have immediate and hard-to-intuit effects on the rest of the elements, and it takes a lot of focused energy to bring everything back into balance once the mobile starts moving around.

At the top of the wheel is the **Strategy** element, a primary coupler in the Adamant Triad. Strategic philosophy will be reiterated and emphasized in the OD and the Strategic Guidelines form the basic guardrails of the design. Another area of your strategy that should be clear in your OD is your appetite for uncertainty (i.e., whether it is embraced or avoided). Value Drivers are emphasized in the Strategy element of DHARMA, as they help clarify the complexity of the environment. Value Drivers are factors that significantly influence the success of your organization, whether you control them or not. In the oil and gas industry, the price of oil has a huge impact on a company's profitability, yet no single company has control over what the price of oil is or what it will be.

The **Value** element clarifies how customer value flows through your organization. It includes your Value Chain, Value Streams, Operating Model, Core Business Processes, and your base philosophy on workflow design (parallel vs. sequential, repeatable vs. varied, etc.). It also clarifies the outer anchors of your value flow, including your suppliers, raw materials and resources, customers, offerings (products, services, etc.), and the competitive positioning of each of your offerings (obligatory, competitive, leader, or game-changing).

The **Image** element is not something normally seen in OD, but I contend that image and brand reputation are just as integral to OD as the rest of the elements discussed here. This is analogous to an architect's consideration of form and of striking the right balance with function. How an organization "looks" is an important part of the design that must be harmonious with all its other elements.

The **Information** element is where one of the two basic organizational flows is defined (the other being Value). Information requirements and processing capacity are of paramount concern to the designer. The Information element clarifies and specifies the sources, collectors, and distributors of internal and external information and the technologies required to support the information management systems. Information is not necessarily data-driven; people exchange information, too, especially when it cannot be neatly codified into a data system. So, in addition to the more obvious data systems, the Information element also clarifies how tacit knowledge is transferred between people (e.g., through structured meetings).

The **Defense** element addresses survivability; it specifies designs that keep the firm alive. It addresses the Darwinian realities of business, such as resilience, adaptability, flexibility, and solvency. Different species survive in different ways: some by strength, some by dexterity, and some by stealth; organizations are the same. Humans are obviously the dominant species on Planet Earth and have been for some time, so this 'survival of the fittest' element of DHARMA is much more than just making sure there is enough money in the bank to pay the bills. However, if the organization was forced into filing for Chapter 11 bankruptcy because it spent too much money on egg pods for its employees to nap in, then the Defense and the Culture elements were way out of alignment.

The **Culture** element addresses the development and well-being of the people in the organization—individually and collectively. It is also where the organization's key capabilities are specified (using Strategic Guiding Principles) and how much each key capability must grow (or shrink) to realize the desired strategy. There is a largely exploratory component in the Culture element called organizational *climate*, which is an assessment of the overall emotional valence of the firm (positive or negative) and how receptive the organization is to change. Climate is assessed rather than directly managed although you can shape culture in an attempt to change climate. We will have a lot of opportunities to discuss culture throughout this book; it is *the most important* element of design consideration when dealing with an organization composed of precocious teams and people.

Contribution is another element that is not traditionally seen in OD; however, as the push for corporate and social responsibility intensifies, I feel we will see these concerns continue to penetrate the OD space. The United Nations has specified 17 SDGs (Sustainable Development Goals) that each modern organization must seriously consider. This element connects the sustainable development goals and responsibilities of the firm to the other elements of OD, ensuring cohesion and proper design balance. I helped a boutique consulting firm build their Sustainability Practice, and it forced them to extend the bounds of their strategic philosophy to explore a more altruistic purpose. Considerations like this may trigger a re-evaluation of your entire strategy and OD.

Finally, the **Power** element is what motivates people to move through the flows defined in the Value element (e.g., business processes and workflows). This is somewhat analogous to electrical circuitry. Even if circuits are wired properly, nothing meaningful happens until the power is applied. The big difference, however, is that people are not as obedient and predictable as electrons. So, we must design Power structures that steer humans to do what we need them to do. Formal authority (i.e., reporting relationships) is one aspect of power; however, there are many other aspects to consider, including expert, referent, reward, and coercive (French & Raven, 1959). This is also where formalization and centralization philosophies reside, like how far down to push decision-making and how much documentation to use with processes and procedures. Of course, there is also a huge cultural aspect to where and how decisions are made, once again illustrating the importance of harmonizing, aligning, and reinforcing all elements before considering the design final.

The eight elements help frame the *constructive* and *exploratory* work that the organizational designer is responsible for performing. Constructive work focuses on shaping the internal mechanisms of the organization, while exploratory work investigates the contextual forces that shape design requirements. Constructive deliverables include operating models, cultural specifications, operating guidelines, and incentive systems, to name just a few. Exploratory deliverables include the environmental assessment, which clarifies the competitive context, and the organizational climate assessment, which reveals internal tensions and evaluates readiness for change (Burton, Obel, & Hakonsson, 2021).

Exploring Different Cultures through the Lens of an Organizational Designer

Confucian teachings emphasize the value of studying the past—not as an exercise in nostalgia, but as a pathway to deeper understanding and future readiness. This is sage advice when considering the design of an organization, especially when culture plays such an important role. Our world's history (and present) provides a rich repository of lessons learned as it relates to culture, social organization, and how power works in different social configurations. Now armed with an effective model for building an organization, let's explore a few cultures through an astute organizational designer's lens.

Despite most leaders' obsession with organizational structure (org charts, etc.), formal authority should only be a significant concern in a strong command-and-control model, as is found in most modern-day militaries. A direct order from a superior must be followed; not doing so is a punishable offense. I joined the United States Army as an enlisted soldier. Therefore, I was required to acknowledge and salute any officer I encountered.[4] This is a culture that is known to have a *high power distance*; one behaves exactly as instructed by their superior(s).

The advantage of a strong command-and-control model (over a strong inclusion model) is that decisions at the top of the hierarchy should quickly and reliably convert to rank-and-file behavior. The downside is that it kills innovation and creativity, since there is no tolerance for even a discussion of a superior's orders. Plus, outside of the military, this is an outmoded and impractical management style, even when creativity and innovation are not valuable to an organization, as in a process-heavy firm.

The Ninja Clans of feudal Japan had a strong hierarchical structure, but rank was based more on skill, experience, and success in missions of espionage, sabotage, and guerrilla warfare. Although clans were structured around key families like the Hattori, Momochi, and Mochizuki, the Jonin (highest ranking ninja) earned their rank in the field. To excel in the field, a ninja needed to be flexible, adaptive, and extemporaneously innovative. Guerrilla warfare never follows a neatly structured plan, so despite a strict hierarchy, the best ninja were very creative, in-the-moment thinkers.

We see high levels of creativity and innovation within a strong hierarchy in Renaissance Florence. This was a different kind of innovation, though, not so much creative maneuvering in the moment to accomplish (or survive!) a clandestine operation, but more out-of-the-box thinking to solve problems that had never been solved before. For instance, Filippo Brunelleschi, a pioneer in the concept of architecture as we know it today, completed the fantastic engineering feat of designing the Dome of Florence Cathedral, a dome without internal supports. This was an engineering marvel of the time that many believed was impossible.

The culture of Florence during the Renaissance period is worth studying if you are trying to design more innovation and creativity into your organization. Although there was an element of old aristocracy, it was often challenged by wealthy merchants and bankers like the Medici family, who exercised a quasi-monarchical style of governance, using their wealth and personal influence to control the city's politics. They used a system of patronage to maintain their power: supporting artists, innovators, and other creative thinkers, and thus gained loyalty. Without this level of support from the influential (referent) power structure that superseded the old aristocracy (formal power), the innovators would not have thrived.

In contrast to the strong hierarchical structures of the cultures discussed so far, the nomadic Mongolian tribes around the period of Genghis[5] Khan used kinship as their basis of social organization: families, clans, and tribes. Mobility influenced their social structures and interactions. The tribe was usually led by a khan or chief, who was often the head of the most powerful clan within the tribe. The khan typically ascended to power through ability and achievements, like the Jonin in ninja clans. Prowess in battle and the ability to protect and provide for the tribe warranted authority and key sources of power. Like the ninja, they were creative and innovative in their ability to adapt and survive; however, the formality of their customs and traditions inhibited the type of creative expression and innovative engineering that we found in Renaissance Florence. Religious rituals and the guidance of shamans (spiritual leaders) reinforced social norms and cohesion in this culture but also prohibited imaginative thinking. We see this happen in many other cultures as well, including ancient Hawaiians where *kapu* (sacred taboo) was strictly observed (until it wasn't).

We have only scratched the surface with a few different cultures to understand how social organization, power, and authority motivate people to behave and inspire (or inhibit) human ingenuity. As we design our organization, we must clarify the culture we need and then understand how the other elements of DHARMA especially Power, support our intended culture. Patrons with power, like the Medici family, understood the value of supporting creative, out-of-the-box thinkers during a vulnerable period of human history. Milieu played a large role in powering Ninja and nomadic Mongolian Tribes into creative survivability (flexibility, adaptability, etc.); however, that does not immediately translate to the type of innovative behavior required to build game-changing products and services. And there is very little utility in deploying autocratic structures and decision-making into a modern-day commercial organization. They stifle creativity and only serve the egos and anxieties of top management. Therefore, leave the org chart alone; there are more important things to contemplate right now.

Evaluating Different Approaches to OD

When dealing with an interconnected multi-variate system, especially one as delicate as an organization, it is best to have some sort of philosophy around how the variables are balanced within the system. A simple example is project management and the application of a technique that I developed called the PLB (Post, Lever, and Balance) Method. Whenever anyone manages a project, there are three variables to consider: scope, time, and throughput[6] (i.e., how fast scope is completed). In most cases, throughput equates to the number of people on the project—more people should increase throughput. The PLB Method helps project managers assign a *management philosophy* to the project. They do this by assigning one variable to Post, one variable to Lever, and one variable to Balance. The Post stays fixed, the Lever is intentionally controlled, and the Balance is allowed to derive from the other two. For example, one could post scope, lever throughput (i.e., the number of people on the team), and allow time to balance. Project managers without a management philosophy fall victim to leaders who incessantly want more done in less time from less people (Figure 5.2).

The significance of having a philosophy amplifies when you have eight variables (elements) to deal with, as we do with OD. There are many, many different ways to approach OD. The best designers will pivot their approach based on the circumstances of the client. A key characteristic of a designer's approach, in any given circumstance, is which element the designer *leads* with. A leading element prevents the designer from perpetually rebalancing element after element without ever obtaining equilibrium, like a hopeless game of whack-a-mole. The leading element acts like a post; it is clearly defined first, and then it stays fixed.

Most organizations that do not solicit professional help (internal or external) follow a structure-led approach to OD. That is because, without the right vaccinations in place, leaders will certainly fall ill to ORD. It's a great misfortune that many leaders *equate* OD with restructuring, but that's the way it is; you know better now. In fact, structure is not even an element in DHARMA (it is tucked away as a component of Power), but you will see it as an element in other models, like the five-star model. It is *never* a good idea to lead with structure. It plays too hard on the emotions of everyone involved, clouding rational judgment of everything else. It is hard for a leader to work on an org structure without "seeing" themselves and their colleagues in it—a cardinal sin of structural design.[7] Plus, it's just not that important in the overall scheme of OD. How many times has your organization performed well *despite* reporting relationships? Structure-led OD is only relevant in strong command-and-control organizations, and we just don't see much of that in business anymore.

Figure 5.2 The Post, Lever, and Balance Method.

Wasabi Moment

Leading amidst a team infected with ORD is extremely difficult. I have seen good leaders blatantly dismiss even the strongest of directives to stay away from org charts until the end of the design process. You must dig in and defend your methods. Expect and prepare for conflict and team dissension—it will happen

Organizations that solicit *good* professional help will likely follow some sort of process-led approach to OD. The idea is to first understand how the organization delivers value to its customers, and then let the other pieces of OD, like structure, fall into place. Practitioners will work with leaders to understand business processes and develop operating models to clarify how work flows through the organization. In DHARMA, this is the Value element; I use the term process-led here because it is more industry-friendly than value-led. Although Process is not a DHARMA element (it is a component of Value), it is an element in other models. This is an extremely valuable approach; I use it all the time: much more effective than structure-led OD.

Culture-led OD is one of my more novel ideas, but the reasoning follows along the same lines. OD starts with what the people in the organization need to thrive, and then the rest of the organization is designed around the culture. In fact, if there is ever a contest between Culture and Strategy, the firm's strategy gets adjusted, not the design of its culture. The same applies for every other element of the design, including Process or Value— Culture trumps all. In many cases, I would follow a process-led approach to OD; however, for an organization filled with precocious people facing a hyper-growth opportunity, that would be the wrong move. It would result in compromises to the culture for the sake of efficient value delivery. This is not an easy tradeoff, so let's be as clear as possible. Culture trumps all—a culture-led approach is the right call.[8]

The Silicon Valley OD Playbook

Just because culture-led OD is novel, doesn't mean we are building our design from scratch. Our earlier cultural journey provides a glimpse into how Culture might connect to Power and other elements, and there are many, many other lessons to be gleaned from our recent and ancient past. Of course, the most valuable lessons come from the Silicon Valley giants that came before us, so let's extricate some themes into what I call the Silicon Valley OD Playbook.

In Chapter 1, we looked at the wealthiest companies on the planet (see Table 1.1); the top ten include five Silicon Valley companies: Apple, Nvidia, Google, Facebook, and Tesla. If you consider the formative and hyper-growth period of each of these organizations, one thing becomes abundantly clear. They all adopted an **allocentric perspective**, with a heavy focus on outputs (effectiveness) and minimal focus on inputs (efficiency). Apple and Tesla have always had a clear vision and direction that emphasized a focus on user experience, Nvidia has a laser focus on catering to the needs of gamers, and Google is on a mission to "organize the world's information and make it universally accessible and useful."

Furthermore, all these companies had **cross-functional teams** that combined expertise from engineering, product marketing, sales, and product development to ensure product offerings were innovative, technically superior, commercially viable, and realistically doable. In all cases, at least one of these offerings was **game-changing** with an **unassailable competitive advantage**.

The teaming principle extended into all these companies, manifesting not only as cross-functional but also **small and autonomous**. Apple and Google were known for launching Skunkworks Projects consisting of small and close-knit teams. This naturally fosters a value of **iterative development**, constantly improving and refining products based on customer feedback. This is exemplified by Facebook's famous motto: "Move fast and break things."

To accommodate allocentric ambitions, they all had **flat organizational structures** with very few levels of management, what's known as low *vertical differentiation*. Coupled with high levels of autonomy, this allowed individuals and small teams to innovate and pivot based on customer demands, without the encumbrance of bureaucratic red tape or over-engineered processes.

Of course, they were all innovative, but their innovation was fueled by an emphasis on **technical excellence**. Nvidia's strong emphasis on engineering excellence has catapulted it to be the undisputed leader in Graphics Processing Unit chip design, affording it a prodigious platform in both the gaming and artificial intelligence arenas. For Tesla, engineering excellence was a key differentiator that allowed the company to disrupt the automotive industry. Google founders Larry Page and Sergey Brin insisted on building a culture driven by engineering excellence and innovation, and even the most isolated cultures in the Congo Basin are aware of Google's innovations.

Data-driven decision-making tends to be a common theme among our icons of consideration. Google has actually leveraged its analytical prowess into a product offering (aptly named Google Analytics). But the real value in embracing advanced analytics for an allocentric organization is in competitive intelligence. These companies are so adept at advanced analytics that they often have insights about their competitors that their competitors don't even know about! And, of course, the player on the field with the best consumer analytics wins ten times out of ten; this is how game-changing products are discovered. For instance, Tesla has collected *billions* of miles of real-world driving data to refine its technology.

Interestingly enough, all of our Silicon Valley icons were tightly coupled with their key suppliers and customers, what's known as **supply chain integration**. This is also what Jack Welch did with GE: physically integrating with suppliers and customers and thereby maintaining a certain level of control over their operations. Walt Disney and Costco are two more examples of companies that have an immense amount of control over their business partners. Partnering with key players in your competitive land-scape to this degree involves re-evaluating the boundaries of your Strategy and Value elements.

Know and Grow

An extreme extension of supply chain integration involves the actual acquisition of business partners to fortify your supply chain. This maneuver, known as **vertical integration**, puts an organization in complete control of their product development and distribution value chain. Vertical integration was used extensively by Silicon Valley giants to dominate their markets

Finally, you'll notice that all these companies had a fairly **clean and positive image** when they went through their initial growth spurt. This is where that Brand element of DHARMA comes in. A clean image is important. Consumers "feel good" about working with companies whose headlines are more positive than negative. More importantly, a good headline a day keeps the regulator away. When government regulators, activist groups, or any other "watch dogs" smell the smoke of bad news, they go looking for a fire. It is difficult, if not impossible, to ascend to greatness while being scrutinized for wrongdoing, regardless of the validity of any claims.

Okay, before we move on, you may be reeling at the fact that I just implied Tesla, and by extension, its very controversial leader had a fairly clean and positive image. Before you hit send on the email you are about to send me, consider this. In 2012, when Tesla entered its hyper-growth phase, the major headlines centered around its viability as a business, not its soon-to-be-questionable image. It wasn't until five or six years later that we started hearing about its employees working unreasonable hours. And it wasn't until 2018, when it *exited* its hyper-growth phase, that we saw the first major controversy where Musk directly got Tesla into legal trouble (with the Securities and Exchange Commission). Between 2012 and 2018, Tesla's revenues went from $413 million to a staggering $21 billion! Now, that's hyper-growth! And yet, at least for the earlier part of that period, it kept its organizational nose pretty clean.

To summarize, here are the themes that emerge when considering the formative and hyper-growth years of our most iconic Silicon Valley giants:

- Allocentric perspective
- Cross-functional teams, often small and autonomous

- At least one game-changing offering (product, service, etc.)
- Iterative development
- Flat organizational structure (wide, with very few levels of management)
- Technical/engineering excellence and innovation
- Data-driven decision-making
- Supply chain integration
- Clean and positive image

Hopefully, this section provides an inspirational playbook to reference as you redesign your organization. Remember—low expectations for now. We still have two more iterations before we arrive at our go-forward design.

Putting It into Practice

Now it is time to *attempt* the first draft of your OD. Please refer to Figure 5.1 as we flesh out your Organizational DHARMA for the first time. For now, just brainstorm your thoughts about each element in the same way you fleshed out your Strategic Framework. Make sure to brainstorm enough details to hold a preliminary conversation with your Strategic Leadership Team. Don't overthink each element, but make sure all the elements balance against each other in harmony, align with your strategic philosophy, and reinforce each other.

Step 1: Define your Culture: We are using a culture-led approach, so in PLB terms, we are *posting* on Culture. The nice thing about taking an iterative approach, though, is that we won't hold fast on to our post until after the third iteration. So, just do the best to answer the question: "What culture must be in place to achieve our opportunity and sustain our strategic philosophy?"

Step 2: Refine your Strategy: Clarify your Value Drivers, which are factors in the environment that significantly affect the success of your organization, regardless of how much influence or control you have over them. Specify how your Value Drivers are interconnected with each other. Adjust your strategy if you have more than a few Value Drivers and/or if they are highly interconnected. It is okay if value drivers are unpredictable (like the price of oil), but they cannot be intertwined such that you are constantly dealing with the compound effects of significantly influential factors in your competitive environment

Step 3: Define your Value Infrastructure: Articulate how your organization delivers value to its customers. Identify your key customers (or segments), suppliers, offerings, and how competitive each offering must be (Obligatory, Competitive, Leader, or Game-Changing). When defining offerings, don't forget about data, insights, and experiences. I helped a global networking and telecommunications company in Silicon Valley improve the way their customers licensed their software. And, although we did introduce some new technology, the key value was in providing a greatly upgraded customer experience

When you are done, construct a simple graphic that illustrates how work flows through your organization to deliver value from your suppliers through to your customers—this is your value chain and your preliminary operating model. Finally, consider the key business processes that deliver value (core processes). If they are too sequential and mechanistic, consider ways to parallelize your activities and unlock more creativity from your teams

Step 4: Define your Power: Reflect on examples from this chapter to define how power will be used in your organization. How will people be motivated to behave their way through your channels of value? Forget about formal power for now; concentrate more on expert, referent, reward, coercive, and information power. How will people know what activities to perform at any given point in time? What will your reward and accountability system look like? What customs and rituals will be installed to maintain social norms, without stifling human ingenuity? How will you install autonomy and decentralized decision-making?

Step 5: Define your Information Systems: What is the nature of the information that needs to be exchanged (tacit and codified). How will critical tacit information flow through the company? What type of data & analytics are required, and what technology will support the flow of codifiable data? How will you control the amount of tacit information that needs to be processed; too much tacit information will overwhelm an allocentric organization. How will you use contemporary technology to mitigate the vulnerabilities of allocentricity?

Step 6: Define your Defense System: How will you make sure your company is resilient, adaptable, and flexible? How will you protect your organization from insolvency? Be diligent but not overzealous with this element. Don't let your Legal and Finance departments scare you into holding a defensive posture as a strategy. The goal with this element is to protect the organization without restricting the other elements. Pull in the best parts of the Ninja and Mongolian Nomads, but don't let creative survivability interfere with your Florentine genius

Step 7: Define your Image and Contribution: These two elements go hand-in-hand, but do not use Contribution to deceptively boost your Image. This is what is pejoratively referred to as greenwashing, a maneuver you do not want to get entangled in. Be purposeful and authentic about how you will contribute to the United Nations' Sustainability Development Goals. And begin designing a positive brand that can be sustained throughout your transformation and beyond

Finally, if you or anyone on your Leadership Team has sketched out potential org charts, please burn them at this time. They are not needed yet.

Executive Debrief

- Organizational design (OD) is a comprehensive set of plans, visuals, and specifications that guide the development and realignment of an organization
- An organizational designer considers the following focus areas: Functionality, Aesthetics, Survivability, People Experience, Competitive Awareness and Sensitivity, Non-Competitive Stakeholder Experience, Sustainable Development Responsibilities, and Application of OD best and emerging practices
- Allocentric (outward-focused) designs are most effective for firms composed of precocious teams and people
- OD should be approached like an architectural design team approaches a new project
- DHARMA is an eight-element OD model that we will use to design our organization. The eight elements of DHARMA are: Strategy, Value, Power, Information, Culture, Image, Contribution, and Defense
- Valuable lessons in OD can be gleaned from different cultures in our past and present, the most relevant and valuable of which can be extricated by examining the top Silicon Valley icons

Notes

1 Take a glance at any one of these structures and you will immediately understand what I mean by stunning visual appeal taking precedence over all else.
2 Invaluable wisdom handed down to us from the late, great Peter Drucker; perhaps the GOAT (greatest of all time) of leadership and management.
3 Currently the Carson, Pirie, Scott and Company Building, this is one of Louis Sullivan's most iconic designs and a shining example of "Form Follows Function."
4 Except in wartime situations. Saluting an officer on the battlefield might be the equivalent of signing their death warrant if the wrong set of eyes witnesses the ritual.
5 Although this is the more common spelling and pronunciation of the great kahn's name, the more authentic spelling and pronunciation is "Chinggis Khan."
6 Some people would consider *cost* as the third variable, but for most intents and purposes, cost is an ineffective derivative of what truly needs to be balanced, which is throughput.
7 The Golden Rule of structural design is: design for the position, not the people.
8 Unless it legitimately threatens the life of the organization. That is why DHARMA has a Defense element. This is the only element that could possibly trump Culture, but if it gets to that point, it is time for a complete strategic overhaul.

Bibliography

Burton, R. M., Obel, B., & Hakonsson, D. D. (2021). *Organizational design: A step-by-step approach* (4th ed.). Cambridge University Press.

French, J. R. P., Jr., & Raven, B. (1959). The bases of social power. In D. Cartwright (Ed.), *Studies in social power* (pp. 151–156). Institute for Social Research.

Galbraith, J. R., Downey, D., & Kates, A. (2002). *Designing dynamic organizations: A hands-on guide for all leaders at all levels*. AMACOM.

Galloway, S. (2017). *The four: The hidden DNA of Amazon, Apple, Facebook, and Google*. Portfolio.

Kane, H. K. (1997). *Ancient Hawai'i*. Kawainui Press.

Strathern, P. (2007). *The Medici: Power, money, and ambition in the Italian Renaissance*. Pegasus Books.

Turnbull, S. (1996). *Ninja: The true story of Japan's secret warrior cult*. Firebird Books.

Twombly, R. C. (1986). *Louis Sullivan: His life and work*. Viking Penguin.

Weatherford, J. (2004). *Genghis Khan and the making of a modern world*. Crown.

Chapter 6

Edison's Boxing Cats

Leveraging Precocity to Weaponize Innovation and Annihilate the Competition

Innovation and the Adamant Triad

One of the greatest contributions to society that the Internet has provided is access to cat videos. Cats are crazy, especially little kittens, and thoroughly entertaining to watch. But did you know that cat videos have been around for as long as movie production has been around? In fact, we have our father of invention, Thomas A. Edison, to thank for the very first cat video, "Boxing Cats." It was released in 1894, for use on the Kinetoscope, another one of Edison's inventions. There was a penny arcade in San Francisco that featured movies like this in a long row of kinetoscopes, where you could get a glimpse of what it was like during the turn of the twentieth century, when the motion picture industry was born. Whenever family and friends would fly in to visit us, we would usually cap off a fun day at Pier 39 with a trip to this penny arcade to play some games and catch a short movie. Good times.

To produce the first motion pictures, Edison built the first film production studio called the "Black Maria" in West Orange, New Jersey, where his laboratories were. This structure was a bizarre contraption, even by today's standards (maybe Edison should have consulted with Louis Sullivan!). Building on the principles of early photography, it included a dark studio room that was covered in black tar paper and an old-fashioned retractable roof that would let sunlight in on demand. One of the more peculiar aspects of this structure was that it was built on a swiveling foundation. Edison and his crew would actually rotate the whole building throughout the day to maximize sunlight exposure through the retractable roof. What kind of person could think this up?

Having the great advantage of historical retrospect, it is easy to understand today how the Black Maria studio worked, and why it needed to be built on a rotating foundation, and how entertaining it would be to see a carefully structured sequence of cat pictures displayed with a quick cadence to simulate what it would be like to watch two cats boxing with

DOI: 10.4324/9781003518181-9

each other. But imagine what it was like for Edison back in 1888, trying to explain the concept of a Kinetoscope to people living in a world where the idea of a motion picture had never been imagined. It was probably similar to Filippo Brunelleschi explaining to the people of Renaissance Florence how he would construct a dome for the Florence Cathedral without using internal supports. It is very difficult to discuss the unimaginable to people with no imagination. Brunelleschi was laughed at and thrown out of the room on the grounds of lunacy. I am sure Edison faced a similar experience many times in his life.

Imagining something that has never been imagined is a unique talent of humans that is often under-appreciated until tangible fruit is witnessed and experienced. Innovators, and their craft of innovation, should be revered by the hearts and souls of all of us who have benefited immensely from their incessant pursuit of a better life experience. Edison never gave up on the light bulb, even after literally thousands and thousands of failed attempts. But with unwavering faith in his vision, tenacious grit, and a growth mindset,[1] he lit the world up in 1879 with the first carbon filament lamp that lasted for almost 14 hours. And then, 15 years later, he gave us "Boxing Cats." What a wonderful man.

Innovation is an integral part of the Adamant Triad that is especially salient for a precocious organization. The Strategic Philosophy of a precocious organization should exude innovation, weaving its way throughout the purpose, mission, values, and vision of the firm. This will, of course translate to Strategic Guiding Principles that shape the development of key capabilities and technologies that are found in the organizational design (OD). The OD is Culture-led, so the prominence of innovation should come through as we define the culture of the organization. And since every other element of DHARMA (Design Harmony, Alignment, and Reinforcement Modeling Approach) either levers or balances against the post of Culture, a culture of innovation should not only be a stalwart of the OD but also radiate into every other element of DHARMA as we harmonize the model and reinforce innovation into all elements of the design.

Lessons Learned from Silicon Valley Royalty

For inspiration, let's revisit the thematic analysis on Silicon Valley greats from the last chapter, with a specific focus on innovation. According to Table 1.1, as of April 1, 2024, Apple, Nvidia, Google, and Facebook had a combined market capitalization of about $8 trillion (that's *trillion* with a T). That is an insane amount of money. For perspective, as of the time of this writing, Japan had a Gross Domestic Product of about $6.72 trillion. So, the entire monetary value of final goods and services (bought by end consumers) produced by Japan *almost* matches the wealth generated by the top Silicon Valley companies. They must be doing something right, and as we know, innovation is at the core of the great success experienced by each one of these icons. Let's take a quick look at how it was done.

Apple, Nvidia, Google, and Facebook all have leaders who espouse innovation. An inspiring *Thing*[2] from Google's philosophy is "Great just isn't good enough." Even from the early days, Google knew that, to succeed, it needed to push beyond the limits of modern imagination, using *great* as a *starting point* for innovation. In the late 1990s, Steve Jobs very publicly evangelized Apple's "Think Different" motto, using it in various marketing campaigns to emphasize his commitment to innovation and creativity. Having this clear and *public* conviction of innovation by top leaders serves as the cornerstone of building a culture and brand of innovation.

Branding is another theme that is consistent with the top five. Not only do they all have a relatively clean image (as discussed in Chapter 5), but they are all *known* worldwide as paragons of innovation. We have already discussed Facebook's early use of its now-famous motto: "Move fast and break things." To add, Nvidia is well known in the gaming world for its "The Way It's Meant to be Played" slogan, signaling its innovation-clad devotion to creating amazing gaming experiences with its cutting-edge technologies. This branding reinforces their culture of innovation inside and out.

Of course, one must do more than just espouse innovation; they must actually *be* innovative in their product offerings and in the culture that they define and nurture for their organization. Silicon Valley companies are so well known for the somewhat esoteric coddling of our employees that we are often ridiculed for it. Hollywood just can't get enough of Google's egg-shaped nap pods, Facebook's barbershop, or Apple's space-age office spaces. Or, all the gourmet food, the high-tech fitness centers, and yes, rock climbing. We get it. Feel free to laugh all you want, while these companies have been laughing on Wall Street for a long time now.

And, although Hollywood sometimes goes a little too far with exaggeration, these seemingly outlandish workplaces are fundamentally real. If you worked at Google, you could actually attempt to scale a rock-climbing wall in the Googleplex,[3] where Google's headquarters is. And if you worked at Facebook, you could not only get a free haircut at their barbershop, but you would also have dry cleaning freely available to you—no charge. It is just one of many tokens of appreciation for being a contributing citizen to their mission, vision, and fortune.

All this is done with the intent to cultivate human ingenuity—the lifeblood of their firms. Workplaces are often open and collaborative to foster spontaneous teaming and creative group problem-solving. However, creative thinkers need private time, so these needs are taken into consideration as well, with private offices and isolated thinking spaces that are far removed from the hustle and bustle of the noisy collaborators. When I was at Silicon Graphics, it was nice to lounge around with colleagues to collectively brainstorm solutions, but it was also nice to return to my private office, shut the door, and quietly focus on my next deliverable.

Another hallmark of innovative cultures is the sanction of time for its members to be creative. Google employees were (and still are) encouraged to spend 20% of their time working on anything they felt might benefit the company. And that is what gave birth to Gmail, AdSense, and Google Hangouts. Facebook and others followed suit by sponsoring Hackathon events every few months, where developers would huddle together for a few days to innovate on ways of improving the Facebook user experience.

Wasabi Moment

Encouraging employees to work on passion projects can be harder than expected. While it may seem like a benefit they'll happily embrace, some need a push—much like with vacation—because they worry about neglecting their primary responsibilities. If time incentives don't work, you might need to take a firmer approach

Finally, we would be remiss if we failed to recognize Google and its dedication to innovation on the world stage with its creation of Google X in 2010, a spectacular innovation lab which is now known as X—The Moonshot Factory. According to their website, their mission is to "create radical new technologies to solve some of the world's hardest problems." How's that for securing innovation into a firm's ethos?

Setting Up an Innovation Factory

Fortunately, you are not required to set up a Moonshot Factory for your firm, unless you intend to compete with Google on the world stage for worldwide innovation bragging rights; an idea I strongly suggest you avoid. You will, however, be required to grow your organizational capability for innovation if you ever hope to create game-changing offerings (see Figure 3.3). The best way to do that is with an Innovation Factory.

As its name implies, an Innovation Factory is a process-driven system that transforms ideas into commercially viable offerings.

Whenever I set up an Innovation Factory, I extend the boundary of the system beyond just insights. To ensure bright ideas actually *benefit* the firm, they must be applied to create commercially superior offerings. Nvidia doesn't stop at publishing ground-breaking research papers about cutting-edge graphics; it creates game-changing graphics cards that create the ultimate gaming experience. So, as illustrated in Figure 6.1, the Innovation Factory extends from Idea Intake and Generation all the way to Commercialization.

Setting up an Innovation Factory for an egocentric organization is straightforward and intuitive. Setting up one for an *allocentric* organization is generally straightforward, with some non-intuitive aspects, the first of which involves the Principle of Unrestricted Progress: Individuals and

Figure 6.1 The Innovation Factory.

teams should never feel like corporate processes are restricting them from pursuing an idea. People intuitively feel like a *factory* should be actively managed, systematically moving widgets from one stage of a structured process to another. However, this approach is more appropriate for an egocentric design, which is the diametric opposite of an allocentric design. So, for allocentric organizations, we still have a structured, high-level, staged process where ideas make their transformation into commercially viable offerings; however, the process is not managed in the traditional sense. Instead, the people working in the process are free to work on whatever they desire. Consequently, for this Value Stream (of innovation) to work, we need an effective Power system that motivates people to move through its value channels.

Small autonomous teams are encouraged to work on any idea in the factory, at any stage of its development. Each stage has clearly defined objectives and guidelines (see Table 6.1), but no strong prescription for how its objectives are achieved. Best practices may be available, but they are not workflows. Teams are free to achieve the objectives of each stage however they wish, as long as they stay within the guidelines. And what would motivate people to spend their time in the Innovation Factory working on ideas? Oh, that's the fun part. Every member involved in a commercially successful offering gets a piece of the pie—a small royalty based on the first year of sales (or something like that). In addition, I suggest setting up a small Delta Force Innovation Team: dedicated resources that are responsible for moving forward the most strategic innovation opportunities.

Finally, it's best to physically isolate the Innovation Factory from the rest of the organization. Creative thinking is easily disrupted by the whirlwind of day-to-day operations, even in the most progressive of organizations. You don't need to house your Innovation Factory in its own building, like Google did—but it's not the worst idea.

Wasabi Moment

The innovation space must be fiercely defended as a space for creative thinking. To generate insights, the human mind must be comfortable, positive, and relaxed. You must protect people in this space from the stress and anxiety that surrounds them

Table 6.1 Innovation Factory Objectives, Guidelines, and Best Practices

Stage	Objective	Guidelines	Best Practices
Generate ideas	Daylight issues, ideas, and insights that could benefit the firm and clearly define the problem or opportunity	Must follow a design thinking approach to explore the problem space	Leverage customers, support services, and professional services to uncover issues, with a keen focus on customer satisfaction
Uncover unmet needs and wants	Translate problems and opportunities into potentially unmet needs and wants	Should affinitize several problems or opportunities into one group of unmet needs or wants Must convert specific product issues into unmet needs and wants	Leverage product or technology specialists to help understand unmet needs and wants based on a specific product issue
Discover deeper-level insights	Generate additional, deeper-level insights from unmet needs and wants	Team must be cross-functional	Lateral Thinking Concept Fan Five Whys
Develop multiple solutions	Generate a set of potential solutions for a deep-level insight	Must follow a Design Thinking approach to explore the solution space Must have three to five solutions Should include some validation of market need	Develop a prototype to help sell the idea Vet solutions with trusted customers or reliable customer proxies
Commercialize innovation	Prove the commercial viability of a solution	Must be validated with market data and analysis Should engage with key business partners (e.g., key customers) to vet the offering's viability	Solution teams pitch their solutions to commercial teams who offer additional rewards for a successful pitch

Making Value-Based Investments in Innovation

A common question I get asked by leaders is, "How much should innovation cost?" This ostensibly fair question is actually quite loaded and also a telltale sign that the leader's philosophy (personal and organizational) should be evaluated. So, no, I am not going to answer this question. This is not the type of question that comes from a leader adopting an allocentric perspective. Cost is an egocentric term; it's an input. Furthermore, this question is short-sighted. As fun as it is, we don't just innovate for fun; we innovate to achieve strategic objectives. And, if hyper-growth is the opportunity in front of us, then our existential need for innovation is to drive hyper-growth. It is important to maintain the line of sight between a commitment to culture and an unassailable competitive advantage (Figure 3.3) and the role innovation (as a key capability) plays when considering the financial aspects of innovation.

I am not trying to dodge the fact that money will be spent on innovation. Even if you succeed in designing an effective rewards-based Power structure to propel ideas through your Innovation Factory, it will still need to be managed. To support your Innovation Factory, you will need both people-based and data-based information systems to process and route tacit and codifiable information, respectively. I also recommend forming an Innovation Center of Excellence to help support the people actively engaged in the Innovation Factory and a Delta Force to reinforce the reward-based structure with a formal structure, specifically as it relates to the firm's most strategic opportunities. This, of course, will be a cost to the firm.

However, don't make the same mistake that many leaders do in structuring innovation as a cost center. As an organizational unit, innovation is neither a division (strategic business unit) nor a supporting function (e.g., Finance, HR, IT). Rather, organizations that have Technology as their Guiding Light should separate Technology off into a separate *profit-centered* organizational unit. This is where innovation and commercialization live. The top line (income) for the Technology unit must be based on an outward-facing metric, like product revenue, market share, or even customer satisfaction. Avoid the temptation to concoct some sort of "funding" scheme for the Technology unit, which will just turn it into another cost center.

The Technology unit holds a portfolio of ideas that are in varying stages throughout the Innovation Factory. Some ideas will go nowhere, some ideas will contribute to marketplace success, and some will be huge hits that contribute to game-changing products and services. The value of the Technology unit at any point of time is based on the cumulative probability of success for all the ideas in the portfolio. Some nascent ideas will be more promising than others but will have wider confidence bands than the more mature ideas. It is not worth getting into the details of the analysis in this text, just know that the simple application of standard probability calculus will help you develop a value model for your Technology unit and the Innovation Factory that drives it. Understanding this concept is more important right now than worrying about how much growing your innovation capability will cost.

Maintaining this Value-Based mindset is important when addressing the financial challenges of setting up an Innovation Factory and many other aspects of designing and developing an allocentric organization. It prevents you from getting trapped by an inward focus, which will just destroy you from the inside out. An allocentric organization does not improve profit margins by driving down costs, it does so by increasing income. And it increases income by taking risks with value-based investments, the biggest of which, for a precocious firm with a Guiding Light of Technology, is innovation.

Our First Attempt at Innovation and Completing the Minimum Viable Product for Our Adamant Triad

We have covered a lot in the last three chapters, and I hope you have kept your expectations low when going through exercises for building out the Minimum Viable Product (MVP) for our Adamant Triad. So far, you have completed a Strategic Framework, an Organizational Design, and a thoughtful exercise on how to grow innovation as a key capability using an Innovation Factory. What we need to do now is put everything in harmony so that we have a *viable* product to show for our first iteration of work.

Since knowledge progresses geometrically through the early stages of discovery, it is likely that your Adamant Triad is out of balance, even though we just got started. So, before we complete the MVP design of our Innovation Factory, which completes our MVP Adamant Triad, let's step back and see if adjustments must be made to your Strategic Framework and OD.

Has anything in your Strategic Philosophy changed after going through Chapters 5 and 6? Does it *exude* innovation as we discussed earlier? My guess is that your purpose and mission are fine, but what about your vision (not just your vision statement, your full-blown vision)? Is there anything that you learned in the last two chapters that either alters or refines your vision of success? And what about your values? Do your values give adequate airtime to innovation? Are any of your values inconsistent with an allocentric perspective? Knowing we are taking a Culture-led OD approach (i.e., posting on Culture), wherein innovation is a prominent aspect, is there a need to alter or refine your Strategic Guiding Principles?

For instance, do you have a principle that is similar to this: "Must grow a key capability of innovation"? Or what about this: "Must develop a people-based and data-based information system to support the Innovation Factory"? You get where we are going with this.

Once you reset your strategy, turn your attention to your OD. Even though you *just* threw together the MVP for your OD, is there anything that you learned in this chapter that would necessitate a revision? Definitely! At a minimum, we must flesh out the Power element to reflect the rewards-based system that moves ideas through the Innovation Factory, and the Information element gets an upgrade with the people- and data-based systems that we just talked about. Plus, there's the Innovation Center of Excellence and the Delta Force—they are all part of the OD that should make an appearance in our final MVP. And what about the Defense element? How will you prohibit your Innovation Factory from sending you into insolvency if too many value-based investments go bust? Put some thought into each element of DHARMA and strive for complete harmony before completing the design of your Innovation Factory.

To finalize the design of your Innovation Factory, simply take Table 6.1 one step deeper. The basic bones won't change (like the five different stages); however, tailor it to your organization, especially when it comes to Best Practices. You might even design what might be considered workflows; however, if you do this, be clear about their intent. Workflows under this type of process design (what I call Business Process *Leadership*, as opposed to Business Process Management) are merely recommended best practices, not prescriptions for what to do when. Then, wrap some context around it to explain its purpose, how the reward system works, etc., so that it can stand alone as its own document. There will be some redundancy between this document and your OD, and potentially your strategy—that's intentional.

Know and Grow

Business Process Leadership is a discipline in which there is a heavy emphasis on defining the process outputs and guidelines for execution, and little to no emphasis on defining process steps. Individuals and teams are granted autonomy to produce the process outputs however they see fit as long as they adhere to the process' guidelines

And there you have it! If everything is still in balance, you have completed the MVP for your Adamant Triad! At this point, you should gather some feedback from trusted stakeholders (on viability, feasibility, and desirability) and then perform a ceremony with your Strategic Leadership Team to formally close the door on Iteration One and formally open the door for Iteration Two. As you will learn, ceremonies and rituals are important for sealing and galvanizing a culture. As a team, review and discuss what you have accomplished. Then, formally align on the decisions, from Chapter 4:

- Have we developed an Adamant Triad that we *could* use (regardless of how much we like it), without another iteration of development?
- Have we captured valuable feedback that we *should* apply to the next iteration?
- *Should* we move forward with another iteration?

Let's hope the answer to that last bullet is "yes!" Because that's where we are going next. Great job!

Putting It into Practice

Now that you have an MVP of your Adamant Triad, you and your leadership team should start practicing how you are going to talk about it with the rest of the workforce. It may seem a bit premature since we have two more iterations to complete before we let the workforce in on what's going on, but it's always good to practice aligning on message. The last thing you want is for two different members of your Strategic Leadership Team giving out two different answers to the same question. So, a good way to crystallize and lock in your messaging is to run this **Break Room Exercise**. It can be the last agenda item in your decision-making ceremony, or it could be a separate, short meeting solely for the sake of aligning on message. Here is how it works:

1 Bring the Strategic Leadership Team together for a short meeting (or schedule an agenda item toward the end of your Iteration One decision-making ceremony)
2 State the objective using a scenario: If someone bumps into you in the break room and asks you why we keep meeting behind closed doors (or how the strategy session went, or what happened at the big retreat last week, etc.), what would you say?
3 Start with yourself, by concisely stating your key takeaways from the iteration and where you and the team landed with your MVP. Target a 30–60-second response

4 The person to your left (or right) tries to improve upon your response. There can be a short group discussion on the difference, and whether the group feels it is an improvement

5 The process continues around the room, member by member, and continues looping to and past you. If someone feels like the message does not need improvement when it's their turn, they just repeat, exactly, what the previous member said

6 The process ends when everyone in the room has stated the exact same response, implicitly signifying complete alignment on messaging

Remember, this is just practice! You should not actually talk with anyone about this just yet, aside from the few people in your inner circle. That said, if you start practicing this ritual now, then it will be much easier to align on messaging when the time does come to engage with the rest of your people.

Executive Debrief

- Imagining something that has never been imagined is a unique talent of humans that is often under-appreciated
- Innovation is an integral part of the Adamant Triad and is especially salient for a precocious organization
- The Strategic Philosophy of a precocious organization should *exude* innovation
- There are a lot of valuable lessons to learn about innovation from the Silicon Valley greats: Apple, Nvidia, Google, and Facebook

  - Leaders must espouse the value of innovation
  - Innovation must be part of your firm's brand
  - Build an outlandish physical environment that screams innovation
  - Sanction time for employees to innovate
  - Dedicate space, specifically for innovation

- An Innovation Factory is a great way to build innovation capability. It has five stages:

  - Generate ideas
  - Uncover unmet needs and wants
  - Discover deeper-level insights
  - Develop multiple solutions
  - Commercialize innovation

- Innovation must not be a cost center. It is housed within a Technology unit, which is a profit center

- The value of the Technology unit at any point in time is based on the cumulative probability of success for all the ideas in the portfolio (i.e., Innovation Factory)
- Maintaining a value-based mindset is important when addressing the financial challenges of setting up an Innovation Factory
- All the elements and components of the Adamant Triad must be balanced for it to be a viable product
- It is important to perform a ceremony to close Iteration One and open Iteration Two; this is when the Iteration One decisions will be formalized
- Running a Break Room Exercise is a great way to align the Strategic Leadership Team on messaging

Notes

1 And he did not even have Carol Dweck available at the time for counsel!.
2 Google's values (what they call their philosophy) are cleverly couched as: "Ten things we know to be true." Brilliant.
3 It is an eerie experience for me to walk into the Googleplex. Google bought these buildings from Silicon Graphics, Inc. (SGI) in 2003, just a few years after my last contract ended with SGI. So, I know the building well, but it has a much different vibe from when it was part of my working playground.

Bibliography

Google. (n.d.). *Ten things we know to be true*. About Google. Retrieved from https://about.google/philosophy/
Musser, C. (1994). *The emergence of cinema: The American screen to 1907*. University of California Press.
X, The Moonshot Factory. (n.d.). *Homepage*. Retrieved from https://x.company/

Accelerating the Adamant Triad with a High-Performing Team

The second iteration of any multi-iteration effort is always my favorite iteration, provided the philosophy is faithfully adhered to: a Minimum Viable Product (MVP) has been presented to the customer, and you have the first opportunity to receive and process their feedback. The magic of iteration comes to life when you are hit with that first wave of knowledge that you could not have possibly known before going through the motions to produce a working product and then handing it over to your customers for the first round of valuable feedback. There is so much discovery that happens throughout the first iteration (including feedback on the MVP), and it is thrilling for any team to know that they have at least one more iteration to apply all this knowledge to make their product better. That is why I call this second iteration the Accelerate Phase.

You will make the greatest improvements to your Adamant Triad in this next iteration, for three reasons. First, although the Strategic Framework, DHARMA, The Innovation Factory, and all the other models that we reviewed in the last three chapters are new to you—they are not brand new anymore. You have been through the process once already, and you now have the benefit of reflection: if I had to do this all over again, what would I do differently? Second, you have very valuable feedback based on a tangible product from trusted stakeholders that you can and should apply in this next iteration. And finally, the next two chapters will advance your knowledge of understanding, nurturing, and leading a precocious organization. This will all be applied to a greatly improved version of your Adamant Triad called a Respectable Effective Product (REP).

Our activities will be guided by the decisions we determined in Chapter 4 that will be made at the end of the iteration:

- Have we applied feedback from the last iteration to develop a significantly better Adamant Triad?
- Do we feel like we are about 60%–70% of the way to a perfect Adamant Triad?

DOI: 10.4324/9781003518181-10

- Have we developed an Adamant Triad that we *might* use, without another iteration of development?
- Have we captured additional feedback that we *should* apply to the next iteration?
- *Should* we move forward with another iteration?

Keep these decisions in mind as you read through the next two chapters. The *significantly better* Adamant Triad referenced in the top bullet will emerge as we take a deeper dive into our human-centered strategy, where people and culture form the center point around which everything else is designed. The next two chapters will provide deeper insights into bringing a *human-centered* strategy to life, an area that is not often discussed in strategy circles.

To help clarify our thinking about people and culture, we will explore the ancient Hawaiians, a culture obviously close to my heart. Of course, I am biased, but that aside, there is a lot about that culture that is unique and especially valuable for the leader of a precocious organization. However, to understand the culture, you must learn some Hawaiian words and names from its history, which brings you into its language, and that may be distracting. If the name of Hawai'i state fish, the humuhumunukunukuāpua'a, is jarring and disruptive for you, I completely understand. Regardless of whether you subvocalize when you read, I suggest taking a quick course on how to pronounce Hawaiian words. It is really not difficult once you learn a few rules. And finally, please don't get too caught up in the precise pronunciation and recollection of some of these names. Nobody is going to test you on the name of our state fish, but you should be able to recognize it when you see it again.

So with that, mākaukau (are you ready)?
Awesome, then let's get into it!

Chapter 7

Manifesting Mana

Cultivating a Healthy, Vibrant Workplace Where People Thrive

Aloha 'Oe

If you stumble upon an ancient Hawaiian idol while hiking in Hawai'i, just leave it alone! I loved watching The Brady Bunch as a kid and I clearly remember the episode when that "tiki idol" wreaks havoc all over their family vacation in Hawai'i. Although this was a family show produced in Hollywood for entertainment purposes, there is a lot of truth in the message they may have been sending about our ki'i (this is what a Hawaiian would actually call a "tiki idol"). There are sacred things about our culture that should not be tampered with, like little wooden idols that are buried with our kūpuna (ancestors). The depth and richness of the Hawaiian culture, especially the *ancient* Hawaiian culture, provide a wealth of insight when considering a human-centered strategy and accompanying culture-led organizational design (OD), where people and culture play such a significant role in the design.

The great advantage of a culture-led OD is that a strong culture provides the framework for the most effective Power structure. In an organization with a strong command-and-control hierarchy, the Power structure relies on formal power, which is very unreliable in most democratic environments because the consequences experienced from any superior are relatively weak. Sure, you might be fired from a company for a provable pattern of disobedience, but that's nothing compared to what you might face if you violated the kapu (cultural laws) in ancient Hawai'i. The installation of a strong culture provides the strongest forms of consequences (positive and negative) because they stem from an individual's base values and beliefs. Consequences of this nature provide the opportunity to design a Power structure—far more powerful than any org chart—that reinforces a culture that favors well-being, community, and human relationships over abstract metrics and impersonal systems.

I loved growing up in a Hawaiian home. Even though I spent most of my childhood physically located in what would be known as Silicon

DOI: 10.4324/9781003518181-11

Valley, my mom brought her culture with her from Hawai'i to the *mainland* (this is how Hawiaiians refer to the continental United States) and made sure we stayed connected to our aloha. In addition, there were a few periods of time when I lived in Hawai'i. I went to grade school and high school there (one year of each), and I would sometimes spend the summer in Hawai'i with my tūtū (grandma), aunties, uncles, and cousins. They all stayed in one big house near Pearl Harbor, so one more keike (child) in the house did not impact them much.

My 'ohana (family) is very loving and welcoming, which is very characteristic of Hawaiians. This is, no doubt, due to our *aloha spirit,* a preternatural force that is endemic to the Hawaiian Islands. You will not find anything like aloha anywhere in the world, but Hawai'i. There is a common misconception that aloha only means hello and/or goodbye. Yes, it is used by Hawaiians as both a salutation and a valediction, but its *meaning* is complex and difficult to translate into English. It is a spirit that radiates throughout Hawai'i and its inhabitants that embodies an unbridled and unconditional care and concern for all humans and nature.

Aloha 'Oe is one of Hawai'i's most popular songs. It was written by Queen Lili'uokalani, the last ruling monarch of Hawai'i, when she witnessed the parting embrace of two lovers during a visit to the Maunawili Ranch on the island of O'ahu. The Hawaiian word *'oe* means, "to you," so when the queen wrote this song, she apparently meant Aloha 'Oe to mean "Farewell to Thee," which is the commonly accepted translation. However, as we just discussed, aloha doesn't necessarily mean *farewell.* Take a moment to think about what Aloha 'Oe might mean, when used in the context we just described in the previous paragraph. This is what we will build our precocious culture around.

There are a couple more Hawaiian words worth noting. We briefly mentioned one earlier: *kapu.* The kapu were the sacred rules of the culture that were adhered to religiously. Violation of the kapu was punishable by death, and a very brutal one at that. Another important concept in ancient Hawaiian culture is *mana,* which essentially means spiritual power. Some people (and things) had more mana than others, like an ali'i nui (head chief) and a heiau (temple). Mana could be accumulated (e.g., by winning battles) or depleted (e.g., by violating kapu). Maintaining or increasing one's mana was an important way to establish status in the ancient Hawaiian society.

For all its merit, it is important to highlight some of the vulnerabilities of the ancient Hawaiian culture. I mean, it is *ancient* for a reason. First and foremost, their aloha left them vulnerable to others with a different belief system, like the Europeans. They were *too* trusting of foreigners. This coupled with their relative inferiority when it came to technology and political savvy is what ultimately caused the demise of their kingdom. Finally, their kapu system effectively controlled behavior, but it also inhibited innovation and creative thinking, much like the Ninja and Mongolians discussed in Chapter 5. These are things to consider as we adopt the elements of the ancient Hawaiian culture that serve our needs, while mitigating the key cultural risks that contributed to its demise.

The Judo of Preempting Attrition, Quiet Quitting, and Employee Burnout

It is no doubt that attrition and employee burnout are perennial migraines for leaders. It is expensive and difficult to find good people, so it is easy to understand why leaders would be incessantly worried about burning them out or losing them altogether. And then there's this old thing with a new label called "Quiet Quitting" that you should be worried about, if you aren't already. However, worrying about what you don't want is the wrong focus. It is like worrying about falling to the ground when walking on a tightrope. If that's where your focus is, you will probably find yourself staring up at the rope from the safety net! It is good to understand why people quit, but it is more important to understand why people *stay*.

In fact, you can leverage the force that drives attrition, employee burnout, and quiet quitting against itself to your great advantage, in the same way judo experts leverage an opponent's own weight and/or momentum to throw them to the floor. Remember the potential energy of attrition that we witnessed during the Great Resignation (see Figure 1.2)? That tension will be in the talent pool for as long as people remember how they felt about their employer during that period, regardless of the circumstances. So instead of doing hand-to-hand combat with that tension, let's flip it on its back using its own force.

As you might guess, I know a lot of other talented management consultants who I consider friends, if not family. So, while writing this book, I asked a few of my esteemed colleagues for their opinions as to why people quit their jobs. With a combined experience of over a century, I am sure you will find this summary of their responses insightful. Donna says people quit when their roles and responsibilities change, outside of their control (e.g., due to a reorganization), to a job that doesn't suit them. Emily says people quit when they feel they have lost all agency, leaving them with no control over their environment. And, Christina says people quit when they feel like they are living to work instead of working to live. Does any of this resonate with you? I full heartedly agree with my colleagues, and, of course, I have a few opinions of my own.

Know and Grow

Anticipatory Anxiety is the stress that builds when you constantly worry about a future event (certain or potential) and all the negative impacts that will result from it. If done too much, it can progress to a serious condition called Generalized Anxiety Disorder (GAD), which requires intervention from a licensed psychologist. It is much healthier, physically and mentally, to focus on the positive

If you focus on building an environment where people love to work, you will intrinsically address all these issues. In simple terms, people will leave your firm when they don't *feel* like working there—it is not more complicated than that. It does not matter why someone would feel like quitting when you know they don't feel like quitting. I know it sounds circular, but I hope it makes sense. Nobody will walk away from an environment where they love to work, so let's focus on building that. Here are ten workplace conditions that naturally prevent attrition, employee burnout, and quiet quitting:

1 **Family Environment:** Use the concepts of aloha, mana, and kapu to build a strong culture and community with high levels of trust, respect, and pride
2 **Tribal Unity:** Once a member of the tribe, always a member of the tribe. Create a community that extends beyond current employees to friends, family, and alumni. Never lose contact with your tribe members
3 **Royal Welcome:** Give newcomers to the organization an amazing first 100 days. Invite them into your family with pomp and circumstance. Develop an onboarding package that ensures they understand your aloha and kapu and kickstart them with a healthy amount of mana
4 **Smooth Turns:** When there is any type of change in the organization that impacts your people, for any reason, partner with them to resolve any roadblocks and ensure a smooth transition or transformation
5 **Persona Ranking:** Use clearly defined personas that align with your strategy to rank people based on level of match or fit. Your best-fit employees should get the most attention
6 **Bespoke Accommodations:** Treat people as individuals, with individual needs and wants. Understand what they like and don't like about their working environment and demonstrate that you are continually working to improve it

7 **Pursuit of Happiness:** Give people the freedom to work on what they love to do. Find jobs that suit people, not people that suit jobs

8 **Rituals of Sharing:** Your system of kapu should include ceremonies (group and one-on-one) where people share their thoughts and feelings, even the undiscussables (Argyris, 1990)

9 **Work-Life Blending:** Blur the lines that separate work and life. When work and life are blended, there is no need for balance

10 **High Exit Barrier:** Make it very difficult to leave your firm, especially for your best-fit employees. Your firm should always be a better option for them than any other option

The Anatomy and Physiology of a High-Performing Precocious Team

It would be foolish to put so much energy into creating a rich environment for your people to thrive without understanding the people who are supposed to be thriving in it, so let's take some time to dissect a high-performing, precocious team. For this, it is best to focus on teams versus individuals, because you should realize more collective value from a team than the sum of its individuals. Furthermore, we need your teams to be both high-performing and precocious. A high-performing, non-precocious team is nice to have but doesn't do much for your strategy of unlocking human ingenuity to create game-changing offerings. And a low-performing, precocious team is just a terrible waste of good talent, like forcing a gifted child to attend a pedestrian public school.

Your evaluation of a high-performing, precocious team should be unambiguous. They will consistently outperform their peers in all the metrics that matter. At the time of this writing, the 2024 Olympics are being held in Paris. It was exciting to watch the opening ceremonies, as it always is, and suspenseful to contemplate who will win gold—for some events. But let's be honest. The 2024 United States Men's Olympic Basketball Team is stacked with *four* NBA (National Basketball Association) MVP (Most Valuable Player) award winners. Furthermore, the United States has always dominated Olympic basketball, even before the "Dream Team" showed up in Barcelona for the 1992 Olympics, marking the dawn of NBA-level competition at the Olympics, and a devastating situation for any other country hoping for gold. It should be obvious that the United States will go home with another gold medal.[1]

And yet, in 2004, during the Olympic Games in Athens, a ridiculously talented roster of NBA professionals made Olympic history—they *lost* three games, the most games ever lost by a U.S. men's Olympic basketball team. We were lucky to hit the podium at all, barely snagging the bronze. Coach Mike Krzyzewski, head coach of the U.S. men's basketball team during the 2008 Olympics in Beijing, built his redemption team based on this valuable lesson from that performance: you cannot just assemble an assortment of great players and expect them to perform like a great team (Krzyzewski & Spatola, 2009).[2] Likewise, you cannot expect to assemble an assortment of precocious individuals and expect them to perform like a precocious team.

That said, their collective precocity should be obvious, so make sure you have clear evidence of how advanced they are, instead of just relying on gut feeling. Precocious teams are so in touch with their craft that they are always several steps ahead of everyone else in their domain. In fact, they are often bored with novel innovations in their space of knowledge, because they've already considered them a long time ago. Matt Damon's character in Good Will Hunting would often get frustrated with his professor when he tried to "work" with him on complicated math problems that perplexed the experts, because, for the precocious kid from South Boston, the answer was always glaringly obvious.

They are very smart high performers, and everyone knows it, including them. Therefore, they occasionally cross the line from confidence to arrogance, but it usually doesn't get too far out of hand. They are generally more fun and playful than stressed and insufferable. They trust and respect each other implicitly, and it shows in the way they interact with each other. There are high levels of communication and interaction, with every member of the team participating equally. You may observe leadership seamlessly passing from member to member as they instinctively tag team to meet a challenge. This demonstrates the level of respect that they have for each other's expertise.

They speak freely and honestly about how they feel and resolve conflicts through duels of intelligence, which is fascinating to witness. Just don't try to interject unless you are prepared to face the entire team in an intellectual battle. They love challenges and will quickly commit to any challenge, especially a tough one. They are creative but tenacious, never giving up until the puzzle is solved. They own the highs of victory and the lows of defeat, but there is typically no in between. A precocious team that is mild-mannered is probably a bored one that needs something more challenging to work on.

One final note that you should be aware of when it comes to high-performing, precocious teams. They can become unraveled when they lose or fall short of expectations, especially when it is public. We will cover this more in the next chapter when we discuss leadership, but this is an especially sensitive aspect of precocious teams that deserves special treatment when (not if) the situation arises.

Cultivating a Rich Environment Where People Love to Work

We have an idea of the environment that we need to create, and we have an idea of the people who will thrive in that environment; now, let's attach all that to our opportunity. Cultivating a rich environment where people love to work touches all five opportunities discussed in Chapter 2:

1 The opportunity to grow exponentially, catapulting the organization into a new level of strategic measures (revenues, costs, profits, etc.), and build much-needed capabilities to ease relentless market demands
2 The opportunity to build and continually nurture a thriving community of skilled workers who love coming to work to do their best work, while simultaneously unlocking precious human creativity and commercializing it for an unassailable competitive advantage
3 The opportunity to effortlessly attract and retain the best people in the talent pool that match clearly defined best-fit personas
4 The opportunity to build a psychologically safe environment where people express their thoughts and feelings without fear of any negative consequences, including normative sanctions from their peers
5 The opportunity to master hybrid working environments that transcend the limitations of physical boundaries and maximize organizational performance through deliberate application of collocated teaming

Opportunity 1 highlights the important relationship between providing an environment where people thrive and serving the devoted fans that buy your products and services (i.e., easing relentless market demands). We have also established a line of sight that clarifies the dependent succession between these two points (See Figure 3.3). As illustrated, the environment should be continually cultivated to support smart *and* happy people—we need the combination of both in every person.[3] To do this, you must have a Prophet Center[4] unlike any other when it comes to the specific technology (Guiding Light) that undergirds your strategy. It should be filled with anything and everything regarding your technology, including proprietary and confidential research your firm has done. You will also need information systems (people- and data-based) for understanding and continually promoting employee well-being (which includes happiness). This is more than just *feel-good* advice. Positive psychology and neuroscience reveal happiness as a key dependency for generating insights.

Of course, Opportunity 2 speaks directly to the continual nurturing of your thriving community; however, it also talks about unlocking human creativity. A robust Prophet Center is important as it provides vital fodder for that "much-needed capability" of innovation that is referenced in Opportunity 1 and illustrated in Figure 3.3. Furthermore, the ongoing operation of the Innovation Factory should stimulate innovation. However, people will need additional help and assistance in unlocking their human creativity. Whether or not driven by an Innovation Center of Excellence (see Chapter 6), the environment should continually expose your people to new and different experiences that have nothing to do with your technology. Recent neuroscience unveils another secret to generating insights: the best ones come when you are not thinking directly about the issue. That is why shower time is an innovator's most valuable period of the day!

We have already addressed Opportunities 3 and 4 in this chapter, so let's jump to Opportunity 5. Hybrid work is a very hot topic at the time of this writing, the controversy of which provides an incredible opportunity for those who seize it while the window is open. If you are pursuing a human-centered strategy, you absolutely *must* create a winning hybrid situation for your people. The best way to do this is to let teams decide what works best for them and not interfere, but hold them accountable for results. It is important to embrace, once again, an *allocentric* perspective when it comes to hybrid work. Focus on what is being produced by teams, not how they produce it. Trust your teams to figure out when they need to come in and when they do not—they know the nature of their work much better than you do.

Wasabi Moment

Defending a hybrid work environment where teams are allowed to determine when and how they work is very difficult. Often, top leadership feel they know what is best, so they use formal power to dictate rules. "Do it because I said so" is the wrong approach if people are your first concern

At the same time, invest energy into, what I call, RW-DEI (Remote Worker Diversity, Equity, and Inclusion). The goal is to have a seamless experience for the team, regardless of each member's physical location. I was working with a multi-national oil and gas company that has several large oil fields in the Central Valley of California (e.g., Bakersfield). It is about a 3.5-hour drive from where I live in Silicon Valley, so I did not exactly drive there every day. I was on-site for some of the time, and when I wasn't, I worked remotely. Unfortunately, the conferencing technology down there was a bit antiquated, and many times, I was the only team member working remotely. As such, there were several occasions when

I felt like an outcast due to my remote situation. This is what you want to avoid. Treat physical work location like any other protected class (race, color, religion, etc.). Continually promote the fair treatment and full participation of all team members, regardless of physical location.

Using Modern Advances in Artificial Intelligence to Build a CybOrg (Cybernetic Organization)

The notion of infusing humans with modern technology to create super-capable beings has been around ever since 1960, when Manfred Clynes and Nathan S. Kline introduced the notion of a Cyborg, which is short for *cybernetic organism* (Clynes & Kline, 1960). And despite the science-fictional romanticism of cyborgs over the last several decades, the seminal proposal of a cyborg was very much science non-fictional. The invention of the cyborg was born out of the necessity of space exploration. Since humans cannot naturally survive in space, the proposal for consideration was to enhance our natural abilities by infusing modern technology (of the time) to unconsciously compensate for our mortal deficiencies, like the way a pacemaker regulates a person's heart rate without any conscious attention.

I submit that we extend this idea into the organizational context, a re-mashup that means cybernetic *organization*. A cyborg, in this context, is an organization that infuses modern technology into high-performing teams to create ultra-high-performing[5] teams. Imagine if you had a tuner car that could sustain a nitrous oxide injection for a prolonged period of time. That is how I envision contemporary technology (nitrous oxide) taking an already high-performing team to an ultra-high-performing team. Since technology tends to advance at such a blistering pace, it is important to constantly stay on the bleeding edge of technology and infuse it, as best you can, to achieve ultra-high levels of performance from your precocious teams. I don't know what the bleeding-edge technology of the day is when you read this book, but in 2024, with the popularity of ChatGPT, it seems to be generative artificial intelligence (GenAI).

Know and Grow

Cybernetics is the study of circular feedback mechanisms, where outputs become inputs in a reinforcing loop, like a thermostat that constantly regulates the temperature of a room. It fits nicely with high-performing teams and GenAI where teams can have a "discussion" with the AI Agent for progressively insightful information

The irrational paranoia that some people seem to have surrounding artificial intelligence is wildly entertaining to me. Yes, it is true that artificial intelligence will displace some people in the job market, but that's nothing new. Technology has been doing that since the Industrial Revolution. But the notion that someday the machines will become sentient and take over the world? That's hilarious. We cannot prevent simple software from crashing every 5 minutes, and somehow the computers are going to overthrow the humans? This is what happens when people let their imaginations run wild.

Anthropomorphism is when we attribute human qualities to something that is clearly not human—like a computer. When "chatting" with a chatbot, it is easy to convince yourself that you are chatting with some sort of pseudo-sentient technology—you are not. Your computer is putting on a well-intentioned magic trick. At the end of the day, they are just following a coded set of instructions, as they always have. It is just that these programs are deliberately coded to mimic human interaction. And they do a pretty good job. But I am not *that* impressed, and neither is anyone else who has been submerged in artificial intelligence for as long as I have.[6]

In today's times, a high-performing team that goes all-in on GenAI has a pretty good chance at achieving ultra-high performance. You should leverage GenAI against your Prophet Center to create a *proprietary AI model* and turn it loose on your precocious teams. Once encouraged, it won't take long for them to figure it out and increase performance; however, specific education and coaching are a great way to accelerate the journey. Plus, I guarantee they will have a load of fun with it. One word of caution, though, GenAI models definitely hallucinate, so be careful. When ChatGPT first came out, for fun, I asked it to give me a list of different OD philosophies, and it spat out a long list of different types of org structures! What a disaster! I guess even artificial humans are highly susceptible to ORD (Obsessive Restructuring Disorder)![7]

Putting It into Practice

One of our key opportunities (from Chapter 2) is to effortlessly attract and retain the best people in the talent pool that match clearly defined **best-fit personas**. But what exactly is a best-fit persona? Personas are traditionally used by Marketing and Information Technology professionals to help clarify the needs, motivations, and objectives of their end consumers or end users, respectively. Let's build one now, given what you have learned in this chapter:

1 Replicate your own version of Figure 7.1 using software that is suitable for your firm. Feel free to add or adjust sections but avoid adding any

Figure 7.1 Best-Fit Persona Template.

protected categories (including physical working location!). We are trying to create a fictional representation of a person that best fits your firm's target environment. You will eventually create several personas, for now, let's just work with the first one that comes to mind

2 What technical skills do they absolutely love and effortlessly excel at?

3 What makes their work meaningful?

4 What kinds of hobbies do they have? What do they do for fun?

5 What interpersonal skills shine through when you watch them work with other people? How do they resolve conflict?

6 What observable leadership skills do they have? How do they compel people to follow them? How do they make decisions?

7 What compels them to follow someone? What is their ideal supervisor like?

8 What motivates them? What demotivates them?

9 What do they like about any given working environment. What do they love?

10 What do they dislike about any given working environment. What do they hate?

Although this might feel like a job specification, it is not. A persona has a much more psychological and emotional hue, which affords you the ability to evaluate people and their environment based on observation. This is an important distinction. You design your organization around people, and then derive job specifications—not the other way around.

Executive Debrief

- The great advantage of a culture-led OD is that a strong culture provides the framework for the most effective Power structure
- The ancient Hawaiian culture is rich with concepts for cultivating a strong, thriving culture

  - Aloha is a spirit that embodies an unbridled and unconditional care and concern for all humans and nature
  - Mana is spiritual power that establishes status. It accumulates or depletes in an individual, primarily based on their behavior
  - Kapu were the sacred rules and rituals that were ingrained in their culture and religiously adhered to

- Although valuable, the ancient Hawaiian culture had vulnerabilities that must be recognized and accounted for

  - They trusted the wrong people who ultimately took advantage of their aloha
  - Their kapu inhibited innovation and creative thinking
  - Their technology (e.g., armament) was inferior and their knowledge was isolated to their area of the world

- The best way to arrest attrition, quiet quitting, and employee burnout is to sustain an environment where people love to work. To that end, here are ten workplace conditions to strongly consider:

  - Family environment
  - Tribal unity
  - Royal welcome
  - Smooth turns
  - Persona ranking
  - Bespoke accommodations

- Pursuit of happiness
- Work-life blending
- High exit barrier

- High-performing, precocious teams have the following qualities:

  - Consistently outperforms peers in all the metrics that matter
  - Collective precocity should be obvious
  - Bored with contemporary innovations that they have already contemplated a long time ago
  - Aware of their performance capability and sometimes arrogant about it
  - Clearly trust and respect each other, it shows in the way they interact with each other
  - High levels of communication and interaction, with every member participating equally
  - Often tag team on taking the lead
  - Speak freely and honestly about how they feel
  - Love challenges and quickly commit to any challenge
  - May become unraveled when they lose or fall short of expectations

- To cultivate a rich environment where people love to work, you should:

  - Develop and maintain a robust Prophet Center
  - Develop and maintain people- and data-based information systems for continually promoting employee well-being
  - Continually expose your people to new and different experiences that have nothing to do with your technology
  - Create a hybrid work environment that fosters diversity, equity, and inclusion agnostic of physical work location
  - Let teams decide when it is best to work remotely or come into the office

- A CybOrg (cybernetic organization) is one that infuses modern technology into high-performing teams to create ultra-high-performing teams

Notes

1 Honest truth—I wrote this paragraph just a few hours before the U.S. Men's Basketball team played Spain for the gold medal. I am glad they actually won!
2 And yes, Coach K and "The Redeem Team" defeated Spain 118–107 for the gold medal.
3 Not that I have anything against happy people who are not smart. They are fun to hang out with. I just don't know about investing in their continued happiness if they are not contributing to my competitive advantage.
4 This is a component of the Strategic Guidance System that serves as an omniscient source of wisdom and truth (see Chapter 4).

5 Ultra- was intentionally chosen over super- when characterizing the level of performance expected out of a cyborg. While super- is Latin for "above," ultra- is Latin for "beyond."
6 I was writing artificial intelligence programs while I was a teenager in high school, to help handicap horse races. The only difference today—I'm not a teenager in high school.
7 ICYMI, we spent a lot of time discussing ORD in Chapter 5.

Bibliography

Argyris, C. (1990). *Overcoming organizational defenses: Facilitating organizational learnings.* Allyn and Bacon.

Clynes, M. E., & Kline, N. S. (1960). Cyborgs and space. *Astronautics, 5*(9), 26–27, 74–76.

Krzyzewski, M., & Spatola, J. K. (2009). *The gold standard: Building a world-class team.* Grand Central Publishing.

Murphy, M., & Burgio-Murphy, A. (2022). *The deadly sins of employee retention: New edition to solve the great resignation, quiet quitting, burnout, and more.* Leadership IQ Press.

Rock, D. (2008). SCARF: A brain-based model for collaborating with and influencing others. *NeuroLeadership Journal, 1,* 78–87.

Chapter 8

I Have a Dream Team
How to Lead a Gifted Team

A Leader That People Will Follow Anywhere

Have you ever witnessed a migrating flock of Canadian Geese in their iconic "V formation"? It is truly magnificent. In March of 2019, I was asked by a business unit leader in Calgary, Canada to help him with some organizational shifts. It was a perfect time of year to be up there, especially if you appreciate, as I do, the majestic nature of these amazing societies of birds in flight. I remember landing in Calgary one crisp Sunday afternoon. To my delight, an amazing spectacle of about 40–50 geese flew by in perfect formation. My wife and I just sat and watched in awe and amazement. They were obviously returning home from, what I hope was, a fun summer visit to the warm climate of the South.

At some point, while preparing for the thousand-mile journey, the geese decided on the one goose who would lead them back home. From what we know about the social organization of geese, it was likely the most experienced and skilled goose who took the lead, as long as they were strong and healthy. The leader was likely not on point for the entire journey, as that would be too exhausting; the point bird in the formation must endure the most drag. Therefore, a few geese were selected to fly in front, just behind the leader, so they could all take turns dealing with the drag. A combination of visual and audible cues kept every goose on track for the long journey until they arrived at their final nesting grounds.

A leader, avian or otherwise, is the individual that the rest of the group decides to follow. Without followers, there is no leader. Furthermore, the greatness of a leader is found in the size and loyalty of their followers. Consequently, leadership is conditional; it will only remain with an individual so long as they have those who choose to follow them. It is not uncommon to find societies in nature where leaders emerge dynamically, based on the conditions of the environment—i.e., when the group decides to follow a different individual. We see this happen in packs of wolves, swarms of bees, and schools of fish.

DOI: 10.4324/9781003518181-12

Therefore, to be a great leader of a *precocious* organization, you must understand the type of person a precocious organization will follow, even when the going gets tough. By definition, precocious people are at the upper end of the academic bell curve, which pushes them out of the "normal" group. Despite the circumstances where this translates to a higher social status, they know the feeling of being "not normal," which isn't always a great feeling. Furthermore, since they are far advanced for their class, it's often difficult to find challenging work for them. They get bored with the challenges most people struggle with and their mind often wanders during conversations, while others struggle to discern what they have already concluded shortly after the conversation started. They may even pretend to struggle with a "difficult" challenge, so it looks like they are working hard, while they're actually relaxing to take a mental break.

Another characteristic of precocious people is the value they place on their status. Status is very important to them, so they often internalize external pressures to be the best. Their identity is tied to their brilliance, so they are very sensitive to being wrong, even in matters that have nothing to do with their expertise. It is hard for them to submit a low-confidence deliverable like a Minimum Viable Product (MVP), so they tend to over-engineer solutions to save themselves from the criticisms that are self-evident in an MVP. And it is hard for them to find people to trust because they are constantly being used for their intelligence.

So, why would a group like this follow someone? Furthermore, what can a leader do to encourage followership from precocious people? Why would these geese choose you to lead the way? Generally speaking, they must trust that you will eventually lead them to a better place and ideally make the journey as frictionless as possible. That means, above all, you must be *trustworthy*. This quality in a leader is especially valuable for precocious people, given their inherent bias against trusting others.

Wasabi Moment

It is common, when exploring behaviors that would improve a design or operation of a group, to deflect the responsibility of change onto other groups, e.g., "they need to trust me more." There is little value to this insight compared to the behaviors you or your group must change, e.g., "I need to be more trustworthy." Focus on what you can control, not how you want others to change

Furthermore, you must take extra measures to keep them engaged in *challenging* work. And finally, they have a special relationship with recognition, so be very intentional about how their brilliance is rewarded. The satisfaction of solving a difficult problem is a very strong internal reward—however, an additional cash bonus usually goes over pretty well, too.

Managing Super-Chicken Personalities

Now that we have laid the foundation for leading a precocious team, let's address some specific peculiarities of dealing with one, starting with Super-Chickens. No, I am not talking about one of my favorite childhood cartoons! I am talking about pretentious little jerks who think they are better than everyone else, so they bully everyone around them into submission to maintain alpha status. You will *definitely* come across these personalities when dealing with precocious people, so you must know how to deal with them.

The term comes from a study that William Muir, a biologist at Purdue University, conducted in the 1990s to understand the egg-laying performance of chickens. He had a control group of typical chickens and a study group consisting of only the highest performers (i.e., those who laid the most eggs). His null hypothesis was that any differences between the two groups were purely due to normal variation. He did, in fact, find a statistical significance between the groups. Over six generations of selectively breeding the highest performers, he found that his study group had an overall *lower* performance than the control group. The aggressive nature of these *super-chickens* turned their henhouse into a caged octagon that proved fatal for a few alphas that really should have reconsidered their perceived social status.

About a decade later, Margaret Heffernan, entrepreneur and CEO, amplified the idea of super-chickens to challenge a popular belief that competition breeds the highest levels of success, advocating for a more collaborative approach to innovation and progress (2014, Heffernan). As much as I love the idea of smart people collaborating to achieve breakthrough success, there is no way I can support the belief that competition is some sort of categorical villain that destroys innovation.[1] We are not chickens! We have a far more advanced neural network that *usually* regulates our primal impulses of pecking threats to death.

However, super-chickens are basically sore losers who resort to bullying when their status is threatened. It starts with a base personality trait of feeling negative emotions under competitive pressure. There is absolutely nothing wrong with someone who does not thrive under competitive pressure; however, people like this should not be forced into competitive situations.[2] Unfortunately, sometimes, that's just the nature of the game. So, in these situations, the high performer must know how to regulate their emotions when they feel their status is threatened. If they don't, they'll start pecking for their lives.

Super-chickens are best controlled with kapu and aloha. Aggressive and bullying behavior must be strictly taboo,[3] especially when it comes to protecting or advancing status, and everyone in the organization should know it. It should be clear that one of the quickest ways to *lose* status is to step on others to advance. This is an anti-behavior to aloha; this is against your culture. And those who do not fit within the culture must be banned from it. You, as the ali'i nui (chief leader), have the ultimate responsibility for holding people accountable when kapu is violated.

Also, keep in mind that the ideal organizational climate for an allocentric organization is one where the emotional valence is positive (as discussed in Chapter 5), meaning there are high levels of happiness, enthusiasm, excitement, trust, morale, and constructive conflict. Super-chickens introduce unhealthy stress into the environment and disrupt

Organizational Climate Survey

For each statement in Table 8.1, mark the box that best describes your personal alignment with the statement

Table 8.1 Organizational Climate Survey

# Statement	Strongly Disagree	Disagree	Neutral	Agree	Strongly Agree
1 I feel like our organization can handle any change that is thrown our way					
2 I am happy, excited and enthusiastic when I am at work					
3 I trust the people that I work with					
4 I feel we handle conflict well as an organization					
5 I feel like I am rewarded fairly for my contributions					
6 My work life does not interfere with my personal life					
7 My company supports my growth as an individual					
8 We love experimenting with new ideas and are open to changing roles based on new technology					
9 Our success is driven more by external factors than internal metrics					

the climate of an optimal allocentric organization. So, one way to identify a potential super-chicken issue is to periodically run an organizational climate survey with your people. The statements that should raise suspicions of super-chickens in the coop are 2, 3, 4, and 5.

Dealing with the "Yips" and Other Feelings of Inadequacy

Holy mother of Mercury,[4] the "yips" are a real pain to deal with, especially with a precocious team that is accustomed to high performance. You will commonly hear this term used with pro golfers when, for some sudden, bizarre, and mysterious reason, their swing is just badly off. In their mind, they are doing everything they would normally do to hit a perfect drive, but you know as soon as the club strikes the ball with a resounding "clank," that ball is either landing in the deep rough or in the water. Although we believe this condition and onomatopoeic term started with golf, it has since spread to various other athletic endeavors, including baseball, darts, cricket, and yes, even cognitive sports like chess.

When the yips strike a precocious team, it can be devastating. It appears to expose a vulnerability that just isn't there. Having an off day is one thing, but when a small pattern of low performance is observed, it starts to look like they have "lost their touch." And as previously discussed, precocious teams naturally *hate* to show up in any way that's associated with low performance. Even with a lot of conditioning, support, and reassurance, it is very difficult for a high-performing team to deal with sudden and unexplainable performance that is decisively lower than expectations.

We do not know exactly what causes the yips, and it is difficult to prescribe a reliable remedy; however, we do know there's a neurological component and that stress seems to be a contributing factor. Neuroscience tells us that higher-order brain functions, like problem solving and decision making, are compromised under threatening conditions. Typically, people who thrive under pressure are not threatened by pressure; this is how they are able to sustain high performance. They have the luxury of operating on unadulterated adrenaline, dopamine, and even serotonin (i.e., they actually *love* pressure). However, we cannot always pick and choose what we are threatened by. So, there may be an unconscious threat at the psychological base of someone experiencing the yips. And, when one member goes tilt, that will likely throw off the rest of the team.

As a leader, it is important to neutralize the effects of the yips with both the team and the observers. Many people don't even know about the yips (did you before you read this?), so simply exposing the concept will help diffuse its effects. Furthermore, reassure them that you are not concerned about their performance and that "these things happen." Talk with the team about their experience with the yips. What you are looking for are telltale signs of the yips, like total confusion as to why this is happening. You should also listen for symptoms of unhealthy stress, like anxiety or self-doubt. Regardless, it is best to take them away from any pressure and send in a coach to help them reset with mindfulness and relaxation techniques. Finally, I recommend establishing a ritual or ceremony for overcoming yips. Even if it seems like an obvious placebo, you would be amazed at what some athletes will do to shake the yips—and swear by it as a cure.[5]

The yips are one of a few conditions that can shake the confidence of a person or team—another one being Imposter's Syndrome. As its name implies, this is a condition where high performers have doubts that their ability is the primary contributor to their success, instead attributing it to luck or external factors that are out of their control. Following from this belief is an anxiety that they will be "exposed" as a fraudster. In almost all cases, these beliefs and fears are unfounded, but the psychology must be dealt with because it is very real for the people who experience it.

Again, it is good to have psychologists and coaches in the wings ready to support people facing conditions like this; however, you have a responsibility as a leader to be a first responder to The Yips, Impostor's Syndrome, and other feelings of inadequacy that precocious people experience sometimes. Fundamentally, all these conditions are a natural threat to the individual's status and relatedness (i.e., to their team). Leaders should compensate by reinforcing a culture where sub-par performance is non-threatening; a psychologically safe environment where the traditional notion of "failure" is replaced by "a discovery of how it won't work."[6] This value must be authentic, and the belief must be real. It's common to see a misalignment between espoused values and observed behaviors when it comes to sensitive areas like psychological safety.

Becoming a Cyborg Leader

We find, in history and nature, a pattern where the most skilled and experienced individuals emerge as leaders if the culture supports it. We have already seen examples of this with Ancient Hawaiians, Mongolians, Ninja, and even geese. There is a good reason for that. Expert power is very strong, and the best way to establish yourself as an expert is to give people a pattern of observable evidence that you are very good at something. Therefore, to whatever extent possible, you should lead by example.

I am sure you have heard this before, but I think most leaders miss the point. Most leaders interpret this as, "I will show you, by my own behavior, how I expect you to act." This is a very egocentric view of leadership that ignores the self-interest of your intended followers. Instead, think of it like this, "I will garner your trust by demonstrating my expertise at something you value." So, in the same way we create cyborgs to elevate high-performing teams into ultra-high-performing teams, we are going to turn you into a cyborg to elevate your leadership to levels never seen before.[7]

The way to approach your transformation into a cyborg is similar to the way Clines and Kline approached it back in the 1960s (see Chapter 7). Remember, they were trying to develop a man–machine system that would seamlessly and unconsciously adapt our bodies to space. Their basis of design was rooted in *regulation*, i.e., a hands-free way to regulate the difference between our natural living requirements and the conditions of space. It was a very serious proposal that, unfortunately, did not produce fruit. If it had, modern-day astronauts would be free to roam around space without the need for an EMU (extravehicular mobility unit), more commonly known as a "space suit." The distinction is important. The vision of the original cyborg was a *fusion* of our natural biology and technology that would automatically compensate for our mortal shortcomings, given the objective of life sustainability in a foreign environment (i.e., space). In a similar way, our goal is to infuse modern technology into your natural leadership capability to seamlessly and unconsciously reset your *hegemonostasis*[8] to a much higher level of performance.

To do this, you need a clear understanding of two things: the elevated state of leadership capability that you should be able to achieve and the technology that will help you effortlessly adapt to that state. This is an iterative process of discovery, which you should be familiar with at this point, so I will start with the latter and encourage you to partner with a good technologist (e.g., data scientist) that you trust. They will understand the best ways to use modern technology to achieve whatever you want to achieve. Which leads us to the first point—what does an elevated state of leadership capability look like? It looks like more followers and more trust from them in your ability to lead. And it also means being outstanding in performing the five non-delegable responsibilities that we discussed in Chapter 3 (see Figure 8.1).

It is important that you continually stay on the bleeding edge of technology to keep apprised of the technologies that you can experiment with. Using the language of Geoffrey Moore and his Technology Adoption Life Cycle (2014), own the role of *Innovator* when it comes to new technologies. Then work closely with your technologist to infuse modern technology into your leadership capabilities to become a super-leader.[9] Here are seven tips I would give to an aspiring cyborg leader who is facing a hyper-growth opportunity with a precocious organization:

1 Develop a Prophet Center incorporating GenAI that has access to both general information (like ChatGPT) and proprietary data that is specific to your firm. Then use it all day, every day, to grow your knowledge and develop your craft as a leader
2 Use your Prophet Center to understand how much trust your people have in you as a leader and to suggest ways that you can become more trustworthy to your people

Figure 8.1 A Cyborg Leader.

3 Use your Prophet Center to understand what motivates and demotivates your people, especially as it relates to the environment that you provide for them, and to suggest ways to improve your inspirational and motivational power
4 Have your Prophet Center constantly probe your external environment and send you regular updates of discovery that may trigger a re-evaluation of your strategy
5 Use your Prophet Center to help you make strategic decisions quickly
6 Use your Prophet Center to help you quickly rebalance your organization after a shift in Strategic Philosophy
7 User your Prophet Center to mine for ideas to put into your Innovation Factory

Remember to partner with an expert on this, at least until you have built enough capability to avoid pitfalls. For instance, at the time of this writing,

GenAI hallucinations are a huge problem until you realize what you're dealing with and how to mitigate them. It's best to have an expert available whom you can rely on when experimenting with technologies that you are not familiar with.

The Heart and Mind of Great Leaders

So far, we have intentionally focused on some specific situations that are faced by a leader of a precocious organization facing a hyper-growth opportunity; that is the focus of this book. However, general principles of good leadership are always in play, no matter what your situation is, so let's step back for a minute to talk about general leadership. I know there are a googol and one books on leadership, most of them ranging from bad to atrocious, so, I'll keep this brief and highly valuable.

In Chapter 4, we talked about the heart of a military general; let's start by briefly extending that discussion. I have admired General George S. Patton ever since I was a 17-year-old trooper in the United States Army proudly sporting my Cavalry Scout insignia (crossed swords) and beret. Patton, like many other brave military generals throughout history, led from the front.[10] He would position himself very close to the front lines, so his troops would *literally* follow him into battle. This is an admirable quality that I feel all leaders should have. Instead of isolating away with your leadership team in an unapproachable ivory tower, showcase your technical skills and expertise directly on the front lines to inspire followership. I have great respect for a leader who can hold their own next to me during a hackathon.

It is best if you have the same skills and talents as the people you are leading. That will allow you to wield expert power in addition to formal power, making it much easier to attract followers. If you are not a technical expert, that's okay, just own it. But don't divorce yourself from the technical aspects of the job; that will only separate you from the group. Instead, get involved and contribute the best you can without getting in the way. For instance, position yourself on deliverables that are not highly critical to the operation. You will earn great respect for your efforts and a great appreciation from your team for your enthusiasm. Of course, if your technical skills are on par with your followers, definitely insert yourself on the critical path with the highest stakes deliverables. This is a great way to command trust, respect, and loyal followers.

While leading an allocentric organization, it is important to stay true to the style of leadership that is best suited for it, regardless of how precocious your organization is. That means pushing decision-making down to the lowest levels of the organization and trusting the people closest to the work to make good decisions. If you micromanage your people, then you will spend too much time cleaning the boat, when you should be driving the boat. Keep your eye on the long-term horizon and take measures to ensure the mid-term and short-term horizons are well-covered without your direct involvement. You should also be curious, constantly seeking out new information and experimenting with new ideas without any fear of failing. As such, good leaders in an allocentric organization are risk takers who are good at recovering when things do not turn out as hoped.

The final piece of leadership advice I will leave you with comes from the world of neuroscience; it is called the SCARF® model, which stands for: status, certainty, autonomy, relatedness, and fairness. This is a model developed by Dr. David Rock that helps us understand the primary factors that drive the threat-reward systems in our brain (2008). I came across this model while studying at the NeuroLeadership Institute to improve my executive coaching skills. I find it useful to leverage the five factors of SCARF when evaluating how an individual might react to a given circumstance or situation. That is why I framed the yips as being a natural threat to an individual's status and relatedness. For maximum followership, strive to achieve the highest levels of all five elements for every follower, potential or actual. If a threat to any of these elements is unavoidable, then compensate by increasing the other areas. For instance, a threat to certainty can be mitigated with increased levels of status, autonomy, relatedness, and/or fairness. I encourage you to learn more about SCARF. Of all the neuro-scientific models I have studied, I find this one to be the most useful.

If you are anything like me, you are an evergreen student of leadership, and this is the most important quality of a good leader. What I have shared are a few of the more prominent thoughts that stand out for me as I reflect over decades of working with leaders. But, what's important for you is to continually learn, experiment, and hone your craft as a graceful and resilient leader, regardless of what life throws at you.

Wrapping Up the Accelerated Design

The Accelerate Phase (second iteration) of our Adamant Triad should feel a little bit easier and a lot more rewarding. We covered some very interesting information over the last two chapters, but not quite the volume that we went through in Chapters 4, 5, and 6. Even so, the jump in value that the design of your Adamant Triad will take is leaps and bounds over where we landed at the end of the Attempt Phase (first iteration). When we are done, we will have moved from an MVP (Minimum Viable Product) to an REP (Respectable Effective Product), which is about 5–6x more valuable (see Figure 4.3). This is very characteristic of the Accelerate Phase as the largest *customer-centric* insights typically happen between the tail-end of the Attempt Phase and the tail-end of the Accelerate Phase.

The decisions that you will align on with your Strategic Leadership Team at the end of this iteration are the ones from Chapter 4:

- Have we applied feedback from the last iteration to develop a significantly better Adamant Triad?
- Do we feel like we are about 60% –70% of the way to a perfect Adamant Triad?
- Have we developed an Adamant Triad that we *might* use, without another iteration of development?
- Have we captured additional feedback that we *should* apply to the next iteration?
- *Should* we move forward with another iteration?

Before your ceremony that ended Iteration One, you did collect feedback from trusted stakeholders on viability, feasibility, and desirability of your MVP, didn't you? I hope so! But if not, you need to do that now— you need this to cover off on the first bullet. However, **do not** share with them what you have discovered over this iteration. You must atone properly for a gross violation of your own kapu.

Speaking of kapu; now that you know the importance of ceremony, rituals, and sacred rules when deploying a human-centered strategy; as a leader, you **must** take your kapu seriously, including these seemingly superfluous ceremonies that formally transition one iteration to the next. You and your leadership team must set the example for the rest of the organization, and the rest of the organization better take your kapu seriously, or you will have a seditious governance problem to deal with.

With stakeholder feedback from the last iteration at the ready and a fresh set of insights from this and the last chapter, go through the process of adjusting your Adamant Triad like you did in Chapter 6, starting with your Strategic Philosophy. Is there anything about your values that should be adjusted now that you have a deeper understanding of aloha, mana, and kapu? Has the discussion of cultivating a rich environment where people thrive altered your mission, or even your purpose? If your Strategic Philosophy stays the same, that is okay. Regardless, it will be more robust after putting it through this lens of new insights.

However, I would be very surprised if your OD stays the same after reading the last two chapters. For instance, elements of kapu should find their way into your Power element as this will be a key component of shaping everyone's behavior. Furthermore, CybOrg insights should drive improvements in your Information element. And, of course, the Culture element should be greatly enhanced after applying learnings and insights regarding the cultivation of greatness in the organization given its precocious nature. What other insights come to mind as you reflect on the information in the last two chapters?

Now rebalance your OD and your entire Adamant Triad so that you can review it with your trusted stakeholders. You should be at about a 60%–70% solution, but let's see how others feel about the design. If you have done this right, you should be almost there—but not quite. Formalize this with your Strategic Leadership Team by holding the ceremony that closes out Iteration Two and opens Iteration Three.

Very nice work. Join me in the next two chapters as we coast over the finish line.

Putting It into Practice

Becoming a super-leader is not for the faint of heart, but I am sure by this point you are up for the challenge—it's time to start your assimilation into a CybOrg Leader! If you are a lifelong learner like me, with an insatiable intellectual curiosity, this exercise will get you into a flow that's beyond your imagination. It's time to get started with your **CybOrg Mentoring Program:**

1 Select a mentor from your organization. Find a front-line supervisor who is a master of cutting-edge technologies that ideally ascended from the ranks due to their technical excellence.[11] Select someone who can be trusted with sensitive information, as you will need to have transparent dialogues with them about your strategy and other company matters

2 Hold an initial relationship-building session with your mentor, wherein you explain to them your intent: to greatly enhance your leadership capabilities by leveraging technology. Use the five non-delegable responsibilities of top leadership to help frame your objectives

3 Ask them to recommend two to three technologies that would best help you achieve your objectives

4 If they are not already familiar with the development of your Prophet Center, fold them into that effort as an advisor. The MVP of your Prophet Center should be ready (or at least close to being ready), so ask your mentor to quickly come up to speed on what it is and how to use it (if necessary)

5 Ask your mentor to develop a mentor-led learning plan that will help you achieve your goals, centered around your Prophet Center and the two to three technologies they recommended. Avail them of your Learning & Development group and any other resources as needed. Instruct them to be agile—you cannot wait for six months (or longer) to start your program!

6 When the learning plan is drafted, interject time in your overall engagement for reciprocal mentoring, where you can mentor them on being a manager and/or leader

Know and Grow

Reverse Mentoring is a practice where senior leaders in the organization are mentored by junior-level people. This gives senior leaders more grounding on what is actually happening in the organization, and lower-level people an opportunity to build relationships with top leaders.

The practice is good in concept, but the labeling and inferred distinction are awful. It implies that senior leaders are the obvious mentors, and that "reverse" mentoring is something that is the opposite of what's obvious.

Mentoring is mentoring, rank is irrelevant

This program will not only facilitate your assimilation into an invincible CybOrg Leader, but the process will give you the opportunity to learn a wealth about your organization and how to lead it—after all, that's the whole point, right?

Executive Debrief

- A leader is an individual that the rest of the group chooses to follow. Without followership, there is no leadership
- To lead a precocious organization, you must understand the type of person a precocious organization will follow
- Above all, the leader of a precocious organization must be trustworthy; this is what engenders followership. Furthermore, they must keep the organization engaged in challenging work and be very intentional about how brilliance is rewarded
- Super-chickens are highly talented but highly aggressive people who achieve status by attacking and bullying others. They are best controlled with aloha (unconditional love) and kapu (strict rules for behavior)
- The "yips" is a very annoying and frustrating condition where a person or group starts underperforming for no apparent or explainable reason. It is important to be very sensitive to precocious teams who

experience the "yips" and provide a psychologically safe environment for their recovery

- A CybOrg Leader is a super-human leader that leverages technology to seamlessly and unconsciously elevate their leadership capabilities. The organization's Prophet Center is a key catalyst in their assimilation. It is necessary to enlist the help of an expert technologist; a leader cannot assimilate themselves into a CybOrg
- The best leaders "lead from the front," wielding some amount of expert power in addition to formal power. This makes it much easier to attract followers
- Ceremonies, like the ceremony that closes one iteration and opens the next, must be taken seriously when deploying a human-centered strategy. It is a leader's responsibility to protect the kapu of the organization

Notes

1 A prefect example of very competitive superstars coming together to form an awesome team is the 1992 U.S. Men's Olympic Basketball team, a.k.a "The Dream Team." Yes, super athletes can play nicely together, given the right conditions.

2 Do not make the mistake of assuming all people cave under competitive pressure. Many people thrive under competitive pressure, and as such, will never feel threatened by competitors.

3 Kapu has its origins in taboo. The sacred rules of kapu were typically formed around what was taboo or forbidden.

4 I have to call out Mercury here, because I feel he is working mischievously behind the scenes when talented people get a case of the yips.

5 Every time I think of the yips, I think of the great movie, Bull Durham with Susan Sarandon, Kevin Costner, and Tim Robbins. In it, Tim Robbins' character is a baseball pitcher that catches the yips. As a cure, Susan Sarandon's character tells him to "breathe through your eyelids, like the lava lizards of the Galápagos Islands." Hilarious! But, as ridiculous as it sounds, it worked!

6 In deference to Thomas Edison who is famously known for reframing his thousands of "failures," when inventing the incandescent light bulb, as thousands of "ways that won't work."

7 If you are wondering, by "Cyborg Leader," whether I mean the leader of a cybernetic organization or a leader who is a cybernetic organism, the answer is—yes.

8 Inspired from the word *homeostasis*, it is a word I coined to describe a leader's ability to effortlessly sustain a certain level of leadership performance.

9 I guess I should have gone with ultra-leader to be consistent, but that just sounds funny.

10 Some notable examples: Alexander the Great, Julius Caesar, Richard the Lionheart, Joan of Arc, Napoleon Bonaparte, and Erwin Rommel. A few examples of great leaders who motivated and inspired their troops from the front line of battle.

11 Although an individual contributor, like a data scientist, might be more technically proficient than a supervisor (maybe), it is better to find a mentor who is already a leader. In this way, you will share common interests in both leadership and technology, making the relationship mutually beneficial.

Bibliography

Burton, R. M., Obel, B., & Hakonsson, D. D. (2021). *Organizational design: A step-by-step approach* (4th ed.). Cambridge University Press.

Clynes, M. E., & Kline, N. S. (1960). Cyborgs and space. *Astronautics, 5*(9), 26–27, 74–76.

Heffernan, M. (2014). *A bigger prize: Why competition isn't everything and how we do better.* PublicAffairs.

Moore, G. A. (2014). *Crossing the chasm: Marketing and selling disruptive products to mainstream customers* (3rd ed.). HarperBusiness.

Rock, D. (2008). SCARF: A brain-based model for collaborating with and influencing others. *NeuroLeadership Journal, 1*, 78–87.

Iteration Three

Arriving at the Final Design

For years, the third iteration of any multi-iteration effort always piqued my curiosity, especially if the effort was launched as an *Agile* project. If you are an Agile maven like me, this is about the time that you start wondering if you are on a legitimate Agile project or a Faux Agile project. On a legitimate Agile project, by this time, the key benefactors (i.e., customers) of your product have been using your MVP (Minimum Viable Product) for a full iteration and are eager to get their hands on a significant upgrade, which is the REP (Respectable Effective Product) that you just handed over to them. On a Faux Agile project, they are still waiting for you to deliver something they can actually use.

The *product*, in our case, is your Adamant Triad of strategy, organizational design, and innovation. So, think about this decision that you just made during the last chapter's ceremony: Have we developed an Adamant Triad that we *might* use, without another iteration of development? I'm hoping the answer is yes!

Of course, the wording is very intentional, specifically the use of the word *might* (refer to the MSmc tool in Chapter 4). Compare this with the decision we will make at the end of this iteration: Have we developed the Adamant Triad that we *should* use? Again, I'm hoping by the time you start reading Chapter 11, the answer to this question is yes!

So, not only *could* you stop, right now, and move forward with the design of your Adamant Triad as-is; but under different circumstances (i.e., not emotionally attached to discovering the wealth of information that's in the remainder of this book), you *might* move forward with the design of your Adamant Triad—as-is. But you would be taking a huge risk. The biggest value of this third iteration is bringing that risk level down by intercepting the most common missiles that blow up the implementation of a transformation-level strategy: poor governance, improper strategic risk management, behavior recidivism, and underwhelming (or non-existent) OCM (organizational change management).

DOI: 10.4324/9781003518181-13

Like the previous iterations, our activities will be guided by the decisions we determined in Chapter 4:

- Have we applied feedback from the last iteration to develop a really lovable Adamant Triad?
- Do we feel like we are at least 80% of the way to a perfect Adamant Triad?
- Have we developed the Adamant Triad that we *should* use?
- Is everyone on our Strategic Leadership Team aligned and committed to making this change?
- *Must* we move forward with another iteration?

Keep these decisions in mind as you read through the next two chapters. Unlike previous iterations, there should be minimal (but not zero) changes to your Adamant Triad. You may adjust certain elements of your strategy, but if you don't, that's fine. Your organizational design will change a little bit, but nothing major. And the design for your innovation (factory, etc.) might change slightly—maybe. But don't be lulled into thinking these small changes are insignificant. The aggregation of all these tweaks is what pushes your decision-making from *might* to *should*. After these next two chapters, you *should* be done with your Adamant Triad. And, not to spoil things, but the answer to that last bullet? Uh, that's a no.

Chapter 9

The Forest Comes into Focus

Clarifying the Strategy and
Preparing for the Transformation

Arriving at the Go-forward Design for the Adamant Triad

I always engage with high-level leaders due to the nature of the work that I do; however, there is no level of an organization that I won't work with. I remember working in the trenches with an individual contributor (an operator) of an oil and gas company located in the Gulf of Mexico whose primary focus is deepwater exploration and production. We had just finished redesigning their entire business unit to align with their newly revised strategic direction, and the operations leader wanted me to work with this bright and talented specialist to help fine-tune the design of a small but powerful corner of the business. The operator's insights from being on the front line were extremely valuable; however, his purview confined him to the lowest levels of organizational design (OD). Therefore, one of the first things we did together was connect the high-level operating model that had just been developed with all the fine design work that had been done over the past couple of years. Once we wired these two levels of OD together, exciting solutions rapidly emerged.

Right now, you have a terrific Adamant Triad designed, which we might have started deploying if it weren't for the fact that we are not quite ready yet. It feels like we are ready, and a lot of leaders would wave the green flag at this point,[1] but based on experience, I would advise that we explore a few more areas before taking off. This path fits with my iterative design experience, which is how I arrived at a three-iteration methodology. Two iterations usually get you almost there—but *almost there*, is not *there*.

Sometimes I refer to the third iteration of a design effort as the Iteration of Perspective. Think of the first iteration of the AAA methodology (see Figure 4.3) as the Iteration of Discovery, the second iteration as the Iteration of Growth, and the third iteration as the Iteration of Perspective. Calling the development of your strategy complete, without the benefit of perspective, will force its implementation into a risky and difficult starting position.

DOI: 10.4324/9781003518181-14

It's not impossible for a racehorse to win from the first or last gate, but why do that when you can start from the middle of the pack (where, all else put aside, you have the best chance of winning)?[2]

Up until this point, we have been deep in the design of our Adamant Triad, much like my good friend in the deepwater operation, but before we wrap up, it's best to step back to see the forest for the trees. This is what Ronald Heifetz, senior lecturer at Harvard and creator of Adaptive Leadership, calls "getting up on the balcony" (Heifetz & Linsky, 2002). According to Heifetz, the balcony is the only place that affords the perspective of patterns, dynamics, and interactions that you wouldn't otherwise see on what he calls "the dance floor." Since we are dangerously close to a mixed metaphor, let's just say we've been dancing on a floor surrounded by a bunch of trees, and we need to step up on the balcony to see the entire forest, to garner our final set of insights.

These final insights will help us error-proof our design, especially our crucial *environment to thrive*, which ultimately undergirds our *unassailable competitive advantage* (see Figure 3.3). In Six Sigma, there's a tool and practice called *poka-yoke*, wherein practitioners systematically explore ways to make it difficult or impossible for humans in the system to cause errors. For instance, a front door that won't lock unless it senses you have your keys with you. Similarly, we will explore the most common areas of strategic implementation that go awry, in an attempt to intercept errors, in design, before they ever cause problems during implementation. The three areas that give leaders the most problems during strategy implementation are: governance, strategic risk management, and behavior sustainability.

Know and Grow

Poke-yoke is a Japanese term that means "mistake-proofing," coined by Shigeo Shinto in the 1960s during the development of the Toyota Production System. It was originally called "Baka-yoke," which means "fool-proofing," but Shinto wanted to avoid any inference that his people were "fools," so he changed the name. Language matters!

Governance and High-Performance Leadership Teams

Governance is one of those areas where I was surprised to discover so many companies that have a large gap between formalized design and the actual, observable operation on the ground. Governance is an element of design that is typically included in organizational transformations and often a specific area of focus when leaders call me for help. And yet, when I ask for documentation on the current state of their company's governance structure, I oftentimes receive something that doesn't feel complete. Most of the focus is on meetings: who is meeting with whom, how often, and when. That's so bizarre to me. Sure, meetings are an important topic to cover when designing governance, but the governance structure of any firm is more than just a collection of meetings! As a result, watching governance in action at most companies is like watching a novice ride a unicycle. It works—somewhat—but it's awkward.

Proper governance provides the organization with the critical lateral capability to set policy, make decisions, and control the execution of key business processes. In foundational OD, *lateral capabilities* are how the organization facilitates coordination and communication between the different branches of the organization (Galbraith, 2002). In an egocentric organization that adopts a functional structure, lateral capabilities are how the different functions coordinate activities between each other (see Chapter 4). In an allocentric organization that adopts a divisional structure, lateral capabilities are how the different divisions coordinate activities between each other. In DHARMA (Design Harmony, Alignment, and Reinforcement Modeling Approach) (see Chapter 5), these considerations are fleshed out in the Value element.

An organizational designer selecting the right lateral capabilities for a firm is like an architectural design team selecting the right building material and construction for their beams. Lightweight lateral capabilities, like a networking group (e.g., community of practice), work well in situations where the organizational requirement is no more than information sharing. If the need for coordination and accountability between groups is stronger, then a stronger lateral capability is required, like a management system or a business process. The benefit of stronger capability comes with this option, but not without a cost. It takes more organizational resources to maintain a business process than it does to maintain a community of practice. Governance takes it all one notch higher. It provides even stronger lateral capabilities than business processes, but that comes at an even higher organizational burden on resources. So, in the same way an architectural design team would not select a steel beam to support the load of a decorative wall, a good organizational designer would not select a governance structure when a simple management system or business process would work just as well. But there comes a point in every organization, where business processes just aren't strong enough, like the oversight of a core value-delivering process. That is when the steel beam of governance gets selected for the design.

Wasabi Moment

Governance is usually over-staffed in organizations because of emotional reasons—everybody wants to be included and feel important. Catering to everyone's psychological need for status begets far too many members of far too many committees that hold far too many meetings. Governance should be designed unemotionally and implemented courageously

Value isn't the only DHARMA element that plays a role in governance. Culture plays an important role as well, especially in a human-centered strategy that embraces culture-led OD. As we discussed in Chapter 7, the sacred rules of kapu heavily influenced the behavior of the Ancient Hawaiians, and we can use the same concept to govern organizational behavior, *without top leadership's active administration*. And because of the influence that this type of culture has on behavior, there is a strong harmonic and reinforcing relationship between the Culture element and the Power element of DHARMA (when certain design choices are made). That's the beauty of a human-centered strategy. It's the only type of strategy where the *culture* of an organization is so strong that it can—in and of itself—drive behaviors through a firm's operating model to deliver great customer value, without direct intervention from leadership. Think of it as a leader's cruise control mechanism.

So, the best way to approach the formal design of governance is to start with the culture, and the design of your kapu, and the implications that it has on your Power. Then, consider all the areas of your Value element where a business process won't be enough to cover the coordination, accountability, and communication required. This is the right place to formalize governance in the Value element. Design in additional elements where leaders must create policy, make decisions, and/or oversee the execution of critical operations. Once the *right* leaders are selected and a clever acronym/name is chosen for the team, determine how that team is going to meet its stated objectives. A meeting is only one of many ways that a team can accomplish its goals.

Managing Strategic Risks and Other Uncertainties

Strategic risks are another area that I've commonly seen mishandled during the implementation of a newly developed strategy, and it is usually because of an underdeveloped (or completely absent) Strategic Guidance

System (see Chapter 4). This is usually coupled with a misunderstanding of the firm's business environment. Once you understand that you are operating in an unordered, complex system, you understand the folly of trying to manage it like an ordered system, which is what most leaders attempt to do.

In this regard, *strategic risk management* is a bit of a misnomer when it comes to managing within a complex system, since the whole environment that you are operating in is one big uncertainty. To reorient our frame of thinking, supplant *strategic risk management* with *the effective operation of your Strategic Guidance System*, given it has been designed to operate in a complex system.

So, how do you ensure the effectiveness of your Strategic Guidance System? It starts with your probing system. You must put a good frame around what, exactly, you are probing for, and more importantly, what you are not probing for. Without a solid frame to operate within, your probing system could conceptually probe for everything in the business universe, and that, of course, is impossible. You cannot design a system to probe for infinity.

At the time of this writing, there is very high tension in the Middle East. It escalated to the point where Iran fired a barrage of ballistic missiles at Israel in retaliation for recent Israeli air strikes that targeted senior leaders of Hezbollah and Hamas. Fortunately, very few lives were lost, as it would have been devastating if those missiles had hit their targets. Israel (with the help of the United States) was able to intercept them, detonating them in the air before they caused any harm to the lives below. Preparation is key in this scenario. Israeli intelligence is very good, and they know what to scan for.

To build the frame for your probing system, start with your Strategic Objectives. Once you have clear objectives, start brainstorming scenarios that could either help or hinder the achievement of your objectives and the elements in the business universe that are involved in these scenarios. This is where the design of your Strategic Guidance System starts to look like traditional risk planning. Anchor on your Strategic Objectives and systematically map out uncertainties that could affect their achievement.

Bear in mind that uncertainty has two hemispheres: negative and positive. Remember the Uncertainty Matrix from Chapter 1 (see Figure 1.1)? It's important to expand your frame to include positive uncertainties, in addition to the more intuitive negative uncertainties. After all, you wouldn't be in this situation if life hadn't handed you the precious gift of your precocious organization, right? Uncertainties with a positive impact are called *positive risks*, and their big-picture importance is to tip the scales back in your favor when it comes to the potential impacts of your uncertain future. If you only probe for uncertainties that deliver a negative impact, then those are the only impacts that are going to strike.

Wasabi Moment

The word "risk" typically carries a negative connotation that infuses an unhealthy bias when discussed. As a leader, it is best to reframe risk in your mind to be more synonymous with uncertainty. Do not try to segment positive risk away from negative risk—it's all risk and both sides must be considered holistically

An insight from my days as a Six Sigma Black Belt that is worth pulling forward at this point is the idea of *detectability*. Most risk planning includes probability and impact, but detectability is rarely seen outside of Six Sigma circles. We add this to help analyze the effects of failure modes and error modes.[3] It becomes relevant in your Strategic Guidance System because your probing system must be able to detect weak signals (i.e., elements in the environment with low detectability), which play a significant role in your Measurement and Analysis system.

Your Measurement and Analysis system includes intuitive components, but it must also cater to *sensing*, which is a special kind of analysis. Whenever you hear the term *sense* in the context of Cynefin (see Figure 2.2), think more in the space of exploratory analysis than the more traditional deductive analysis. Sensing is about observing data and recognizing patterns, the most valuable of which are inconspicuous (Snowden & Boone, 2007). The real power of your Measurement and Analysis system comes from its ability to spot a little cluster of outlier activity that warrants your response.

The final pitfall regarding strategic risk management that stands out in my mind is the actual *management* part. I wish I had a dollar for every time I've witnessed a lot of energy going into a strategic risk management plan, only for it to sit untouched on a virtual and/or physical shelf during implementation. Just make sure you have a regular cadence in your Strategic Guidance System that activates the probe–sense–respond sequence, then *follow through on the process*, and you will be fine.

Begin with Behavior Sustainability in Mind

I was working with the Vice President of a $3 billion oil and gas exploration and production business unit in Bakersfield, California, when a rare thing happened—I was caught flat-footed during an important phase gate meeting. It was very early on in the project, and we were clarifying the opportunity to get his alignment. Oil production was declining, so the business unit needed a new strategy to sustain long-term viability. Transactional change was out of the question, and transitional change would have only bought us a few years, so I worked with some of his key leaders to develop a transformational change strategy. During our meeting, we reviewed the opportunity, and the Vice President looked very pleased. Then, he turned to me and asked, "Where is your Sustainability Plan?" After an awkward pause of dead silence that seemed to go on for several minutes (even though I know it was only a few seconds), he knew what the answer was. He broke the silence that he inadvertently instigated with the directive, "Schedule a meeting with me for tomorrow to review your Sustainability Plan." I never made that mistake again.

To be clear, he was referring to a Behavior Sustainability Plan—a plan to ensure people do not revert to old ways of working, once the new strategy goes live. For our strategy to work, we had to break down long-established silos of behavior that culturally reinforced the identities of three major sub-geographies of the region. Once we went live with the new strategy, if people continued to identify with the location they had long been associated with, it would be disastrous. So, this acute and insightful leader was well justified in his enthusiasm to see a plan for how to prevent this phenomenon that we call *behavior recidivism*.

To be fair, I always knew I would need to develop a Behavior Sustainability Plan; I just didn't think I needed it to pass through a phase gate this early in the process. But the leader was right. Especially with transformational change, where life in the organization can potentially look and feel very different from what it does today, it is so important to begin with behavior sustainability in mind. Even if you establish new processes, people will remember the old processes. And, even if you establish new technologies, people will probably have access to the old technologies, or at least figure out a way to work around the new technologies to get back to something that resembles the old technologies.

And why would people do this? Because the old way worked for them. And it is very, very hard to move people away from behaviors that have suited them well for years, or even decades.

The key to sustaining behaviors is understanding the Full Life Cycle of Behavior Management (see Figure 9.1). Working back from right to left, the end goal is stability of desired-state behaviors. This goal must be *operationally defined*, meaning clear enough to measure and interpret without ambiguity. You will learn more about measuring change in the next chapter. For now, just know that clear targets of behavioral stability must be established for the organization during the *Planning* stage, not after behavioral interventions begin, or even worse, complete![4]

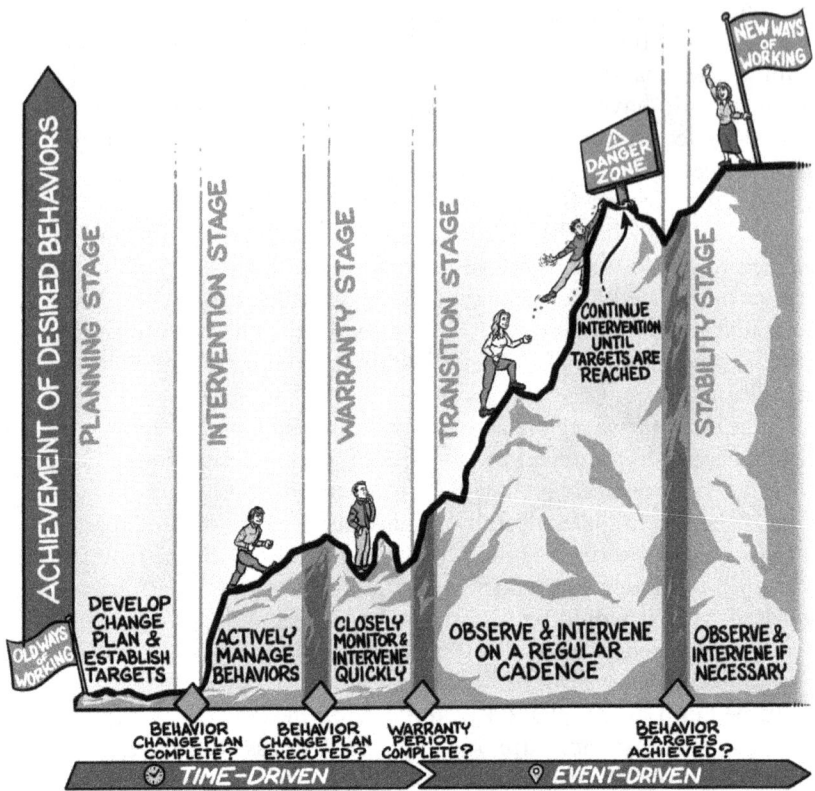

Figure 9.1 The Full Life Cycle of Behavior Management.

Prior to the Stability Stage is the Transition Stage (still working back from right to left). This is the stage where desired organizational behaviors are on the right track to obtain, but they clearly have not obtained yet, as evidenced by your operational definitions of sustainability. You cannot let go of your change management levers before you exit this stage. Furthermore, the passage between the Transition and the Stability stages is not based on time—it is based on operational definitions of organizational behavior, the progression (and regression) of which is a human process, not a business process. There are many times when leaders are pressed to "move on," and wrap up a transformational change effort before the Transition Stage has a chance to complete. This is a sure-fire way to invite recidivism.

A final note on the Full Life Cycle of Behavior Management (while we are here), the Warranty Stage, which immediately succeeds the Intervention phase where behaviors are actively being shifted, is a relatively short period of time where a heightened level of change management is required to ensure organizational behaviors ever find the right track to be on in the first place.

The Planning and Intervention stages are fairly intuitive and self-explanatory, which is why it's so important to understand the *full* life cycle of behavior management to avoid sustainability problems during implementation, when it's too late to plan for mitigations.

Appreciating the Genius of Pareto

Before we close out our discussion of the forest—which can easily be seen from the balcony—I feel a closer examination of the Pareto Principle is appropriate, because it is consistent with the idea of maintaining a wider, big-picture purview to avoid getting trapped in the very attractive, but time-consuming minutiae that doesn't provide enough value for the effort expended.

It reminds me of the roads of Tennessee. In 2023, my niece decided to get married in hills of Tennessee. A short distance away from Gatlinburg, as the crows fly, you will find a charming set of cabins neatly nestled away in the hills of Tennessee. The area is absolutely beautiful; the mountainous valley accented by a slow-flowing creek provides the perfect canvas for a stunning display of flora and fauna. My wife and I flew into North Carolina a few days early and stayed at a nearby casino, before making the drive to the site. The drive to Gatlinburg, which covered the bulk of the driving distance, was nice and easy. When we weren't driving on the wide, paved interstate, we were casually winding through the well-maintained, serpentine roadways of the Great Smoky Mountains. However, the "short" drive from Gatlinburg to the cabins was a completely different experience: single-lane, gravel-paved (and I use the term *paved* liberally) trails with hairpin turns and near-vertical grades made this expedition a lot more harrowing and time consuming. There was one point in the single-lane journey where the incline-to-decline grade was so acute that you just had to pray there wasn't an oncoming vehicle on the other side of the incline. But on this occasion, it was worth it. The setting was absolutely perfect for a wedding.

Metaphorically, I call that 35-mile, 45-minute, easy-going drive from the casino to Gatlinburg the *road to success* and the 12-mile, 30-minute, death-defying drive from Gatlinburg to the cabins the *path to perfection;* inspired by a key practice I learned from strategist Alan Weiss, "Success, not Perfection." This is a clear and concise expression of Pareto's 80–20 Principle. In most situations, the relatively easy cruise on the road to success will garner 80% of what you are looking to achieve, with only 20% of the effort. However, if you are not satisfied with *just* an 80% outcome, then you must turn onto the path to perfection and expend the remaining

80% of your effort for only a 20% increase in value. So, unless you are looking for the perfect spot to get married, it's best to avoid that turnoff and just have a great time in Gatlinburg.

One very important note about the Pareto Principle is that the model supporting this axiom is based on *two* variables: inputs and outputs. What we are discerning is the relationship between inputs and outputs, not a percentage split of any one variable. I highlight this because I often hear evidence of the wrong frame being applied to the Pareto Principle. For instance, when I was down in Bakersfield trying to shift the organizational behavior of engineers from a pursuit of perfection to a pursuit of success, I would often hear, "I feel uncomfortable just stopping when we are only 80% of the way through a project." This language is coming from an input-based frame of mind and completely misses the point. It is very unfortunate that Vilfredo landed on the two numbers 80 (for outputs) and 20 (for inputs), because it's too easy to put these two numbers together and think that we are splitting up some kind of 100% pie into an 80-piece and a 20-piece. This is, of course, not the case. It would have been easier to intuit if it were the 75–5 principle or the 95–12 principle, but we can revise neither history nor the observable phenomena of nature.

The AAA methodology (see Figure 4.3) was inspired by the Pareto Principle. The iteration that we are in now, the Arrive iteration, is where we cross the 80%-value threshold. This is where success lives; this is your Gatlinburg. You will see the signs pointing to the path to perfection, and you may actually take the turnoff to see what it's like. But as you see, feel, and hear the stark contrast between the paved road and the gravel trail, step up on the balcony for a minute and make an intentional decision on whether the path ahead is worth the additional silver coins.

Putting It into Practice

When it comes to organizational behavior, you cannot manage what you cannot measure, and you cannot measure what cannot be physically observed. We talked, in this chapter, about the importance of establishing organizational targets for desired behavior; however, they won't have any purpose if you don't clearly define the behaviors that are to be desired. In this exercise, we'll walk through the process of **defining target behaviors**:

1 Re-read the current version of your Strategic Vision (the long version) and take note of anything that describes or alludes to the desired behaviors of the organization
2 Affinitize your notes into three to five behavioral themes.[5] Resist the urge to compare them to your current organizational behavior. This exercise is completely about the future, not the present

3   Spend a moment in contemplation of the themes that have emerged. Are there any more themes that should be added to the set for completion? If so, add them to the list

4   Starting with the first theme, write down five to eight bullets of what you would physically see if someone were performing that behavior. Be critical in the wording of each bullet to ensure the behavior is *observable*. For instance, you cannot see someone "not" doing something

5   Repeat this process for each behavioral theme

6   Review your behavioral themes, including bulleted details, with your Strategic Leadership Team, and revise based on feedback. Ensure everyone on the team is aligned

7   Revise your Strategic Vision to include insights from this exercise. Improve and re-balance the rest of your Adamant Triad if needed

8   Store the final, detailed behavioral themes as an appendix in your Strategic Philosophy. You will need them soon, so keep them close by

The starting point for any structured behavior management effort is clearly defining desired behaviors. On the surface, the exercise seems simple, but in practice, it is more difficult than it appears. When I facilitate this exercise, it usually takes a few rounds of discussion before the group hits the right groove of defining *observable* behaviors. You may want to have an organizational behavior specialist look at your work before you call it done. Glancing ahead, these operationally defined target behaviors set the foundation for the next chapter's discussion on managing behavior change.

Executive Debrief

- Calling your strategy complete without the benefit of stepping back for perspective will force its implementation into a risky and difficult starting position
- "Getting up on the balcony" is another metaphor for stepping back to get perspective
- Insights from a big-picture perspective will help error-proof the design of your strategy
- Three common areas of strategy implementation that benefit from good initial design are: governance, strategic risk management, and behavior sustainability
- Proper governance provides a robust lateral capability for the organization to communicate and coordinate activities between branches
- Establishing a governance structure must be a very thoughtful decision. Do not use governance when a simpler form of coordination will suffice
- Governance plays a role in multiple areas of organizational design. In terms of DHARMA, it impacts the Value, Culture, and Power elements

- When operating within a complex business environment, strategic risk management is synonymous with effective execution of the Strategic Guidance System
- It is important to define a solid frame for our feedback or probing system. You cannot feasibly probe for *everything* in the business universe
- When structuring the frame for your probing system, make sure to include positive risks, which are uncertainties with a positive impact
- Your Measurement and Analysis system must have the capability to do proper *sensing*, which is exploratory analysis that looks for patterns
- A Behavior Sustainability Plan is a tool used to prevent people from reverting to old ways of working when a new strategy is deployed
- The key to sustaining behaviors is to develop a clear definition of how people should behave in the future, then continue managing until those behaviors obtain
- The Pareto Principle is a valuable guideline to achieve success with minimal effort, but it takes a commitment to stop early (20% of the effort) when success (80% of the value) is achieved

Notes

1 The waving of the green flag is a universal signal to start a motorsport race, like the iconic Indianapolis 500.
2 Unfortunately, for trainers and owners, you cannot choose what gate your horse starts from. That's another aspect of the game that's left to the luck of the draw.
3 An FMEA (Failure Modes and Effects Analysis) is a useful tool in Six Sigma to systematically analyze the way a system could fail and mitigate the impacts of failure. It's close cousin, the EMEA (Error Modes and Effects Analysis), is typically used to understand how humans or software might produce an error and mitigate those impacts.
4 If you are in the Warranty Stage of Behavior Management and you do not have clear targets defined for behavioral stability, you have made a huge error. At this point there will be an implicit and almost unavoidable bias on sustainability targets that carries forward from the Intervention Stage.
5 "Success, not Perfection" was one of five critical behavioral themes that emerged during my work down in Bakersfield with the oil and gas organization. Petrotechnical engineers are very bright, but tend to exhibit perfectotropism: a strong tendency to pursue perfection.

Bibliography

Galbraith, J. R. (2002). *Designing organizations: An executive guide to strategy, structure, and process*. Jossey-Bass.
Heifetz, R. A., & Linsky, M. (2002). *Leadership on the line: Staying alive through the dangers of leading*. Harvard Business Review Press.
Snowden, D. J., & Boone, M. E. (2007). A leader's framework for decision making. *Harvard Business Review*, 85(11), 68–76.

Chapter 10

Metamorphosis
Transformational Change in Animals and Organizations

The Complexity of Transformational Change

"You are not fine."

It was around two o'clock in the early morning of August 16, 2024. The glow from the television and soft groans from my wife nearby woke me out of a light sleep. She was obviously having a bad dream. It seemed like she was terrified in her dream, shaking and moaning as if she desperately wanted something to stop or someone to go away.

Although I knew it was just a bad dream, my worry for her extended beyond just a nightmare. She hadn't been feeling well for a while, and it concerned me. It started with problems doing strenuous activities, like exercise, and progressed to difficulties with simple tasks, like walking up the stairs. When it got to the point where she struggled getting up from the couch, I got really worried. I kept urging her to see a doctor, but she consistently brushed me off. She understood her own situation, and there was no need to see anyone else. It was allergies; the same ones she had dealt with her whole life, and there was nothing the doctors would say that she hadn't heard before. She knew how to fix it, and she would get better soon—she promised.

So, I left it alone—until then.
I gently laid my hand on her shoulder and squeezed softly. "Are you alright?"
She slowly raised her eyelids and stared at me with a dazed look. "Yes, why?"
"You don't look alright."
"You just woke me up."
"That's a good point." Touché. "Okay, but I want to keep talking with you for a few minutes."

DOI: 10.4324/9781003518181-15

"What for?" She was visibly irritated at this point, but still had a glazed look in her eyes.

"Because I want to make sure you are alright."

"That's silly, and I'm tired. Can we do this tomorrow?"

"No. I want to keep talking for a few minutes."

We went back and forth for a few minutes, but her general condition did not change. This was not normal. Although she had been struggling with physical issues, she was always cogent. This was different. She looked dazed and spacey.

Concern now turns to fear. "Something is not right, I'm calling 9-1-1."

"Don't do that. Please? Can we talk about this tomorrow?"

"No, there's no more talking about this tomorrow. I really hope I'm wrong, but I need to call 9-1-1 and we need to figure out what's happening with you."

"Stop it. Don't call 9-1-1. I'm fine."

I just stared at her, trying hard to believe her.

"You are not fine." A single tear slowly made its way down my cheek. Those were the last words we ever exchanged. I never had the chance to say goodbye.

On August 26, 2024, after a fierce 11-day battle for her life in the ICU (Intensive Care Unit), my wife passed away from acute idiopathic pulmonary fibrosis. It is an insidious disease that slowly imprisons the lungs until they cease to function. It is very hard to detect, impossible to cure, and lethal to our cardiopulmonary system—our central life support.

My sincere hope is that neither you nor anyone else reading this, now or in the future, ever has to deal with this type of transformational change. It was Kim and me against the world for over 30 years, and in the blink of an eye, all that was gone. The change process for me felt like a rabbit punch followed by a gut punch. August 16 came out of nowhere—I was completely blindsided. August 26, I saw it coming, but that didn't stop it from landing a devastating, visceral blow.

The dual nature of change (in my case, the one-two punch), is the insight that struck me throughout this process. This type of change has two parts: letting go of the status quo and then normalizing to a new future. Many conceptual models present this journey as a singular change process, but it is actually two related but different changes, with a very uncomfortable and sometimes prolonged state of limbo connecting the two parts. During the 11 days when my wife was in the ICU, I knew the status quo was gone, but my future could take on one of a few very different scenarios, so I had no solid future to anchor on before August 26. This is a very turbulent and emotional period that is seldom explored. It is like a trapeze artist suspended in the air, anxiously hoping for a strong grasp on the incoming bar but knowing that's not the only possible outcome. For me, the insight brought further illumination on the change management model that Kurt Lewin introduced in the 1940s, where change follows the progression of unfreezing, transitioning, and then refreezing (Lewin, 1947). I now have a greater appreciation for the separation between unfreezing and refreezing, and an elevated respect for the challenge of transitioning when there is no stable vision of success.

As discussed in Chapter 2, with transformational change, there are no easy answers in sight. We don't know exactly what we are going to look like when we get to wherever we are going, so we don't know how we are going to get to—wherever. Therefore, despite the solid foundation that John Kotter espouses with his well-known eight-step change model (Kotter, 1996), we need something more robust for handling the complexities of transformational change.

August 16, 2024, changed my life forever.[1] The man you see looks the same, but the man inside has metamorphosed into something very different. Not necessarily better or worse—different.

Inspirations from Nature

Have you ever wondered why we cannot survive without air for very long, when we were doing just fine in our mummy's tummy without air just seconds before we were born? Think about it. Just before you were born, your lungs were filled with liquid, and you weren't disturbed about it at all. It's hard to argue that this is just part of the development process, because by the time you start telling mom that it's time to come out, you have pretty much developed into a bona fide citizen of the world. Yet, in just a few moments, your whole cardiopulmonary system will quickly and irreversibly morph from liquid-based to air-based. Then, over the next 24 hours, although onlookers will just see the cute baby that you are, internally, your body will undergo the most rapid and aggressive transformation it will likely make for the remainder of your life. And, although some may argue that this is a far stretch from *metamorphosis*, the argument would not be tenable.

Since the dawn of humankind, metamorphosis has enchanted our imaginations with an aura of mysticism and wonder. The word itself was born from Greek mythology as a way to describe legendary gods, heroes, and creatures who "changed form," like almighty Zeus changing into a Swan to seduce Leda or Narcissus' eventual fate as a flower. The word was later adopted by the natural sciences to describe the same phenomenon observed in insects, amphibians, crustaceans, and other animals. The natural world around us is rife with inspirational fodder for leaders facing a change that alters their organization's fundamental form—i.e., a transformational change.

The quintessential metaphoric celebrity from everyone's childhood is, of course, the adorable caterpillar. Let's quickly enjoy a flashback to the days of lunch pails and recess and the four stages of *complete* metamorphosis: egg, larva, pupa, and adult. Eggs are pretty boring, but things get interesting when a caterpillar (the larva stage) emerges. Caterpillars molt, like many others in nature. When they grow too tight for their exoskeleton (skin), they essentially walk out of it. What's interesting is that its new exoskeleton forms *before* it molts, inside the old exoskeleton. When the caterpillar emerges from its old exoskeleton, the change has already happened. This is more visually dramatic when the caterpillar transforms into a chrysalis (the pupa stage). A caterpillar transforms into a very different-looking animal, *while, to onlookers, it still looks like a caterpillar.* Of course, the same metaphoric process happens between the chrysalis and the butterfly, but because a chrysalis is visually similar to a moth's cocoon, it doesn't seem as remarkable (even though it is). Concealing internal transformation from the external world is a notable survival tactic in nature—and in business.

Whereas a caterpillar undergoes a complete metamorphosis, a dragonfly undergoes an *incomplete* metamorphosis. It is called incomplete, because its form doesn't radically change, like a caterpillar. The larva and pupa stages are replaced by one nymph stage, and the naiad (nymph dragonfly) resembles the adult but does not have wings or reproductive organs. So, is this still considered transformational? Absolutely! Just because the naiad resembles the dragonfly doesn't mean that a major transformation hasn't happened. Not only are there significant physical differences between the two, but adults have a very different lifestyle from nymphs. Like the caterpillar, the naiad metamorphoses for survival. They need the mobility of wings and changes in dietary needs to avoid depleting surrounding resources with their kin. The point of a transformation is not in the degree of physical change, but in the need for change.

An even *less complete* metamorphosis (in strict biological terms) can be found when a grasshopper changes to a locust. Only a small percentage of grasshoppers can shift to locust, but when they do, watch out! What's interesting is that there is not much about the physical appearance of a grasshopper that changes when it becomes a locust other than its color.

Table 10.1 Summary of Business Insights from Nature on Metamorphosis and Transformational Change

Animal	Nature of Metamorphosis	Insight from Nature
Caterpillar	Complete metamorphosis	Concealing internal transformation from the external world is a notable survival tactic in nature—and in business
Dragonfly	Incomplete metamorphosis	The point of a transformation is not in the degree of physical change, but in the need for change
Locust	Behavioral metamorphosis	A radical shift in behavior and culture is as much a metamorphosis as a radical shift in form
All	Fundamental building blocks (DNA)	It is your job as a leader to understand the essence of your organization and ensure it never gets lost throughout its many metamorphoses

But its behavior radically changes! It morphs from a quiet individualist to a gregarious fanatic, joining the mosh swarm of other locusts for a frantic flying feast. This type of transformation is, for all intents and purposes, completely behavioral. A radical shift in behavior and culture is as much a metamorphosis as a radical shift in form.

Despite differences in how different species metamorphose, there is one commonality—the fundamental DNA of an organism never changes. The primal essence of the organism carries the same program throughout its entire life cycle, regardless of its shape, composition, or behavior. It is your job as a leader to understand the essence of your organization and ensure it never gets lost throughout its many metamorphoses.

Twelve Best Practices for Managing the People-Side of Change

John Kotter's eight-step change model works well for transitional change; however, it is deceptively facile for transformational change. If you are not familiar with this model, I strongly encourage you to learn and understand it. It is fundamental learning for anyone involved with OCM (Organizational Change Management) and provides a solid and necessary foundation for managing transformational change. However, we need something more robust for our purposes.

Know and Grow

In the 1990s, John Kotter introduced his eight-step change model, which is now foundational in the domain of OCM:

1. Establish a sense of urgency

2. Create a guiding coalition

3. Develop a vision and strategy

4. Communicate the change vision

5. Empower employees for broad-based action

6. Generate short-term wins

7. Consolidate gains and producing more change

8. Anchor new approaches in the culture

The model works well for transitional change, but must be enhanced for transformational change due to the uncertain nature of both the destination and the path to the destination

Attempting to manage transformational change using nothing but Kotter's eight-step model is like trying to drive an 18-wheeler two weeks after obtaining your first driver's license. You might be able to fumble your way along, but you will eventually do more damage than good. Kotter's change model is too simplistic to handle the complexity and uncertainty of transformational change. You will need to lead an organization when there are no clear answers in sight. To do this, consider these 12 OCM best practices that I have learned over decades of dealing with very difficult change efforts.

OCM Best Practice #1: Help people embrace the uncertain nature of the change. The sooner people accept that the vision is dynamic and the path to get there is emergent, the easier the journey will be for them. Kotter's model begins to break down on steps 3 and 4, where you create and communicate a vision. Unless you clearly articulate the shifting nature of this vision, your credibility will be compromised the first time it changes—and it will change.

OCM Best Practice #2: Put more effort into OCM upfront than you initially feel necessary. Studies show that the biggest regret leaders have after reviewing a significant change effort is that they did not do enough change management (Prosci, 2023). This aligns with my personal experience as well. Dedicate resources to managing the change and hire experts if you don't have the capability in-house.

OCM Best Practice #3: Begin with the end culture in mind. Do not extrapolate from the present culture. Design the ideal culture and then compare it to the current culture to uncover gaps. When the vision changes, start by redesigning the culture to align with the new vision.

OCM Best Practice #4: Strongly manage all leader behaviors. Clearly define what leaders at each level of the organization must do and how they must behave (e.g., open and honest communication always), and take great measures to ensure leaders do what they are expected to do. Set leaders up for success by providing coaching, tools, and, most importantly, time to effectively lead the change. Effective sponsorship of the change effort will make or break it.

OCM Best Practice #5: Find sources of informal power and authority to help influence behavior. There are likely influential people in your organization that don't have a high-ranking title or salary. Identify who they are and enroll them in your sponsorship workstream as change leaders.

OCM Best Practice #6: Move quickly to establish a thriving environment where people love to do their best work. Identify high-impact, low-effort wins for building a thriving work environment and implement them right away. This will prevent people from leaving when the waters turn turbulent.

OCM Best Practice #7: Broadcast metrics (targets and progress) for well-being, community, and human relationships. Make their importance very clear to everyone in the organization and constantly communicate actions you are taking to improve these metrics.

OCM Best Practice #8: Aggressively encourage everyone to protect, reinforce, and grow their mental health. Always have coaches and psychotherapists ready and available to support the workforce throughout the change journey. Lead by example; publicly express your appreciation for your EMT (Executive Mental Team).

OCM Best Practice #9: Develop and install one-way locks along the Emotional Journey (see Figure 3.1) to prevent regression. Pay particular attention to the Gulf of Resistance. Once people have successfully crossed over to the Base of Exploration, make it difficult for them to regress back to the gulf.

OCM Best Practice #10: Clearly document the difference between the current state and the future state. This will help people understand exactly what's changing. When the future state changes, clearly document the new changes for the same reason.

OCM Best Practice #11: Overly manage the first 100 days of change. This is a very vulnerable stage of the transformation that must be very tightly monitored and managed.

OCM Best Practice #12: Actively manage the firm's Emotional Journey. Do not get too attached to timelines on a project plan. Stay in tune with the emotions of the organization and take actions based on how people feel, not on when activities are *supposed* to happen.

When it comes to change management, Kotter gives us a very nice foundation with his eight-step model. Learn it. Love it. Use it—as a base to build upon. But don't think for a second it alone will work for *transformational* change. For that, we need to step up our game, especially when it comes to that last best practice on managing the firm's Emotional Journey.

Measuring and Managing Emotions and Behavior

One of the greatest things you can do to effectively manage any kind of change is to honor and respect the emotional aspect of the change journey. After you understand Kotter's eight-step change model, one of the best follow-up reads is his book on the emotional side of change, *The Heart of Change*. This is still one of my all-time favorite books on change management. It should be clear by now that it is dangerous and irresponsible to treat any kind of process involving humans like a process that deals with widgets or machines. And yet, I see so many change management methodologies that ignore the fact that *people* are the fundamental subject of the system. As such, when managing organizational change, emotions must be the *primary* consideration.

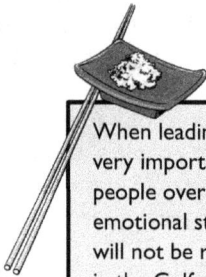

Wasabi Moment

When leading transformational and transitional change, it is very important to prioritize the emotional journey of your people over everything else. Interventions must align with the emotional state of any particular group. For instance, people will not be receptive to behavior change when they are mired in the Gulf of Resistance

Managing emotions is not as paralyzing as it may seem, as long as you authentically care about the people in your organization. When I engage with a leader considering (or facing) a transformational change, and the reality sinks in that organizational emotions will need to be managed, I can almost predict the point when fear and anxiety will manifest throughout their whole body; starting with the discoloration for their face, down to clenched fists and white knuckles, and finally incessant fidgeting with legs and feet. Because the management of human emotions is so foreign and uncomfortable for most leaders, they typically ignore it, thereby making a colossal change management mistake. If you put your head in the sand, you'll likely suffocate like the rest of us who require oxygen to survive.[2]

The emotional aspect of change management applies to all types of change but is most relevant and important for *transformational* change. Emotional management during *transactional* change is more of a light-weight control measure, just to make sure everything is going as expected. You must be more intentional and proactive with *transitional* change, since the path to the destination is unknown. However, the actual destination *is* known, and that is a huge advantage; you can use a clear and unwavering vision as an anchor to significantly ease the emotional journey. Kotter's eight-step model is very effective in these situations. Of course, with *transformational* change, the vision is not so stable, and that's why it's so difficult to manage.

To effectively manage emotions, you need three things: some literacy, a few experts, and a measurement system. This book provides a decent base of literacy, but I encourage you to continue learning about humans and emotions; the more you know, the less frightening they are to manage. We have already talked about your EMT (Executive Mental Team), who will be a fantastic source of information and advice. In addition, consider a change management expert if your advisor is not fluent in OCM. They should be able to help you build a behavior measurement system; if they cannot, you have the wrong change management expert.[3]

Your measurement system should instrumentalize the Emotional Journey (see Figure 3.1). At any point in time, you should know where different groups of your organization are in their emotional journey. That means you must stratify your organization in a way that makes sense, e.g., department/function, geography, level of leadership, and/or career group. Then, you need a probing/sensing method that gives you the best indication of where, along the Emotional Journey, everyone resides. The best way to do this is by asking them how they feel about the transformation (using a survey, interview, or focus group), then using a tool similar to Table 3.1 that maps feelings to stages of the Emotional Journey. With emotional insights in hand, engage your leaders to assist with emotional progression, using the tips provided in Table 3.1.

Managing emotions makes it much easier to manage behavior. Once you have *operationally defined* your desired behaviors (see Chapter 9), you can measure and manage them to ensure they are obtained. A model for managing behaviors that I have fine-tuned over the years is presented in Figure 10.1. Let's walk through it.

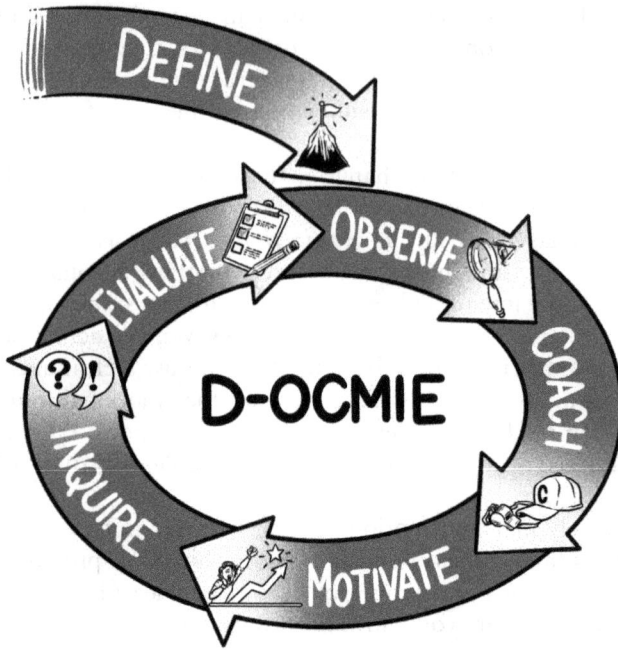

Figure 10.1 Managing Behaviors with the D-OCMIE Method.

Define: You have already defined your future-state behaviors in Chapter 9 for sustainability purposes; now, you must engage with each performer[4] to clarify expectations and bridge alignment. This is best done with a one-on-one supervisor engagement, so you will need to cascade this effort down successive levels of management.

Observe: The most accurate way to measure behaviors is to personally observe them. Since most supervisors work closely with their team members, this should not be too difficult. However, in those situations where you cannot physically observe behavior, you may need to delegate the responsibility (e.g., to a hired performance coach), ask others who work closely with the performer, and/or ask the performer to self-report.

Coach: Use the gap between observed behavior and desired behavior to prepare feedback for coaching. Once again, coaching should be done one-on-one with the performer's supervisor. Enlist the help of professional coaches, if needed, to help design the coaching program.

Motivate: Deploy positive and negative consequences to assist the performer in meeting behavioral objectives. You need both but be cautious with negative consequences. This is a tricky area in today's litigious environment, so make sure to cover your bases before bringing out the stick.

Inquire: Have a follow-up discussion with the performer to understand their experience with the coaching program and the new motivators. Are the motivators working for them? Do they feel optimistic about making the change to the new behaviors?

Evaluate: Step up on the balcony and evaluate overall progress. Enlist the help of experts to help through troublesome and confusing evidence. Refine your lens as you re-enter the Observe step for another cycle through the process.

    Managing behaviors and managing emotions are two different but very interlocked practices that are essential to managing transformational change. This should give you a good base with which to work. In addition, surround yourself with the right experts, and you will be fine. There's no need to be fearful or anxious; it's just part of this crazy movie we are in right now.

Incorporating Final Insights into the Design of the New Organization

And here we are at the end of the Arrive Phase, the third and final iteration of our design journey! That wasn't so bad, was it? Note that we did not discuss any new design concepts, which were covered in the first two iterations. However, we did look at *implementation*, specifically the areas that give most leaders problems during a transformational change, to garner *design* insights. This is a sophisticated management move that I hope will resurface more times throughout your experience as a leader.

Our goal, as we wrap up the design of our Adamant Triad, is to land with a LOP (Lovable Optimal Product). The value boost with this version of the product is small when compared to the large value differential that comes with the REP (Respectable Effective Product); however, from a management perspective, it is more significant than the REP, as it puts us over the magic Pareto threshold of 80% value. We have passed the critical junction that joins the *road to success* with the *path to perfection*; there is no point in pursuing the treacherous path to an absolutely perfect design.

Now that you have been through this closing ceremony twice, there shouldn't be any surprises. As before, the decisions that you will align with your Strategic Leadership Team at the end of this iteration are the ones from Chapter 4:

- Have we applied feedback from the last iteration to develop a really lovable Adamant Triad?
- Do we feel like we are at least 80% of the way to a perfect Adamant Triad?
- Have we developed the Adamant Triad that we *should* use?
- Is everyone on our Strategic Leadership Team aligned and committed to make this change?
- *Must* we move forward with another iteration?

To finalize the design, review the stakeholder feedback from the end of the second iteration and contemplate what we have covered over the last two chapters. Our discussion of governance should have triggered some insights into your OD (organizational design), specifically in the areas of Value, Power, and Culture. Has our discussion of risk management triggered any insights regarding your Strategic Guidance System?

There was a full discussion on OCM (Organizational Change Management), including the Full Life Cycle of Behavior Management (Figure 9.1), management of the Emotional Journey (Figure 3.1), and my D-OCMIE method of managing behaviors (Figure 10.1). As you look at the design of your Adamant Triad and reflect on these concepts, do any design improvements come to mind? What about our discussion of metamorphosis? Refer back to our summary of insights in Table 10.1. Does this trigger any potential adjustments to your Strategic Management System and the way it addresses all three types of change (see Figure 4.1)? These are just a few questions to get blood flowing to your PFC (pre-frontal cortex). Spend some time generating insights from the last two chapters and combine them with the feedback that you received earlier from your stakeholders.

Once the brainstorm is completed, carefully adjust your Adamant Triad, paying particular attention to maintaining balance. You should go through thoughtful cycles of adjusting and rebalancing until all the adjustments are incorporated and the design is completely balanced. Note that rebalancing will generate additional insights, so stay with it, like a complex logic puzzle, until the design is fully settled.

This last design ceremony with your Strategic Leadership Team should be very rewarding. So we are clear, the answer to that last question is no, and we will not be moving forward with another iteration for this design. However, you will, on rare occasions, when using the AAA methodology, move forward with a fourth iteration. But only when you and your leaders and your stakeholders feel like the product is not at 80% value, and you *must* give it one more try to land the right solution.

Otherwise, you have crossed the finish line. Congratulations! You will, of course, share the final design with your key stakeholders, but the objective of this engagement is more of a showcase than a feedback session. Make sure they are clear on the objective; you are not processing any more feedback. Also, align with them that we have, indeed, crossed over the 80% value threshold. If they disagree, you just might need that fourth iteration![5]

Putting It into Practice

As the leader of your firm, you must set an example when it comes to managing behaviors. It is fine to rely on behavior management professionals for help when you are first starting out, but they should not be a permanent dependency. At some point, you must master this skill. So, no better time than the present to start. Let's start building fluency in D-OCMIE.

1 Select a coachee from your leadership team that you spend a lot of physical time with and feel psychologically safe around
2 Agree on one behavior development objective from the final list of behavioral themes that you created in the last chapter
3 Engage with your performer one-on-one to clarify the desired behavior and address any issues or roadblocks they perceive in its obtainment. Agree to a weekly cadence of engagements
4 Actively observe their behavior for the first week and record specific observations as they relate to the desired behavior. Make sure to record date, time, situation or circumstance, observed behavior, and perceived impact. Make sure to record all observations, including desired behaviors, anti-behaviors, and missed opportunities
5 Prepare for your first weekly engagement by developing a coaching program, based on your observations. Enlist the help of a performance coach or other behavior management expert as needed. Your coaching program is a list of recommendations, based on your observations, coupled with positive and negative motivators (i.e., consequences)
6 Your first weekly engagement is a coaching session. Review your observations and your coaching program (recommendations and motivators) with the performer. Check for understanding and alignment, and raise/resolve any issues or concerns
7 Implement your motivators (quickly) and continue to observe passively
8 Your second weekly engagement is an inquiry session. Gather feedback from them on their experience with the coaching program. Does it seem to be working? Is the behavior starting to obtain (from their perspective)? Are they optimistic about fully obtaining the behavior?

You are just gathering feedback at this point; do not provide feedback or coaching

9   Evaluate your coaching program and adjust if needed. Enlist the help of professionals when you get stuck

10 Actively observe performer behavior again, like you did in Step 4. Your third weekly engagement is another coaching session, Step 6. This cycle repeats until you and the performer both agree that the behavior has fully obtained and there is little risk of recidivism (i.e., back to old behaviors)

It is important that you learn in a safe environment, so that you can stumble without negative consequences and stay positive in your growth. Select a coachee that you trust and have your coach and advisor (from your Executive Mental Team) nearby as a safety net. Behavior management seems daunting at first, but it's really not that hard once you practice a few times with a good method.

Executive Debrief

- Transformational change has two related but very distinct parts: letting go of the status quo and normalizing to a new future. Each one of these parts has its own localized change journey
- If the change starts (letting go of the status quo) before the new future is defined, people will be forced to endure a very uncomfortable limbo between the two change journeys
- Metamorphosis, as it is observed in nature, provides a wealth of insights for transformational change. Here are a few to consider:
  - Like the caterpillar, concealing internal transformation from the external world is a notable survival tactic
  - Like the dragonfly and its incomplete metamorphosis, the point of transformation is not in the degree of physical change, but in the need for change
  - Like the locust, a radical shift in behavior and culture is as much a transformation as a radical shift in form, operating model, or structure
  - It is your job as a leader to understand the organization's DNA and preserve it throughout its many transformations
- Kotter's eight-step change model is sufficient for transitional change, but for transformational change, consider these additional 12 best practices:
  - Help people embrace the uncertain nature of the change
  - Put more effort into OCM upfront than you initially feel necessary

- Begin with the end culture in mind
- Strongly manage all leader behaviors
- Find sources of informal power and authority to help influence behavior
- Move quickly on establishing a thriving environment where people love to do their best work
- Broadcast metrics (targets and progress) for well-being, community, and human relationships
- Aggressively encourage everyone to protect, reinforce, and grow their mental health
- Develop and install one-way locks along the Emotional Journey (see Figure 3.1) to prevent regression
- Clearly document the difference between the current state and the future state
- Overly manage the first 100 days of change
- Actively manage the firm's Emotional Journey

- To effectively manage emotions, you need some literacy, a few experts, and a measurement system
- Your emotional measurement system should instrumentalize the Emotional Journey. At any point in time, you should know where different groups of your organization are in their emotional journey
- Managing emotions makes it easier to manage behaviors
- To manage behaviors, consider the D-OCMIE Method: Define, Observe, Coach, Motivate, Inquire, Evaluate
- At the end of the third iteration (the Arrive Phase), you should have an Adamant Triad design that represents at least 80% of a perfect design. If you have not crossed this threshold, you must execute a fourth iteration before continuing

Congratulations on a job well done! We have come a long way, and we are finally ready to deploy our strategy

Notes

1 On August 15, the day before we rushed my wife to the Emergency Room, I nearly finished writing Chapter 8 of this book. Despite my deep experience, training, and knowledge in matters of this sort, I could not bring myself to start writing again until exactly one month after her passing. Of course, this Chapter turned out quite differently from what I originally outlined. It is what it is.

2 It is clearly a myth that ostriches bury their head in the sand when trying to avoid an uncomfortable or dangerous reality. No animal can survive with their head buried in the sand! They often lower their head to eat, rest, and check on their eggs, which gives off the illusion of a sand-buried head; this is likely how the myth started. How it persists is beyond me.

3 Not all change management experts are created equal. Some of the less-expensive experts deal primarily with communications and tactical engagements (town halls, lunch-and-learns, etc.). The more sophisticated ones will have a background in psychology and/or organizational behavior, but they may not have much business acumen. The best change management experts will understand both human behavior and business, but even some of those won't know how to measure behaviors. You need a real solid change management expert on your team if you are attempting a transformational change. Choose wisely.

4 Using the term "performer" may sound aloof and clinical; however, it conveys the level of professionalism that must be taken when managing behaviors. I like it when leaders use this term because it signals their seriousness and competence with applied behavior science.

5 Seriously, if this ceremony does not go as planned and/or your stakeholders don't feel like you have an 80% design, collect more feedback with the specific intent of crossing over the 80% value threshold. Ask your stakeholders what it will take for them to feel like they have an 80% solution. Then, proceed with a fourth iteration to complete the design. Do not continue until this last ceremony confirms the design is completed.

Bibliography

Horowitz, B. (2014). *The hard thing about hard things: Building a business when there are no easy answers*. Harper Business.

Kotter, J. P. (1996). *Leading change*. Harvard Business Review Press.

Kotter, J. P., & Cohen, D. S. (2002). *The heart of change: Real-life stories of how people change their organizations*. Harvard Business Review Press.

Lewin, K. (1947). Frontiers in group dynamics: Concept, method, and reality in social science; social equilibria and social change. *Human Relations, 1*(1), 5–41.

Prosci. (2023). *Best practices in change management* (12th ed.). Prosci Inc.

Scott, K. (2017). *Radical candor: Be a kick-ass boss without losing your humanity*. St. Martin's Press.

Going Live and Making the Transition

Even with the best design in hand, going live with a new strategy, organizational design, approach to innovation, or any combination thereof is scary. I lost count of the times I have walked into an organization to help implement a strategy that was unimplementable. The popular approach is to hire a very expensive, big-brand consulting firm to design one, some, or all of these components. Then, once the voluminous set of slides is handed over to the recipient organization, the big-brand consulting firm bids adieu, and the proud owners of said slideware enthusiastically embark on implementation. After meandering aimlessly for several months in the Enchanted Forest of Good Intentions, they reach out to a consultant like me to help them find their way to meaningful progress. In almost all cases, they were doomed to fail from the beginning.

In all fairness, consulting firms are not in the habit of setting organizations up to fail. I have reviewed countless strategies from all the major consulting firms (and some of the minor ones). Most of them are really good—on paper. However, in most cases, it is either not appropriate for the receiving organization (e.g., pushing an innovation-heavy strategy into a company that is clearly risk-averse and process-driven) or the receiving organization is not capable of successfully deploying the strategy (e.g., not enough resources to simultaneously transform and run the business). So, the strategy, in and of itself, is good; however, for all intents and purposes, it is unimplementable. Unfortunately, this happens a lot.

Lucky for you, if you have been following along with the last ten chapters of this book, you have already mitigated a lot of common implementation risks by designing with the end in mind. This is a lesson I learned very early in my consulting career while cutting my teeth in high-tech. Back then (early 1990s), the prominent SDLC (Software Development Life Cycle) methodologies were very linear (i.e., waterfall). Analysts would gather requirements, developers and architects would build and test the software, the software would be deployed into production, where it was handed over to Operations, and then the end users would use the software while

DOI: 10.4324/9781003518181-16

Operations provided end-user support. With this approach, Operations often inherited software that was very difficult to support. So, I started adding Operations people to my project teams so they could influence the design of the software before it was actually developed.

However, designing for implementation doesn't mean you are *ready* for implementation. As eager as you are to get this new strategy, organizational design, and approach to innovation implemented, let's spend a few more chapters rolling it out the right way. I would hate for you to spend all this time doing great work on the design of your Adamant Triad, only to stumble out of the gate and throw your jockey off before the race even gets started. Remember this metaphor from Chapter 3? Most implementations fail because of emotions (the horse), not logic (the jockey). If you push forward without being ready and stumble out of the gate so hard that you get thrown off, the emotions of the organization will take off without you, and you won't have the reins to steer the organization in the right direction. This is an unforced error.

We have already spent a lot of time getting ready. Now, let's get set— and then go!

Chapter 11

The Final Approach

Going Live with the New Organization

Countdown to Day Zero

The best laid schems o' Mice an' Men Gang aft agley

This line from Robert Burns' eighteenth-century poem, "To a Mouse," inspired the opening of John Steinbeck's classic novella, "Of Mice and Men." And, in case you weren't around in eighteenth-century Scotland, "Gang aft agley" roughly translates to "often goes awry." I happen to agree with Burns (and Steinbeck), who states that the best-laid plans are often rendered worthless by the time the final outcome makes an appearance.[1] I have spent most of my adult life studying execution excellence. It's a topic that caught my fascination as a very young adult, and I have never stopped contemplating what causes the gap between plans and outcomes. My insights and opinions could fill an entire book of their own, but I'll share my favorite one with you here: you should never plan with the expectation that the plan will execute as expected—you should plan with the intent of uncovering what to do next.

I have *never* seen a plan for transformational change executed as originally expected, because, in the complex milieu where transformations live, there is no hope for any plan to execute as expected. But this law of complex systems does not render the planning process valueless. Planning is a critical activity. Without a plan, you will aimlessly meander in the Enchanted Forest of Good Intentions with all the leaders who just bought a new strategy from a big-brand consulting firm. The planning process is not where leaders go wrong; it's in managing to a plan that has no hope of staying relevant for longer than two shakes of a lamb's tail. Your plan is only relevant until new insights are discovered. And this is where the watershed moment lives. Either you adjust your plan, or commitment bias kicks in and you blindly manage to an outmoded plan.

DOI: 10.4324/9781003518181-17

Wasabi Moment

A commitment bias, also known as the sunk cost fallacy, is an emotional filter on rational judgement that favors consistency with prior decisions, actions, and resource investments. This is a tricky area for leaders. You must defend good decisions; however, acknowledge when prior decisions are not appropriate anymore and forgo any investment in time, money, or other resources that seemed appropriate in the past

The trick to succeeding with an organizational metamorphosis is understanding the first principle of transformational change management: the first layer of management is emotions; everything else builds from there. The sequence for layering plans, from foundational to topside, is: Emotional Journey Management (see Figure 3.1), Behavior Management (see Figure 9.1), Organizational Change Management, and then Implementation Management (i.e., the actual nature of the change). I often joke with leaders, while going through a transformational change effort, that we are actually running a behavior management effort, and along the way we will make some change to our strategy and organizational design—only, in truth, I'm not joking.[2] When you begin with Emotional Journey Management and all the principles that apply (e.g., continuous discovery and event-driven management), you avoid most of the landmines that leaders trigger during a transformational change.

Using the Emotional Journey Management Plan as a base, layer on the Behavior Management Plan. Decision-driven management continues to apply, even after the three iterations of the design phase are over. Although plans will often change, key decisions at each stage of the process should not. Use the Full Life Cycle of Behavior Management (see Figure 9.1) to anchor your decisions. What decisions must be made at the end of each stage? Determine these now *before* you complete the Planning Stage. The key decisions that should be included are found in Table 11.1. Use this as a starting point and add a few decisions of your own, if needed.

Your Change Management plan, which includes sponsorship, communications, engagements, and talent development, is layered next. Sponsorship should be the main emphasis of your Change Management plan; it lays out the plan for how *all* leaders and influencers in the organization will support the change. Of course, a communications plan

Table 11.1 Key Decisions For Each Stage of the Full Life Cycle of Behavior Management

Stage[3]	Key Decisions
Planning and Readiness	Do we have a solid plan with a comprehensive set of objectives and deliverables that extend through the Stability Stage?
	Are there mitigations in place to compensate for expected lower performance during the resistance and exploration stages of the Emotional Journey
	Does our Organizational Readiness Assessment indicate a move to implementation?
Implementation/ Intervention	Are all implementation objectives and deliverables completed?
	Is our scorecard and measurement system ready to deploy, including clear targets for stability?
Warranty	Have implementation issues and interventions shifted from urgent to non-urgent?
	Do we have a baseline of metrics from which to start our Transition Stage?
Transition	Do our scorecard metrics unequivocally indicate stability, based on predefined success targets?
Stability[4]	Do our scorecard metrics trend in a stable range?

(one-way communication) is expected, and an engagement plan (two-way dialogue) is a must; however, I can tell if a change management plan will fail or succeed purely based on its Sponsorship Plan. Leaders at different levels will have different responsibilities, but *all* leaders must be involved in some capacity. I led a large transformational effort that went live on January 8, 2018, so we assembled *every* people leader in the organization for a mandatory all-day meeting on December 15, 2017, to prepare them for the following year's go-live event. This was just one of several structured leader engagements that comprised our Sponsorship Plan.

Once the Change Management plan is in place, layer on an Implementation Plan to manage the deployment of all the details (ceremonies, systems, structures, processes, etc.). Start by taking inventory of everything that must be true *before* you go live with the new strategy, organizational design, and approach to innovation (your Adamant Triad). Manifest this inventory into an Organizational Readiness Assessment. Then, create an execution and control plan that includes a comprehensive set of objectives, deliverables, and activities. Your Organizational Readiness Assessment will be used in the management ceremony that moves you from Planning to Implementation. Your plan should ensure there are no surprises during this formal gateway into the gauntlet.

Surviving the Gauntlet without Breaking Apart

Welcome to the Gauntlet

Everything that we have done so far is in preparation for this moment. Once you enter, your only focus until you exit the gauntlet is survival! Are you ready for this? You should be—so let's do it!

If you lived in seventeenth- or eighteenth-century Europe, *running the gauntlet* was not something to rejoice over. This draconian ritual was used for punishment, accountability, and atonement. Violators of laws, rules, or other social norms would be forced to run through a terrifying human boulevard formed by two rows of weapon-wielding disciplinarians who would strike as the convict sailed by. In some tribal societies, the ritual was used as a rite of passage, instead of a public punishment, to demonstrate bravery and resilience. Although it could serve today as a powerful negative consequence to reinforce social order, the practice is generally frowned upon in modern societies.[5] However, the illustrative language and graphic metaphor persist to represent any challenging and treacherous endeavor— like a significant transformational change.

Ever since watching the 1994 movie, "The River Wild," with Meryl Streep, I have used dangerous white-water rapids as my mental imagery for a gauntlet (see Figure 11.1). In the movie, The Gauntlet was the name of a particularly perilous section of the river that Meryl Streep's character attempted to navigate while under duress from the criminals in her raft. It's a fitting metaphor for the early stages of the implementation of a major transformation. Surviving the gauntlet, which we will define as the Implementation/Intervention and Warranty stages, is not easy, but I'll give you my best advice for making it through in one piece.

Structured communications and engagements developed in the Planning Stage should set you up for success in the Implementation (and Intervention) Stage, where communications and engagements become very critical. It is important that you remain open, transparent, and timely with your communications, paying particular attention to your plan. Everyone must understand all the stages of the plan (Implementation, Warranty, Transition, and Stability) and all the nuances that go along with each stage. It is a natural tendency for people to ask questions that can only be answered in a future stage, so your plan serves as a valuable tool for managing expectations.

Regarding your firm's Emotional Journey, there will likely be people who are still stuck on the Bridge of Denial when you go live. That is why going live should include a "shock factor" to hopefully shove anyone who is stuck on the Bridge of Denial into the Gulf of Resistance. This could be as simple as over-the-top pomp and circumstance about going

Figure 11.1 Surviving the Gauntlet.

live, or it could be very direct and strong language to known obliviouists or both and more. Regardless, do not let this last contingent of holdouts slow down your go-live plans; the point is to make it painfully obvious to anyone who is still clinging to the status quo that those days are definitely gone.

That should put most people in the Gulf of Resistance, where it is very important that people feel heard. This is where some finesse will serve you well, because you must also help people understand, in a delicate but firm way, that you have a solid plan that will not change until the firm safely arrives at the Transition Stage. It is far too risky to change plans while dealing with the Level 5 rapids of early-stage transformational change, so as grateful as you are for people who volunteer feedback during this period, you must stay the course until the waters calm down a bit. That said, let people know that feedback is encouraged and will be considered as soon as the firm reaches the Transition Stage.

Knowing that performance and morale are difficult to sustain while people struggle with resistance and exploration, you should have mitigations in place to compensate (considered and readied in the Planning and Readiness Stage). This can manifest as lower performance expectations and/or compensatory measures to offset expected lower performance (e.g., additional contingent staff). Communicate these mitigations to your people. They need to understand that you are not expecting the same performance from them while they are dealing with difficult emotional challenges.

One way to mitigate low performance and morale, worth strong consideration, is to fast forward quick wins that build a rich environment where people thrive and do their best work (see Figure 3.3). We have already discussed its importance in previous chapters; there is no better time than the most difficult part of this journey to put your money where your mouth is. Installing a new, shiny gym for people to play with during this treacherous time might seem like "guilt spending," and maybe it is, but who cares? It will make them feel better about their situation, and that's what matters.

When you listen and engage with people, do more than just active listening—develop solutions with them that will be implemented once you reach the safer waters of the Transition Stage. Talk to them about what they are passionate about and match their passions with your needs. If you see the opportunity for their passion to contribute to your plan, without changing or disrupting the Implementation Stage, take advantage of it. The more people are part of the solution, the better.

However, some people won't be part of the solution, or even part of the new organization. That's okay. You changed on them, not the other way around. So, do your best to find them a home, whether it is somewhere else in the new organization or even outside of your organization. It may seem odd to put effort into finding a new home for people who don't fit well with your new organization, but they were part of a great team that brought you great success—you owe them at least that much.

Once you formally transition to the Warranty Stage (by way of a formal ceremony), closely monitor the organization and prepare for rapid-fire interventions. When semiconductors are newly manufactured, they must be "burned in" for a few days to ensure reliability. Similarly, it is not uncommon for serious and urgent issues to surface shortly after implementation. That's why you must retain critical resources for rapid response and resolution. This is also when you should accelerate efforts to collect feedback from the people and work with them on solutions to be implemented in the next stage. After your "burn-in" period is completed, it is time for the transition to stability.

Measure, Inspect, and Adapt until the Organization Tells You the Transition Is Completed

Whenever I order a pizza for delivery from a good Italian restaurant, I prefer to order it half-baked. That way, I can finish it off in my oven and enjoy freshly cooked, piping-hot pizza instead of taking the risk that my pizza is delivered cold, forcing me into the no-win situation of either eating a good pizza cold or an overcooked pizza hot. Plus, as a cooking enthusiast, I like having contribution rights to the finished product, even if it's only heating it up to completion. The goal of the Implementation Stage during a transformational change is to deliver a half-baked solution to your people so they can help bake it to completion during the Transition Stage.

The typical connotation for "half-baked" in this context is not positive, so avoid that language when addressing your people, but hold on to that concept internally as a good mental frame for how to manage transformational change. There are three reasons why you should hold this somewhat non-intuitive conception. First, in a complex environment, the best you can hope for is about a 50% solution, even with a solid design. Second, you will never get full buy-in from your people if you don't engage them in the solution. And most importantly, you need their insights to arrive at the best destination.

As you move into the Transition Stage, you will shift your management philosophy from time-driven to event-driven, because this is when the unpredictable nature of human processes dominates. In terms of the PLB (Post, Lever, and Balance) Method (see Figure 5.2), your post will switch from time to scope. More completely, you will post on scope, lever on throughput (people), and allow time to balance. Allowing time to balance is unnatural and unsettling until you get used to it, at which point it is liberating. It is a concept that you will not only need to embrace but also lead your people through, as it may also be unnatural and unsettling for them to be managed this way. You cannot communicate when the Transition Stage will be over; you can only communicate how your scorecard will look when it is time to move to the last stage.

Cadence plays an important role throughout this period. I recommend you set up a regular and reliable cadence of inquiry, analysis, planning, and adjustments that is consistent, in concept and timing, with the probe-sense-respond approach suitable for complex environments. In practice, to manage the Emotional Journey of the organization, I usually set up a quarterly process that involves a survey, response analysis and recommendations, decision-making and planning for adjustments, and then implementation. Concomitantly, there is a probe–sense–respond cycle against the business environment to ensure proper strategic adjustments are made. The workforce is fully involved at this point in helping to steer the emerging organization to its final destination. How do you know when you have reached your final destination? Listen to the organization and it will tell you. Scorecard metrics will hit target ranges and neither strategic nor emotional change will seem necessary anymore. It's a good day when it arrives—believe you me.

Getting through the Transformation Blues

I hope, by now, you understand how emotionally taxing a transformational change can be on the great people who make up such a significant part of your success. Despite all your efforts to neutralize the punishing elements inextricably tied to metamorphic change, your people will be exposed and vulnerable. It is very common during the Transition Stage to experience the Transformation Blues, a sort of melancholy and malaise that sets in after prolonged exposure to unhealthy stress and anxiety. This is very different from an acute cause that deserves a targeted intervention. When the Transformation Blues set in, there's no identifiable root cause. After a while, people just start feeling—to use a technical term—bleh.

It is very difficult to stave off the Transformation Blues, but not impossible. First things first, make sure you have an adequate staff of licensed therapists available to help and make sure people are encouraged to talk with them. They are not only very helpful for private, individual discussions, but they can also facilitate group discussions, which are extremely helpful during challenging times. If you have already established an Employee Assistance Program (EAP), promote it. If not, consider starting one, or at least standing up a temporary program with similar services specifically for the purpose of surviving the transformation.

As you structure your engagement plan (as part of your Change Management plan), weave in sessions that are led by your therapists and coaches. You can even use your own EMT (Executive Mental Team) to facilitate relevant mental wellness sessions, especially with top management. It is so important that your leaders do everything they can to prevent contracting the Transformation Blues, as it tends to bring out the worst in them and those they influence. An ounce of prevention is worth a pound of cure, so get in front of it early.

Know and Grow

Engagements differ from communications in that they allow the target audience to engage in a meaningful dialog with the person or people delivering the message. They are very effective at bridging alignment, garnering buy-in, and resolving issues. Small groups of about 7-10 people work best, but they can be larger if the dynamic in the room is right. Once the room gets so big that conversation is inhibited, the purpose and power of an engagement diminishes quickly

We talked earlier about bringing forward efforts to install a rich environment where people thrive and do their best work. This will help with the Transformation Blues, as long as people live in and enjoy said rich environment. It does no good to bring in egg pods if they stay empty all day. So, have your leaders "walk the halls" once your rich environment starts to take shape, to observe how the intended inhabitants respond. This is another situation where they may need a little nudge into the playground—for their own good.

Finally, do your best to create a *fun* working environment and simply—decide to have fun. It's a choice. Find a reason to celebrate, whether it is a small win, a new member of the tribe, or even a made-up holiday. I worked with a client who would periodically host employee appreciation events, and they were so much fun! It was an all-day event outside that resembled a carnival or a fair. Food trucks would come in with a variety of carnival food, and there were games to play and contests where great prizes were given out. We even coerced some of the leaders to get involved, often seeing one awaiting their fate while sitting in a dunk tank. What a day! I have worked with some great clients.

That is the spirit you should maintain throughout the transformation. It does not have to be so serious all the time. It can be fun if you choose to have fun. And people should know that help is available if they are feeling down or just not having fun. The more you can keep those Transformation Blues away, the easier it will be to make it to the other side.

Celebrate, Rest, and then Relax for a While

Celebration serves a much higher purpose than just staving off the Transformation Blues; celebrations are seriously fun business. Not only do they provide an excuse to have fun, but they also play a valuable role in showing people they are appreciated. Sure, it is nice to have a good-paying job with perks. And many leaders would assume that, in and of itself, it is enough reward to keep people motivated. And they would be wrong.

On a logical level, the calculus works; however, on an emotional level, everyone needs a boost of appreciation occasionally, even when they have a great job. Additionally, isn't it fun to throw a party? Most leaders I know, once they pull themselves away from the whirlwind that spins us around every day, are thrilled at the opportunity to make their people feel happy and appreciated. So, it's a win for everybody involved!

However, you must make it a *must*, not a nice-to-have, or they won't get planned, and they won't get done. I led the organizational design effort for a firm that went through a radical shift in strategy, which we deployed over a grueling timeline due to unavoidable time constraints. The whole team put in a monumental effort to meet unreasonable deadlines. And when everything was said and done, we didn't get so much as a box of cupcakes. A 30-minute meeting was held to debrief and say thanks and goodbye. The next day, everybody went back to their day jobs, and I went on to a new client. That's how it goes sometimes. Say what you will, I think that's a missed opportunity. A lot more should have been done to thank and reward that team.

There are four types of events that show up on your plan that must be celebrated: small wins, major milestones, the end of the Transition Stage, and one year into the Stability Stage. It is important to maneuver a small win shortly after the Warranty Stage. I am not suggesting you manufacture a small win; it must be legitimate. However, do everything in your power to select a prospective win that has a very high chance of succeeding close to the end of your Warranty Stage. This is a critical period when people need a morale boost, and a celebration is usually the right prescription. Be sure to recognize and reward everyone in the organization for surviving the gauntlet and celebrate the team that brought in the organization's first victory.

The level of milestone celebration depends on the significance of the milestone; however, pull out all the stops when it comes to the celebration that marks the end of the Transition Stage. This is an amazing feat of accomplishment, and it demarcates the beginning of a new era for the firm. In fact, it would not be unreasonable to etch this date into the memory of the organization as a day to remember. A lesser but still fantastic celebration should be thrown one year later, on the anniversary of its major metamorphosis.

Use celebrations to reinforce your culture with rituals, folklore, and ceremonial reinforcement of your *kapu* or sacred rules (in a positive way). Since culture is such a prominent aspect of our OD (organizational design), it should play the leading role in all your celebrations. It is a time for expression and a time for sharing and a time for learning and passing on learnings to the young, future leaders of the firm. They are intended to be fun, but also much more, so take them very seriously—in a fun way.

Putting It into Practice

In this chapter, we built out our plan using a technique that I call **plan layering**, starting with a plan for managing the Emotional Journey as the foundation. It is a step up in sophistication from segmenting your plan (e.g., into work streams) because it intentionally sequences the development, and more importantly, the mental precedence of the plan's construction and subsequent execution. Let's walk through the process of assembling your layered plan.

1 Start by creating the scope for your Emotional Journey Management Plan, using Figure 3.1 as a reference, starting with a scope statement. How will you shepherd people from denial, to resistance, to exploration, and then finally commitment? Then, think through objectives (about 4–7) and then deliverables needed to accomplish those objectives (about 3–8 per objective).

2 Develop a measurement plan to go along with your scope, including what data to collect, how you collect it, and what good looks like as you pass through each stage. These are *events* that trigger work packages of deliverables (and supporting activities), and sometimes entire objectives. For example, when 80% of the organization has cleared the Gulf of Resistance, it starts the objective of engaging with the organization to explore and implement solutions while mitigating expected low performance.

3 Develop a schedule that maps out the process and cadence for your data collection and analysis. This is how you will know if an event has been triggered. The schedule can *float* for now until we can anchor it to the next plan.

4 Create the scope for your Behavior Management Plan, using Figure 9.1 as a reference, in the same way you did in Step 1. Make sure it is aligned with the scope for the Emotional Journey plan. If there are any inconsistencies, adjust *this* scope, not the underlying scope.

5 Map objectives and deliverables onto a schedule for the time-driven stages of the plan (Planning, Intervention, and Warranty). For alignment with the underlying plan, assume that the event that signals transition from denial to resistance sits just after the decision point between the Planning and Intervention stages.

6 Develop events based on a measurement plan, like you did in Step 2, for the remaining stages (Transition, Stability)[6].

7 Develop a schedule that maps out the process and cadence for your data collection and analysis, like you did in Step 3.

8 Anchor and align the schedule that you developed in Step 3 to this schedule. Holistically, you should have only one measurement plan that is executed on one cadence.

9 Create the scope for your Change Management plan, including considerations for sponsorship, communications, engagement, and talent development. Make sure it is aligned with the underlying scope. If there are any inconsistencies, adjust *this* scope, not the underlying scope.

10 *Hook* your objectives and deliverables to time and events as appropriate for the stage (on the Behavior Management Plan) in which they occur. It is okay if your Planning, Intervention, and/or Warranty stages "grow" in schedule due to insights from change management planning.

11 Create the scope for your Implementation Plan, including all the specifics of the Adamant Triad and any other non-people-specific changes. Check for alignment with the underlying scope and adjust if needed. Hook on objectives and deliverables like you did in Step 10.

12 Take one or two more passes through the entire process to ensure cohesiveness and alignment. Always start from the bottom (the Emotional Journey Management Plan) and work your way up.

Plan layering and event-driven management are advanced techniques that take some time to master, but are absolutely necessary when faced with managing through complex terrain. And the technical skills are not the hard part—it's the leadership. Leading people through the complexities of methods like these is an art and a science worth pursuing.

Executive Debrief

- You should never plan with the expectation that the plan will execute as expected—you should plan with the intent of uncovering what to do next

- The planning process is not where leaders usually go wrong; it is in managing a plan that is outmoded and irrelevant

- To best accommodate transformational change, practice *plan layering*. Build your plan in layers, starting with the Emotional Journey Management Plan, then the Behavior Management Plan, then the Organizational Change Management (OCM) Plan, and finally the Implementation Plan (the actual nature of the change)

- The stages of transformational change management follow from the Behavior Management Plan, with only slight modifications:

  - Planning and Readiness Stage

- Implementation/Intervention Stage
- Warranty Stage
- Transition Stage
- Stability Stage

- Decision-driven management continues to apply after the design phase; see Table 11.1 for key decisions to make at the end of each stage
- The OCM plan includes sponsorship (how leaders and influencers will lead the change), communications, engagements, and talent development
- The Implementation Plan contains all the tactical changes deployed into the organization as a result of the new Adamant Triad design (ceremonies, systems, structures, processes, etc.)
- An Organization Readiness Assessment is a checklist that is used to formally move from the Planning Stage to the Implementation Stage
- To survive the "gauntlet" of transformational change, or the Implementation and Warranty stages, follow these best practices:

  - Communicate frequently, honestly, and transparently with everyone
  - Conspicuously, "shock" everyone who is still stuck in Denial into Resistance
  - Listen to people and make sure they feel heard
  - Stick to the plan until the Warranty Stage is over
  - Fast-forward quick wins to build a rich environment where people thrive and do their best work
  - Engage with your people to collect feedback and start developing solutions for when the Transition Stage starts
  - Help people find a new home, even if it is not in your new organization

- Closely monitor the organization during the Warranty Stage and prepare for rapid-fire interventions
- The goal of the Implementation Stage is to deliver a partial solution that your people feel comfortable completing with you during the Transition Stage
- Your management philosophy shifts from time-driven to even-driven as you enter the Transition Stage
- During the Transition Stage, set up a regular and reliable cadence of inquiry, analysis, planning, and adjustments
- Transformation Blues set in after prolonged exposure to unhealthy stress and anxiety. To stave them off:

  - Strongly encourage people to talk with licensed therapists who are always ready to help
  - Pay particular attention to your leaders, make sure their mental health is protected

- Have leaders "walk the halls" to see how people are responding to your "thriving environment"
- Decide to have fun

- Use celebrations to reinforce your culture with rituals and folklore. *Insist* on celebrating small wins, major milestones, the end of the Transition Stage, and the one-year anniversary of entering the Stability Stage

Notes

1 It is a bit of a misnomer that plans go awry. Plans do not go awry, it's the execution of a plan that goes awry if your expectation is that things will go as planned.
2 Per the first principle of transformational change management, it would be more accurate to joke about actually running an emotional management effort, but that sounds too esoteric and weird.
3 Note that once the Behavior Management Plan is overlaid with an Implementation Plan, the first two stages are augmented slightly, adding "Readiness" to the Planning Stage and "Implementation" to the Intervention Stage.
4 There is technically no *end* to the Stability phase; however, you should look back after a certain period of stability (e.g., one year) to check on the organization, ensure its stability, and capture additional lessons learned.
5 This is why you *must* review all behavior management programs that involve negative consequences with your HR and Legal departments!
6 It is not necessary to build out a robust plan for stability; however, at a minimum, you should have quarterly checks, an intervention plan in case the organization starts drifting back to old behaviors, and a one-year review and celebration.

Chapter 12

Our Building Has a New Shape

Institutionalizing Lessons Learned from an Exciting Journey

Let Culture Do Its Job

May 10, 1941, was a dark day for Great Britain's dignitaries that plunged them into ruins (literally and figuratively) and violent divisiveness. Germany's strategy at the time was to weaken the United Kingdom's resolve through a sustained bombing campaign known as the Blitz—an unrelenting barrage of night raids that started with the bombing of London on September 7, 1940. Despite its ineffectiveness as a strategy, the Blitz did succeed in forcing the government into a Pyrrhic decision. The Palace of Westminster was struck by incendiary and high-explosive bombs, igniting both the House of Commons and the historic Westminster Hall. They could not save both, so they saved Westminster Hall and helplessly witnessed the House of Commons disintegrate into a pile of ashes and rubble. The business of Parliament could not be conducted without a House of Commons, so a new one had to be built—but how should it take its new form? The debate that ensued from this seemingly simple question is not for those of low constitution.

Some politicians, like George Thomas, believed they should use these unfortunate circumstances to "improve" the design and even the location of the House of Commons, largely warranting their position with then-modern theories of democratic architecture. Prior to the bombing, the House of Commons was built using an adversarial design, with several rows of benches directly facing opposing rows of benches. The design fostered a culture of vigorous debate against two clear contingents—the government and the opposition. Thomas and others holding this point of view argued that it should be redesigned as a semicircle, fostering a more inclusive and consensus-building culture.[1] There was even some collective passion to construct a new House several miles outside of London so that it would be more inviting to and inclusive of the world outside of the palace.

Winston Churchill, then Prime Minister of the United Kingdom, violently disagreed. He argued that the House of Commons must be rebuilt to

DOI: 10.4324/9781003518181-18

its original form to preserve the culture that had been shaped by its original design. There was no reason to abandon their cultural value of adversarial discourse and therefore no reason to abandon the design that shaped it. Furthermore, he felt government consensus, with all its merits, was fatally flawed when it opposed popular opinion. In these circumstances, there is no influential "voice of the people"—that is how revolutions start. So, Churchill stood his ground and eventually won the day. In his famous speech to Parliament on October 28, 1943,[2] when Churchill stated, "We shape our buildings; thereafter they shape us," he indelibly cemented the relationship between the architecture of the house and the culture of the House into the spirit of Parliament. By preserving its rectangular, opposing-bench design, Churchill preserved the integrity of their democratic culture.

Know and Grow

Architectural Determinism is a theory developed in the 1960s that posits human behavior is directly affected by the physical layout of the structures they inhabit. When applying to management theory, consider how leader behaviors are shaped by the design (architecture) of the organization

While Churchill decided to preserve the incumbent culture by restoring the House of Commons to its original design, we have decided to grow our leaders by implementing a new Adamant Triad. In both cases, the future culture of leadership is a direct result of the architectural design decisions made during the planning stage. With the deployment of and successful transition to your new human-centered strategy, culture-led organizational design, and innovative capabilities, you have built a new house; now, it is time to let the culture emerge and shape you into a better leader.

The transformation is over, so please give the organization a break and let it breathe for a while. It is wonderful to step back and experience the new organization come to life, so embrace it. For some reason, after surviving a grueling and successful transformation, some leaders start looking for the next transformation! If you happen to be one of those leaders, resist the urge and find another hobby to pour your energy into. The last thing your organization needs, right after a transformation, is another transformation! That is like dumping a tank of water on a garden of seedlings. Everyone will drown, and they will hate you for it. You have put a lot of work into getting the organization where it is. Just leave it alone and let the culture do its job.

The Insanity of Repeating Past Mistakes

In 1981, during the seventh annual Woman to Woman conference, featured speaker Jessie Potter, a prominent counselor on family relationships and human sexuality, offered the following sage advice to the attendants: "If you always do what you've always done, you always get what you've always gotten" (Ahern, 1981). Doing the same thing over and over again and expecting a different result is not the definition of insanity; it's a symptom of SSMI (short-sighted myopic ignorance)—a condition, unlike insanity, which is easily corrected. That said, intentionally allowing SSMI to go untreated is—well—insane. There is no sense in sticking a fork in a light socket after you have done it once. And yet, to my bewilderment, I see this metaphorically happening with organizations all the time.

I was working with a project team at a high-tech data systems firm in the early 2000s. They had just completed a self-imposed gauntlet—a grueling implementation to deliver a product in three months that should have taken at least six months. They delivered on time, but the experience was torturous, and it was their own fault. At the initial chartering of the project, the team committed to a three-month delivery, based on their estimation of the effort. Of course, they were way off. They grossly underestimated the project's risks. But, as they say, you live and learn—or do you? Once the product was delivered, we moved forward with the next deliverable, which was very similar to the one that had just been delivered. And do you have a guess as to what the team estimated this time? Three months! Unreal. When I tried to explain to them all the risks they ignored during the last chartering exercise—just three months ago—they argued with me, defending their position with statements like, "Yeah, but that won't happen this time." Times like that really make me question why I do this for a living.

Very early in the twentieth century, philosopher George Santayana said, "Those who cannot remember the past are condemned to repeat it." That is why it is so important to understand the history of our world, the history of your country, and especially the history of your own organization! However, understanding your organization's history is not as easy as it seems. It is one thing to learn your own lessons as a leader during the tenure of your leadership. But an organization, like a country, has many leaders throughout its history, all with different temperaments and styles. Furthermore, almost all modern-day organizations are led by a collection of leaders, not just one autocrat at the top. So, the collective leadership of an organization, at any point in time, is very dynamic and fluid as leaders continuously precede, succeed, resign, and retire. Consequently, consolidating and organizing all the decisions made by and lessons learned from all the leaders that have shaped and are shaping the organization is no easy feat. But it must be done. Otherwise, you will keep making the same mistakes, over and over again, and that's insane.

After we completed a massive transformational effort in the San Joaquin Valley of California, for the leader of a strategic upstream oil and gas business unit, the Vice President engaged with my team and me for a very important follow-up deliverable. He charged us with creating a web-based archive that detailed our journey and insights, from beginning to end, and he personally overlaid his own lessons learned from the experience. He wanted to make sure the leaders who succeeded him knew exactly what we did, how we did it, and most importantly, *why* we did what we did. We spent a few months developing this archive, and what an incredibly valuable use of time. Our journey is now indelibly memorialized in the history of that oil field.

Wasabi Moment

It is difficult but important to defend your decision to capture lessons learned after a significant change is implemented. Although the idea of capturing lessons learned will not be met with much resistance, the bias of the organization will be to move forward, not look back. This is a common failing of organizations that you must avoid. It's the only way to inoculate your organization against SSMI

Prominent archives of past journeys, lessons learned, and key insights are part of the organizational architecture that guides the growth of your culture. Stories of the past will often turn into organizational folklore, which establishes folkways (simple, informal norms), mores (morally significant norms), and *kapu* (see Chapter 7) that govern and maintain social control. Leadership is relatively easy under these circumstances, provided decisions are consistent with established norms. The justification for decisions is not required while strong social norms are in power.

Techniques for Collecting and Documenting Lessons Learned

Committing to and defending the decision to do a robust job at capturing lessons learned after a significant change effort is the hard part. After that, execution is easy. It is delightful and enriching to reflect with a great team of talented people on a significant challenge that was accomplished. Surviving a gauntlet comes with a great deal of adversity, which is the fodder for wisdom. But it will not obtain organically. Once the transformational dust settles, and before the memories of the journey fade, the critical question for your team to answer is, "How do we memorialize the adversity we just endured?" Let me share some ideas from my past experiences that are worth considering.

The web archive that we built for the leader in the San Joaquin Valley turned out beautifully. Instead of building it from scratch, we converted the Microsoft SharePoint site that we used to manage the program into an online museum and library. Our Sponsorship Plan included the production of about a dozen leader videos that were very useful in helping the organization understand what we were doing and why. They then served a later purpose when we built the archive to help draw interested people into our challenge and the circumstances we faced. We reorganized our file structure from management to discovery, given the shift in intended audience. For instance, we created indexes to make it easier for people to find information and supplemental references to explain concepts and rationale that did not need explanation to the program team during implementation. Finally, we added reflective insights from those who were closest to the leadership and management of the journey, including valuable takeaways from the Vice President himself. I will admit, this is an extreme, but it is worth every minute we put into it. It has been several years since we released this archive, and people still talk about it.

At the other extreme is a simple Quick Reference Guide of key lessons learned. Although it won't have the same impact as a robust web archive, it still serves as a valuable tool, and it can be produced in a fraction of the time. The best outcome is a double-sided one-pager, either letter- or legal-sized. These documents are easy to produce, distribute, and consume, so they are good for reaching a wide audience. Fill the document with eye-catching infographics and concise lists (bulleted, numbered, etc.). Avoid long paragraphs of tiny-font text. It's not about cataloging everything that you know about the transformation; it's about synthesizing that into valuable information that others will need to know if they attempt a similar or related transformation.

Videos are one of my favorite tools for communicating lessons learned. They are easy to consume and highly impactful, especially when leaders and other influencers deliver the message. Whether they are produced in a studio with expensive equipment or on the fly with a personal phone, a short montage of key leaders and stakeholders sharing reflections and insights is a powerful way to build and reinforce long-term institutional memories. Produce these as interview-style clips with an off-camera interviewer. Pre-production (the work done before filming) is important, even with a low-budget production. Make sure each interviewee is prepared, giving them adequate time to rehearse their answers to a set of predetermined questions. During production, multiple takes are acceptable, even expected.

You are not a reporter on location trying to break a story; you are producing a meaningful video that will be valuable to future leaders.

Lastly, you would be remiss to overlook your Prophet Center when collecting and documenting lessons learned. By design, your Prophet Center is where people go to find answers. So, why would your most valuable lessons learned be absent from such a central source of knowledge? Regardless of your approach and the materials it produces, ensure your lessons learned make their way into your Prophet Center. Imagine a future leader engaging with your Prophet Center to ask questions about your transformation. How would you want your Prophet Center to respond? Or imagine a future leader contemplating another organizational transformation and turning to your Prophet Center for advice. Wouldn't you want your Prophet Center to reference the key lessons learned from this transformation when organizing its response? That's a rhetorical question; you know the answer.

Using Governance to Protect the Organization against Itself

As your culture emerges, governance plays the most influential role in its trajectory and final state. In Chapter 9 we discussed how to select the right materials for governance. Here, we will discuss the best practices for executing it once deployed. If culture is a grapevine, governance is the trellis system that guides its growth. It is also the pruning and canopy management that ensures a high-quality culture is produced by efficiently using organizational resources. Most importantly, it keeps the culture from becoming unruly, ensuring it grows in a predictable and manageable manner.

The practice of governance is underwhelming in most of the organizations I've worked with—and I have worked with a lot of them. A key failing pattern I have observed is in the decision-making process, perhaps the most critical responsibility of governance. I typically see diversity and inclusion, which is good; and logical reasoning, which is good; and diligent fact-gathering, which is good. It's all good, but it's not enough. The problem with most governing bodies that I have come across is that they don't learn from their past decisions, and that's bad. If you don't learn from your decisions, then you run the risk of repeating the same bad decisions from the past. Does that sound familiar? Of course it does. It's the governance variant of SSMI.

Like all SSMI variants, this is easily corrected. It starts with documenting the *reason* for each decision, as soon as the decision is made. When a governing body makes a decision, everybody in the room understands why that decision was made—until approximately five minutes after everyone leaves the room. Unless measures are taken to record the reasons supporting the decision, they will be lost along with all future opportunities to learn from it. So, make it a governance practice to record the reasoning for each decision each time a governing body makes one.

The next best practice is to record the *dissenting* opinion. It is rare to find a significant decision supported by a unanimous opinion. That's why most governing bodies have a consensus process, a way to bridge unanimous support in the face of divergent opinion. What often happens, though, is that once the decision is made, the arguments supporting the dissenting opinion are dismissed. This is a huge mistake! Just because the opposition concedes doesn't mean that their arguments are invalid. In fact, just the opposite is true. The dissenting opinion and the arguments that support it are extremely valuable inputs to future decisions. Plus, they prevent the organization from rehashing old arguments. I have witnessed an organization rehash the exact same debate over the exact same issue using the exact same arguments and arrive at a different decision! It's silly.

Next, draw insights from a decision after each decision is made and record them for future reference. The more you debate issues and arrive at decisions, the more you learn about the nature of the decisions and the experience of making them. There are great gleanable insights that should be carried forward; however, they won't if they are not remembered, and they won't be remembered unless they are recorded.

Finally, once again, leverage your Prophet Center. Every time a governing body makes a decision, the Prophet Center should be consulted for sage wisdom and advice. And where does it get this sage advice from? You guessed it, from your governing bodies! Every decision made by every governing body in the organization should be housed in your Prophet Center, along with supporting reasons, dissenting opinions, and lessons learned. That way, when each governance team convenes to make an important decision, their starting point is the wisdom from the past. Learning and continual improvement becomes endemic to the organization's governance, which plays such a prominent role in shaping your culture.

Continual vs. Continuous Improvement

You may have heard of continuous improvement, but what about *continual* improvement? It is the lesser-known and more efficient cousin of continuous improvement, with the key distinction being that continual improvement is decision-driven, whereas continuous improvement is constant. Continuous improvement is a driver with a lead foot pinning the gas pedal to the floor; continual improvement is a driver who only accelerates when necessary. Continual improvement involves a little more management; however, the payoff in efficiency is well worth the additional management tax.

I wish I could take credit for the concept and the term, but I am glad I stumbled on it. In 2016, I worked with the Global Manufacturing Center of Excellence of a large, privately held agribusiness (food company). They needed an Operational Excellence advisor to help simplify their organizational model, and given my expertise in both OD (organizational design) and PI (process improvement), my skills fit nicely with their needs. They were very mature in their PI organizational capability, as most manufacturing operations are, and the TQM (Total Quality Management) geek in me quickly emerged as I pored over their process maps. Having spent over a decade as a practicing Lean Sigma Black Belt, I was surprised to come across a term I had never heard before—continual improvement. In working with them, I quickly came to know they used that term intentionally, in explicit contrast to continuous improvement. The insight was so bright that I have spent the last eight years evolving and developing the model as I conceptualize it (see Figure 12.1).

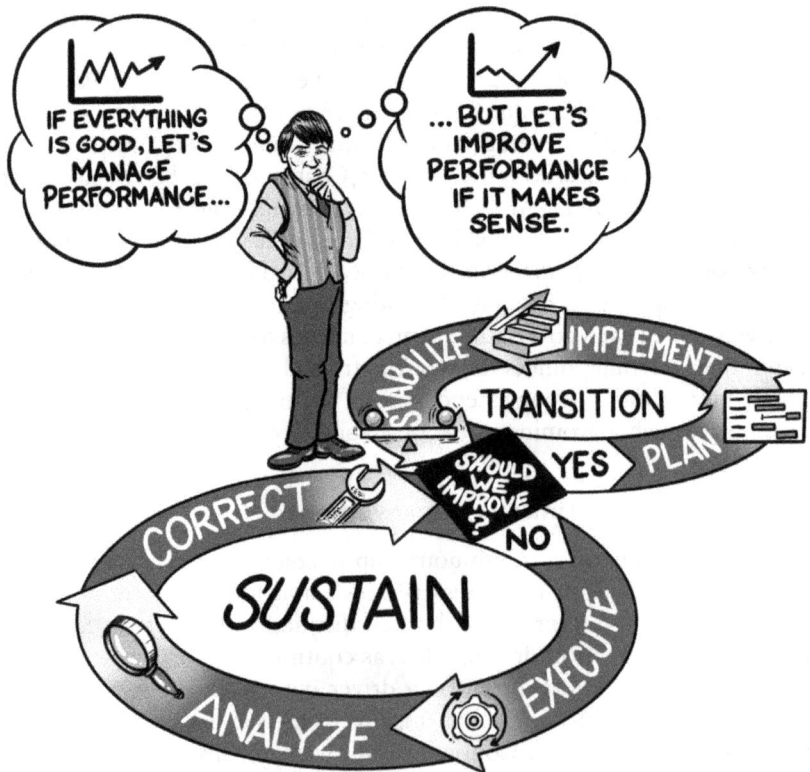

Figure 12.1 The Continual Improvement Cycle.

Key business processes are a vital component of how your firm delivers value to your customers. As such, they require significant focus when building and rebalancing the Value element of your OD (see Figure 5.1). As discussed in Chapter 5, an *egocentric* organization puts more emphasis on business processes than an *allocentric* organization; however, that doesn't absolve the allocentric organization from process development and subsequent improvement. All organizations need some degree of process management, and that is where the continual improvement cycle adds tremendous value to the run-state firm. In fact, continual improvement is more appropriate for an allocentric organization, as it must be more judicious in how much energy is spent improving its processes. An example of continual improvement can be found during a NASCAR race, like the Daytona 500. Drivers circle around the track and only enter the pit when it is absolutely necessary. There is no way a driver could win the Daytona 500 if they practiced continuous improvement on race day!

The continual improvement cycle is broken down into two different states: Sustain and Transition. The Sustain state resembles Deming's PDCA (Plan, Do, Check, Act) cycle (Deming, 1982) with a few nuances, most notably the absence of a *Plan* step. Any time you deploy a process into an organization, you must have a measurable way of knowing whether that process is performing as expected. This is typically done by developing and operationalizing a Control Chart (Gitlow, Levine, & Popovich, 2006). So, while a process stays in control, there is no need to plan. You will know whether the process is in control when you execute the *Analyze* step—basically, update and analyze your Control Chart. Regardless of whether the process is officially out of control,[3] if you suspect there is an opportunity to nudge the process in the right direction, take that action during the *Correct* step. Then, instead of planning, you will make that all-important decision: *should* we improve this process? The intentional use of *should* clarifies the guideline around this decision (see Chapter 4 if you need a refresher on MSmc).

Like all other decision-driven processes, you must clearly define the decision criteria for this turnout upfront to simplify the decision of throwing the switch.[4] In most cases, you will improve performance when the process is clearly out of control or when its CTQ (critical to quality) metrics must be changed (e.g., for strategic reasons). These are the typical circumstances for switching the process from Sustain to Transition. That said, in this case, the decision criteria should inform the decision, not make the decision. It is ultimately up to the decision maker, regardless of what the decision criteria suggest.

The Transition state is where process improvement occurs following a simple three-step process: Plan, Implement, and then Stabilize (very intuitive, no explanation needed). It is called the Transition state because, when your continual improvement cycle is operational and effective, the maximum degree of change that should fall out of the Strategic Management System (see Figure 4.1) is Transitional. Only under rare circumstances would you find yourself in another Transformational Change (e.g., extremely disruptive market conditions). Most organizations that face Transformational Change are doing so because they were not practicing continual improvement.

Putting It into Practice

In this chapter, we discussed how lessons learned shape culture when captured, documented, stored, and used properly. Most organizations grow naturally, but it can be slow and unpredictable. To accelerate and influence the shape of your culture, be more intentional about how lessons learned are applied. One valuable application of lessons learned, especially in a culture-led organization, is **establishing folkways**. Folkways are informal norms that are rarely written down, yet widely adopted by the community, like saying "please" and "thank you" as a way of being polite. They are not heavily enforced and carry only minor social consequences if violated, but they serve an integral role in the fabric of your culture. Here is how to build folkways from lessons learned:

1 Capture and document lessons learned (i.e., from your transformational journey), as described in this chapter
2 Work with your team to discern and define desired behaviors that apply these lessons learned. Ask your team, "How should we behave differently, knowing what we now know?" Use the exercise in Chapter 9 as a reference for clearly defining behaviors
3 Assess the overall importance (of making sure the behavior obtains) and impact of each behavior, then segment them using MSmc (must, should, might, could)
4 Set aside all the behaviors in the *must* and *should* categories. We will only build folkways from the behaviors in the *might* and *could* category. Don't let their category dissuade you from spending effort to obtain these behaviors. Even though they are lower in importance and impact, they are still valuable in the overall taxonomy of your culture
5 Weed out any behaviors that are complex or difficult to obtain. Behaviors that build folkways are simple and sensible (e.g., like saying "excuse me" after a loud belch)
6 For each resultant behavior, clarify its reason. In some cases they are practical (like removing shoes before entering a house to keep the house clean), in some cases they are adaptive (like holding up an umbrella when it rains so you don't get wet), and in some cases they are symbolic

(like waving hello to show that you are unarmed and pose no threat), but in all cases there is some reason for behaving a certain way[5]

7 Develop a story for each behavior that narrates its history and reason for existence. Folkways are built from folklore, and folklore is simply the collection of stories that encapsulate the beliefs, customs, and practices that make up your culture

8 Work with your leaders and other influencers to model these behaviors and diffuse these stories into the organization at every opportunity. Modeling a behavior will typically serve as a prompt for telling its story; however, this is not the only opportunity. Meetings, ceremonies, and large company events provide perfect opportunities to establish folklore

Over time, these simple behaviors and the folklore attached to them will form folkways that effortlessly reinforce the stronger norms of your culture, like mores and kapu.

Executive Debrief

- Architectural Determinism is a theory that suggests human behavior is directly influenced by the physical structures in which individuals operate. When applying to management theory, the design of an organization ultimately shapes the behavior of the leaders who deploy it
- Once the transformation is over, give the organization space for its culture to emerge. The last thing it needs is another major change!
- SSMI (short-sighted myopic ignorance) is a condition that organizations suffer when they ignore valuable experiences and lessons from their past
- SSMI is easily treated by intentionally capturing, documenting, storing, and utilizing lessons learned from past efforts and decisions
- It is difficult but important to defend your decision to capture lessons learned after a transformation
- A few useful techniques for capturing and documenting lessons learned are web archives, quick reference guides, and videos
- Ensure lessons learned eventually make their way into your Prophet Center
- Good governance will guide and accelerate the growth of your firm's culture
- A common failing of governing bodies is not learning from the decisions they have previously made
- Three things should be recorded for each decision a governing body makes: reason, dissenting opinion, and insights
- Ensure the complete record of each decision makes its way into your Prophet Center

- Your Prophet Center should be consulted each time a decision must be made by a governing body
- Continual improvement is a more efficient alternative to continuous improvement. Where continuous improvement is constant, continual improvement is decision-driven. That is, processes are improved only when they should be improved
- The Continual Improvement Cycle is broken down into two different states: Sustain and Transition. In the Sustain state, performance is managed. In the Transition state, performance is improved
- At the end of every Sustain sub-cycle, a decision is made on whether the process should be improved
- The Transition sub-cycle is typically entered when the process is either out of control or when there is a strategic change in the process's quality metrics
- Most organizations that utilize a Continual Improvement Cycle avoid transformational changes
- Folkways are simple, informal norms that are highly effective in reinforcing stronger norms like mores (morally significant norms) and kapu (the strict cultural laws of the organization)

Notes

1 Interestingly enough, this happens to be the design of choice for most democratic governments around the world, including the United States of America.
2 Churchill's speech to Parliament on October 28, 1943 regarding the rebuilding of the House of Commons is available on YouTube here: https://youtu.be/k8rbpai905I. It is worth reviewing to get the full impact and meaning of his famous quote on the matter.
3 There should be very clear rules that officially indicate an out-of-control process.
4 A *turnout* is the mechanism on a railway that guides a train along one of two possible tracks. *Throwing the switch* is the activity of moving the switch blades from one track to the other track.
5 Don't let logic stand in your way of attaching a reason to a behavior. Every time I line up in front of a golf ball, I do a little bounce. There's no good reason for doing that, it just feels good.

Bibliography

Ahern, T. (1981, October 24). Search for quality called key to life. *The Milwaukee Sentinel*, p. 5, col. 5. Retrieved from Google News Archive.

Deming, W. E. (1982). *Out of the crisis*. MIT Press.

Gitlow, H. S., Levine, D. M., & Popovich, E. A. (2006). *Design for six sigma for green belts and champions: Applications for service operations–foundations, tools, DMADV, cases, and certification*. Pearson Prentice Hall.

Zooming In on the Luck, Skill, and Grit of the First 100 days

Fortune Favors the Brave

The Bellagio Casino in Las Vegas is magical. It has been quite a while since I stayed there, but strolling into the opulent lobby and gazing up at the dazzling blown glass floral display that adorns the ceiling is a memory that will never fade. One summer, we vacationed there with my sister-in-law, Debbie (Kim's sister), and a fun group of her Chicagoland friends. Las Vegas was a curious choice for them, since they don't gamble that much. It didn't matter; we had a blast! Las Vegas these days has everything for everyone: dazzling entertainment, relaxing pools (the one at the Bellagio is spectacular), incredible restaurants, all the shopping you can handle, and of course a 24-hour open invitation to dance with Lady Luck. However, one thing you won't find in Las Vegas is a building with a 13th floor. In fact, according to the Stress Management Center and Phobia Institute in Asheville, North Carolina, more than 80% of high-rise buildings in the United States do not have a 13th floor, and the vast majority of hotels, hospitals, and airports avoid using the number for rooms and gates as well. It has been 400 years since Sir Francis Bacon laid the groundwork for empirical scientific methods, and yet one hemisphere of the world is afraid of the number 13 and the other one is afraid of the number 4.[1] As a rational, scientific-minded leader, does it make sense to hold on to irrational, non-scientific superstitions? Well, if you haven't figured it out yet, try finding a Chapter 13 in this book.

There are many great leaders in our past who behaved in superstitious ways. President Franklin D. Roosevelt was highly triskaidekaphobic, actively avoiding anything related to the number 13. For instance, he disliked sitting at a table with 13 guests, so he would either invite a 14th guest or skip the event altogether. Also, he never traveled on Fridays and reportedly carried lucky charms. He may have picked up this last superstition from his cousin, President Theodore Roosevelt, who was known for carrying a rabbit's foot for good luck. Prime Minister Winston Churchill would go out of

DOI: 10.4324/9781003518181-19

his way to avoid black cats, as did Napoleon Bonaparte, who feared them outright. And then there is Hitler, with his fascination for lucky charms and numerology. Maybe he should have looked closer at the numbers when he decided to turn south for Stalingrad in 1942. On that note, why Stalingrad? Because it was named after Soviet leader Joseph Stalin? Sure, that's a good reason to make a series of horrible decisions. For the record, it wasn't superstition that brought Hitler down; it was poor decision-making.

I encourage leaders to embrace superstition because it pairs well with risk. To be a good leader, you must take risks. And, if you take risks, then you should be superstitious, provided your superstitions don't interfere too much with rational leadership. Carrying a lucky charm, avoiding black cats, or wearing a red handkerchief on Wednesdays won't affect your ability to make good decisions or to motivate and inspire your people. However, overruling your Chief Operating Officer because your astrologer disagrees with them is probably not a good idea.

I grew up around gambling, so taking risks is a natural way of life for me. My dad taught me how to handicap horses at a very young age, so we have been playing horses together for over 40 years now.[2] I have fond memories of sitting around the dinner table with my dad, aunt, uncle, and family friends, going over the Racing Form for the next day's races. The following morning, the whole family would pile into Dad's Cadillac and enjoy the golden tunes of the 1950s and 1960s as we made our way up Highway 101 to Bay Meadows Racetrack. It was a great day of fun for everyone. My dad knew a lot of trainers and jockeys, so we were always treated well at the track. I was too young to place bets, but I had my own money, and I knew what I was doing, so I had a *special arrangement* with my dad. Some days we would win, and some days we would lose, but we would always have a great time. We had everything you could ever want: laughs, thrills, food, sun, and most importantly, family. But the one thing we never had was a $50 bill. Why would we? They're bad luck.

Using Luck to Tip the Scales

The rational person's balderdash is the astute person's edge. Nonsense is only nonsense until it makes sense. Some things don't make sense because we are not technologically advanced enough to understand them—yet. Before the nineteenth century, if you washed your hands to prevent the spread of disease, you would be ridiculed for following a senseless, superstitious ritual. The idea that tiny, invisible germs could transmit disease was too fantastic for most rational-minded people of the time. But some people, like Ignaz Semmelweis, a Hungarian physician and scientist who worked at the Vienna General Hospital during the mid-nineteenth century, thought differently. And, despite clear evidence that his hand-washing policies would drastically reduce maternal mortality rates,[3] his ideas were met with strong skepticism and resistance from the medical community. To his critics, Semmelweis just got lucky somehow with his silly hand-washing ritual.

But, you may say, that was a long time ago. We are far more intelligent now, with our ChatGPT, our drones, and our same-day delivery of liquid detergent. Fine. But don't be so naive to think that you are blessed to be born in the golden age of enlightenment when humans have figured out everything that can be figured out—because we haven't. We still don't know how anesthesia works, why cats purr, or why we get hiccups. And on that last point, I have not met a person who doesn't have their favorite ritual for stopping them once they show up.[4]

It is good to be science minded; I strongly encourage it! However, if you confine your perspective to the rational, scientific world, you run the great risk of self-limiting to suboptimal outcomes known as *local maxima*. To achieve the greatest outcomes, or the *global maxima*, you must embrace preternatural concepts like emanations, superstitions, and faith.

Gradient Ascent and the Global Maximum.

Gradient Ascent is an algorithm that showed up early in my life as an AI (artificial intelligence) enthusiast and then later in life when I became a Lean Sigma Black Belt. It is a sophisticated mathematical technique that helps practitioners find the optimal solution to a multi-variate problem. It is useful for training a neural network because that's essentially what a neural network is trying to do: take an input set, which usually has a large number of elements, and produce an optimal output set based on a large variety of input-set examples and a clear way to differentiate whether one output set is better than another output set. It does this iteratively. Each time it takes a step, it evaluates whether the outcome was better or worse than prior outcomes. If the outcome is better, it will keep going in that direction. If the outcome is worse, it will try another direction. Once it realizes that it cannot go in any direction without improving the outcome, it is done. It has found the answer. Or has it?

The well-known vulnerability of the Gradient Ascent algorithm is *local maxima*. The global solution space for most multi-variate problems is not that simple and straightforward. It has peaks and valleys and higher peaks and higher valleys, and gorges, and cliffs, and everything else. So, when Gradient Ascent starts you on an uphill trek to a peak, there is very little chance you are somewhere on the *highest* mountain in the land. Therefore, when you reach the peak of whatever hill or mountain you are climbing, there is very little chance that you are at the *highest* peak possible. So, how do AI specialists, data scientists, and Lean Sigma Black Belts[5] deal with this situation? Simple. Just relocate somewhere else and start again. If Gradient Ascent happens to take you to a higher peak after relocation, awesome! I guess you got lucky, right? Maybe. It depends on how you chose your new starting point. Did you wash your hands first? Did you rub your lucky rabbit's foot?

Know and Grow

Emanations are the essential auras that flow from your thoughts into the universe. They are the way outcomes are manifested from the metaphysical to the physical world. They are inherently authentic; they cannot be manufactured, altered, or suppressed. Remember, thoughts are things! What you emanate through your thoughts influences your reality

Applied superstition is not that hard, but you must first accept and embrace preternaturalness—the quality of being beyond what is ordinary or natural. That's where faith comes in. Authentic faith in your superstitions is essential to ensure you emit the right emanations. You can manifest an outcome; emanations are real! And finally, don't worry about what other people think of your superstitions, especially when there is little to no downside. I can't tell you how often my highly educated colleagues have looked down on me after I spent a fun-filled weekend gambling in Reno or Vegas. *If* I lose, I usually come back having lost less than a thousand dollars, including gambling, food, hotel, and other entertainment (shows, etc.). I wonder how much that weekend vacation with the family in Disneyland cost them?

A Closer Look at the First 100 Days

When President Franklin D. Roosevelt (FDR) took office in March of 1933, he was handed a country in desperate need of a transformation. It was a dark and scary period in the history of the United States. The country was mired in the Great Depression, its worst economic crisis in history. Unemployment was a staggering 25% (one in four Americans was without a job), industrial production had fallen by almost 50% (compared to 1929 levels), GDP had fallen by about 30% from its peak in 1929, 60% of Americans lived below the poverty line,[6] about 40% of the banks had failed taking with them the life savings of millions of people, and the stock market lost **90% of its value** since the start of its ten-car pile-up of a crash in October of 1929. Americans had about had it with Hoover and the Republicans, eagerly handing FDR and the Democrats a landslide victory,[7] but it came with an ultra-high expectation—*get us out of this mess!*

And that's exactly what FDR did. Regardless of your opinions on whether his strategies and policies were appropriate for the beacon of democracy and the land of the free, one thing is unequivocal. FDR used his executive power and uncontested congressional support to get his country back on track. He took swift and immediate action, moving so fast even Mercury[8] was impressed. And he delivered on the promise of his "First New Deal," a series of legislation and executive actions aimed at relief, recovery, and reform. The amazing catalog of what FDR accomplished in just 100 days is summarized in the table on the following page.

In a radio Fireside Chat on July 24, 1933, FDR publicly reflected on all his accomplishments during his early days in office. This would cement the idea that his first 100 days were extraordinarily successful and establish a very high bar for future presidents and other leaders—like you. FDR did not create and execute a 100-day plan because he didn't have the foresight at the time. He just took explosive action to pull his country out of a tailspin, then, upon reflection, handed great leaders to come with an invaluable insight. Given the chance to do it all over again, I am convinced he would have carefully constructed and then skillfully executed this 100-day

President Franklin D. Roosevelt's Accomplishments in His First 100 Days in Office

Legislation	Category	Impact	Date Passed
FDR takes office			March 4
Emergency Banking Relief Act[9]	Reform	Stabilized the banking system	March 9
Beer-Wine Revenue Act	Recovery	Ended Prohibition by legalizing the sale of beer and wine	March 22
Economy Act	Recovery	Cut government salaries to reduce the federal deficit	March 20
Civilian Conservation Corps	Relief	Created jobs for young men in conservation projects	March 31
Abandonment of the Gold Standard	Recovery	Allowed the government to expand the money supply and combat deflation	April 19
Federal Emergency Relief Administration	Relief	Provided $500 million in aid for unemployment relief	May 12
Agricultural Adjustment Act	Recovery	Raised crop prices by artificially suppressing production	May 12
Tennessee Valley Authority	Recovery	Built dams and hydroelectric plants in the impoverished Tennessee Valley region	May 18
Securities Act	Reform	Laid the groundwork for regulating the stock market	May 27
Home Owners' Loan Corporation	Relief	Assisted homeowners in refinancing mortgages to prevent foreclosures	June 13
National Industrial Recovery Act	Recovery	Established the National Recovery Administration to set industrial standards like minimum wage, reasonable work hours, and the abolishment of child labor	June 16
Glass-Steagall Act	Reform	Created the Federal Deposit Insurance Corporation (FDIC) to insure bank deposits	June 16
FDR marks his first 100 days in office			June 16

plan, broadcasting his intentions to all the Americans through his Fireside Chats. Fortunately for us, we have a long history of leaders to learn from, starting with the OG (Original Gentleman) himself, FDR.

Your first 100 days start when you "go live" and enter your Gauntlet (see Chapter 11), so you must have a solid plan ready. That is why we have a Planning and Readiness Stage ahead of the Implementation/Intervention Stage. But your plans are not just for you and your implementation team; they are for everyone. You should still be in your Gauntlet on Day 100, either wrapping up the Implementation/Intervention Stage or just starting your Warranty Stage, so let's review what should be accomplished by that point:

- Robust communication (including your Fireside Chats) with the workforce
- Multiple workforce engagements to make sure everyone is heard
- A shock campaign to move any remaining Luddites from denial into resistance
- Solutions ready to explore and implement during the Transition Stage
- Boosters for anticipated low performance and morale
- New homes for people who no longer fit in with the organization

With this in mind, make sure you have an *extremely* detailed plan ready to share with the organization that covers your first 100 days. It should clarify what *everyone* in the organization is expected to do, week by week, and month by month, until the first 100 days are completed. Segment your organization by management level and make sure you have a separate plan for each level of each major group, from the top level (that would be you) all the way down to the individual contributors. Then, as we discussed in Chapter 11, make it very clear that this plan is locked down—no changes. Subsequently, proceed to crush the execution. How will people feel about you and the transformation on Day 100? Do everything in your power to make sure that narrative is flattering, even for the future historians who tell your story decades later.

How Compelling Is Your Business Case?

As soon as you enter the Gauntlet, the most haunting question you and your team will face is: "Why are we doing this?" In fact, this one question is so significant and powerful that when we talk about managing emotions (e.g., with Emotional Journey Management), we are fundamentally attempting to mitigate the consequences attached to this seemingly innocent question. The question isn't innocent at all; it is fully loaded with emotional bullets that can easily pierce logic and strike your vital emotional organs.

A good executive coach will never ask you a *why* question (although a psychotherapist might). The objective of coaching is to assist the coachee with generating actionable insights. To do that effectively, the coachee must stay in a slightly positive mood. Negative emotions inhibit insight generation due to the physiological reactions that happen in your PFC (pre-frontal cortex), or your executive brain, when you start to experience negative emotions. That is why we tend to stay away from the word *why*. It is a trigger word that tends to route humans to a negative emotional space.

Unfortunately, we don't need to be prompted by someone else to enter a negative emotional tailspin triggered by *why*. We often do it to ourselves, especially during stressful situations—like the Gauntlet that starts your first 100 days. In fact, it's unavoidable. As soon as the real stress of the transformation sets in, despite all your good upfront work to communicate your case for change, people will instinctively start to spin: *why, exactly, are we doing this again?*

The answer should have been well documented long before Day 0 when you articulated the business case for your transformation. It should clearly lay out all the reasons why the transformation makes sense: the market demand is overwhelming, customer expectations have exceeded our current capabilities, hyper-growth is our only option, etc. Most of the time, it is very well structured, presenting a perfectly logical case. However, logic is not the issue during an emotionally taxing time. If your business case lacks emotional appeal, it will serve no good during the perilous journey through the Gauntlet. That's why you must create something better than a solid business case; you must create a *compelling* business case. It is the compelling aspects of your business case that will support your people through the first 100 days. If the compelling aspects of your business case are weak or nonexistent, then you won't make it to Day 100.

A compelling business case has two components: a pull toward the future and a push away from the present. Your people must believe, with all of their hearts, that there is a better future in front of them. Your Clarion Call (see Chapter 3) should help with this, but it needs to be tested with your people before you can call it compelling. If they find your future compelling, then you are halfway there. If not, then you have some work to do to find out what inspires them about a potential future state. The second half of your compelling business case is a push away from the status quo. If we do nothing, what will happen? Once again, your people must believe, with all of their hearts, that doing nothing is not an option. This is where most leaders fail. They don't build a strong enough emotional case for why change must happen now. If you are on a sinking ship, there's no question in your mind that the status quo is not working. However, if you are blissfully sailing on tranquil waters, why in the world would you want to be "saved."

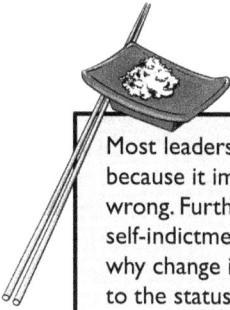

Wasabi Moment

Most leaders eschew speaking negatively about the status quo because it implies that the current organization is doing something wrong. Furthermore, it may be perceived as a damning self-indictment! Nonetheless, you must give people a reason why change is an exigent concern, or they will hold on tightly to the status quo

Compellingness is in the eye of the beholder, so your business case must be tested and validated before you know how compelling it is. Engage your people in the early stages of your transformation (i.e., when you are designing your Adamant Triad) to understand how compelling your business case is. You can do this with interviews, focus groups, surveys, or some combination thereof. And make sure it scores high on the compellingness scale *before* you enter your Gauntlet. If you are not ready with a strong, *compelling* business case to inundate your people with by the time you enter the Gauntlet, you won't make it to the other side.

When to Assemble and Diffuse Your A-Team

When we started down this journey in Chapter 1, it was really about you and understanding your Scaling Dilemma. Before long (Chapter 2), we brought in your SLT (Strategic Leadership Team) to help clarify and shape the opportunity. By the end of Chapter 3, you had your EMT (Executive Mental Team) assembled to help you manage the emotional side of the transformation. And before you wrapped up the first iteration of the Adamant Triad in Chapter 6, you gathered some feedback from trusted stakeholders on your MVP (Minimum Viable Product). You cannot implement a strategy, design an organization, or build organizational capability (e.g., for innovation) in a vacuum. You must engage the right people at the right time to help you lead and manage the transformation.

At some point before the Planning Stage begins, you must assemble your implementation team. These are the managers, experts, doers, approvers, and leaders (MEDAL) that will help you realize the organization's new strategy, design, and innovation capabilities. You can bring some of them on as early as opportunity framing, but they should all be on board for the Planning Stage. It is good to bring higher-level leaders on earlier in the process so they can influence the organization's strategy and design.

However, too many people will slow everything down. So be judicious on the timing of when to onboard whom.

The team that you select for your transformation must be your A-Team; the very best leaders, managers, experts, doers and critical thinkers (for reviews and approvals) in the firm. It is critically important that these people are *dedicated* to the transformation effort. To be effective, they must step away from their day jobs for a significant amount of time. This is a very difficult decision to make. Who is going to run your organization while your best people are busy with the transformation? Well, it must be your B-Team. That is your only option. Once your A-Team is identified, you must identify where they will *fully delegate all* their day-to-day responsibilities. It's a tough reality, but it's the only way I have seen it work.

Naturally, despite my admonitions and irrational outbursts, I have been in many situations where great people are *voluntold* to be on the transformation team—as long as they handle their existing job too. In the most egregious cases, they are told they are "dedicated" to the transformation team; however, no backup is assigned, and day-to-day responsibilities are never transferred. This is completely unfair and wildly ineffective. Nobody will turn down the opportunity to be on the transformation team, so they will accept. And they will kill themselves trying to do two demanding jobs at the same time. Unfortunately, they will not succeed at either. I've seen it a hundred times, it never works, and it usually puts the transformation in jeopardy. Most people are more committed to their day job than any "and-job," even one as important as the transformation. So, when push comes to shove, meetings are missed, deliverables are dropped, excuses fly, and everyone just lets it happen—it is what it is (I'm sure there's an Argyris-style undiscussable undiscussables thing going on here).

I have also been on teams with dedicated people and, simply put, it works. The organization doesn't run as well because your best people are working on something more important, but performance is usually acceptable. Sure, your B-Team is not your A-Team, but they're not benchwarmers! They're good—good enough to run the organization while the A-Team focuses on the transformation. Just let the B-Team hold the reins for a while and rest easy knowing that the transformation is in the hands of your best people.

Do not put your B-Team, or worse whoever happens to be available, on your transformation team. The stakes are too high, and the work is too difficult. Plus, you need your A-Team's buy-in and commitment to make it through the transformation, especially the Gauntlet. Who is going to capture their hearts and minds, your B-Team? Probably not.

Most of your A-Team, especially leaders and key influencers, should move back into the run organization (potentially with a new role) once the new organization goes live and you enter the Gauntlet. They will play a key role in your Sponsorship Plan to help lead the organization through the difficult change. They will also play a key part in helping fellow tribe members deal with the Transformation Blues. Their intimate knowledge of the new strategy and design will give them an added boost of expert power to go along with the influential power they already wield. Your B-Team at this point are key advisors to the A-Team, as they are now more intimate with the day-to-day operations of the firm and probably understand some nuances of the culture that are hidden from the transformation team.

Key elements of your management team and your entire change team should stay on the transformation team until well into the Transition Phase to ensure the organization stabilizes properly. It's best to release everyone left during the celebration that marks the end of the Transition Phase; however, it's wise to retain some of these resources in your Strategy function, just to make sure someone is keeping an eye on the organization's stability.

Putting It into Practice

FDR set a high bar of accomplishments for a leader's first 100 days in office. Whether you like it or not, you will be graded on your leadership ability about 100 days after you go live with your new strategy and organizational design. Given that, you might as well stack the odds in your favor. Here's how to make your first 100 days legendary:

1 Toward the end of the Planning Stage, gather all the information that you know about the first 100 days of your upcoming transformation and write a first draft of the Fireside Chat that you will deliver on Day 100

2 Review and dissect FDR's Fireside Chats[10] for style and format, if you haven't already. Notice the depth of explanation for every decision that was made (logos). Notice the constant push and pull from his compelling business case (pathos). Notice targeted reminders of how they (the American people) put their faith in him and his administration (ethos)

3 Revise your Day 100 Fireside Chat to boost its logos, pathos, and ethos. Use the techniques of Cinematic Visionography explored in Chapter 2 to crystalize your vision of Day 100

4 Write the first draft of the Fireside Chat that you will deliver on Day 0, using the same process

5 Using your Day 0 and Day 100 Fireside Chats as anchor points, work with your planning team to create a detailed, week-by-week action plan for you and your L2 (level 2, your direct reports) leaders that spans the period from Day 0 to Day 100 (15 weeks total)

6 Charge every one of your L2 leaders to create a similar 15-week plan
   for them and the L3 (level 3, your skip-level) leaders that report to
   them. It is best if they personalize their Day 100 and Day 0 visions to
   anchor their exercise, even if they won't be delivering a Fireside Chat[11]
7 Charge every one of your L3 leaders to create a 15-week plan for them
   and their entire organization, all the way down to their front-line leaders and individual contributors[12]
8 Have your transformation team consolidate all of the First 100-Day
   Plans and review them for feasibility, consistency, and alignment
9 Have your best critical thinkers review the plan to make sure everything is covered and *everyone* in the organization has a plan of action. Remember, you will not change this plan for any reason once it is
   locked down, so triple-check to make sure you have covered everything
   for everyone
10 Write the rest of your Fireside Chats. You will have either 8 or 16 total,
   depending on your cadence. You will eventually revise each one to reflect the current state of affairs when they are each delivered; however,
   write them all now based on what you know, to push the right emanations into the universe for go-live

When it comes to legendary first-100-day execution, planning excellence
is the key. China's Broad Sustainable Building (BSB), a subsidiary of the
BROAD Group, constructed a 57-story skyscraper in just 19 days using
modular construction techniques and superior planning (Peng & Tang,
2015). What will be the lore of your new organization's first 100 days? It's
fine to embrace superstition, but don't leave this one to chance.

Executive Debrief

- Many great leaders in our past behaved in superstitious ways
- Embrace superstition because it pairs well with risk
- The rational leader's balderdash (nonsense) is the astute leader's edge
- Sometimes nonsense seems nonsensical because we aren't technologi-
  cally advanced enough yet to have an explanation; there are many phe-
  nomena that we cannot scientifically explain today
- If you confine yourself to the rational, scientific world, then you will be
  limited to suboptimal outcomes called *local maxima*
- To find the most optimal outcomes, or *global maxima*, you must occa-
  sionally abandon rational thought
- Applied superstition is not hard, but you must first accept and embrace
  preternaturalness
- Trust in your superstitions, especially when there is little to no downside

- President FDR set a high bar on how much leaders should accomplish during their first 100 days
- Your first 100 days start when you go live with the new strategy and organizational design, essentially when you enter the Gauntlet
- You must have a compelling business case to survive the Gauntlet
- A business case is not compelling unless it moves the hearts and minds of the people impacted by the change
- A compelling business case has two components: a pull toward the future and a push away from the present
- Your transformation team must be comprised of your A-Team, the very best people in your organization
- Your A-Team must be dedicated to the transformation effort; let your B-Team run the company while they focus on the transformation
- Key leaders and influencers on your A-Team should return to their leadership roles when you go live with the new organization
- Key managers and your entire change team should remain on your transformation team until the Transition Phase completes
- Create a comprehensive and detailed action plan for your first 100 days that clarifies what everyone in the organization should expect and do. This will be a significant part of your legacy, so take every measure to make sure it is done with excellence

Notes

1 The number 4 is very bad luck in many East Asian cultures due to its phonetic similarity to the word "death." This is especially prevalent in China, Japan, Korea, and Taiwan. In the same way you won't find a 13th floor in the West, you won't find a 4th floor in the East.
2 On the day that I wrote this, my dad and I hit a Pick 5 at Gulfstream Park. True story.
3 Using very scientific studies, Semmelweis was able to reduce maternal mortality rates from about 18% to less than 2%.
4 I hold my breath for 30 seconds and hope for the best.
5 In Lean/Six Sigma, only Black Belts deal with Gradient Ascent, which is used during DOE (Design of Experiments). It is an advanced technique that is usually reserved for the higher-skilled practitioners.
6 In 2025, the poverty line in the United States for a household of two is $20,440. Imagine if 60% of Americans today were trying to make it on that much money or less.
7 FDR won 42 out of 48 states, securing 472 electoral votes out of 531.
8 In addition to his reputation for cunning and mischief, the winged messenger of the gods was also known for his incredible speed and agility.
9 The Emergency Banking Relief Act was passed just *five days* after FDR took office.
10 The University of Santa Barbara's American Presidency Project has a nice archive of FDR's Fireside Chats. See Wooley & Peters (n.d.).

11 They may, however, plan to address their organization after your Fireside Chats. This vision work will come in handy for those engagements.
12 By this time, you should have all your L3 leaders on your transformation team, or at least the key ones. If you have L4 leaders on your transformation team, feel free to cascade this exercise down one more level, charging them with creating a detailed plan for their front-line leaders and individual contributors.

Bibliography

Maranzani, B. (2024, September 13). *What's so unlucky about the number 13?* History. https://www.history.com/news/whats-so-unlucky-about-the-number-13

Peng, P., & Tang, D. (2015, April 30). Chinese builder puts up 57-story skyscraper in 19 days. *Associated Press News*. Retrieved from https://apnews.com/general-news-finance-business-finance-business-82ebe4bf0a8b4c079c7a3e8932b6936f

Woolley, J., & Peters, G. (n.d.). *Fireside chats (F. Roosevelt)*. The American Presidency Project. Retrieved from https://www.presidency.ucsb.edu/documents/presidential-documents-archive-guidebook/fireside-chats-f-roosevelt

Epilogue

Bon Voyage!

A proud and grateful leader quietly reflects on the incredible story of her organization over the last few years. It has been a full year since the organization celebrated the end of the transformation and its full transition to stability. That was quite a party! Tomorrow, she celebrates the one-year anniversary of this historic event with the amazing precocious organization that continues to sustain its unassailable competitive advantage. At this level of maturity, should they still be considered precocious? Does it matter? Probably not. What matters is that they are special, they know it, and she knows it.

Your organization has transformed, and as a result, so have you. You have shaped your building, and now it shapes you. Your organization underwent a forced and unwelcome growth spurt, but that's all folklore now. There are a lot of things you can laugh about now that weren't so funny when the Gauntlet was trying to rip your organization apart. Your firm is stable again, but operating decisively better than it was a few years ago. The transformation has brought it into a new realm of performance and taught you lessons you will never forget. And you are a different leader, a better leader, more Solomonic and mercurial (in a good way).

Tomorrow's celebration will be spectacular, second only to the one you threw one year ago. Your tribe will engage in another day of serious fun as you share stories of the birth of the Adamant Triad, the perils of the Gauntlet, and the rise to new and uncharted levels of growth and performance. You will reminisce about all the victories along the way—small, medium, large, and fantastic. You will brag about the greatest innovations and laugh at all the "brilliant ideas" that didn't turn out to be so brilliant. You will reinforce your kapu, spread your aloha, and build your mana with ritual and ceremony. You will express your gratitude for the precious gift of being in this place, at this time, with these people. The great journey has left an indelible impression on the organization's fabric. We will never forget.

DOI: 10.4324/9781003518181-20

Mahalo nui loa (thank you very much) for embarking on this journey with me, and I hope you found it informative, insightful, and entertaining. Although this is the end of our time in this book, your story has just begun. Your organization is destined for greatness, and your journey to become a great leader has no endpoint. Many of the concepts and techniques you have learned in this book are foundational. Use them to your advantage as you face the complex world in front of you. Probe, sense, respond. Attempt, accelerate, arrive. Must, should, might, could. Post, lever, and balance. Use these and other insights from this book as building blocks to become an even greater leader.

Strategize like a military general, design your organization like an architect, and channel your inner Thomas Edison when you are in the innovation factory. This is the almighty Adamant Triad, a fusion smithed with the hardest metal in the universe. Brandish this secret weapon to annihilate anyone who dares to come close to your competitive position.

Lead at superhuman levels like a CybOrg and inspire others to be superhuman. Build a Prophet Center, the likes of which the world has never seen. Nurture it, learn from it, and constantly seek its advice, but respect its known limitations. Pay attention to your people, as they are the lifeblood of your organization. Treat them like they are special, because they are. Shower them with luxury and privilege. Make it unbearable to leave the tribe.

Meet life head-on, especially during the challenging times that force you to transform internally. This is when you grow the most. Learn to handle the uncomfortable space between letting go of the past and grabbing on to the future. Sometimes life forces us to let go of something we really don't want to let go of. It's okay. You'll be alright.

Be grateful, humble, and wise. Know your limits, but never let them limit your potential. Continually improve. If you don't grow, you die. And whatever you do, don't touch any $50 bills—they're bad luck.

Bon voyage, my friend. I wish you well, and I hope to see you someday in the show.

Index

Note: **Bold** page numbers refer to tables; *italic* page numbers refer to figures and page numbers followed by "n" denote endnotes.

Adamant Triad 59, 74, 133–134, 157, 180, 205; Go-forward Design for 135–136; innovation 44, 95–96; minimum viable product (MVP) for 96, 98; OD *see* organizational design (OD); respectable effective product (REP) 101; strategy 51, 53–54
AdSense 91
allocentric organization 82, 85, 92–93, 96, 120, 121, 125–126, 137, 187
allocentric perspective 81, 83, 95, 96, 110
Alphabet (Google) 7, **8**, 21, 81
Amazon **8**
ambidextrous organization 71–72
Angelou, Maya 39
Anticipatory Anxiety 106
Apple 7, **8**, 22, 81, 89–90
architectural determinism 180
Aristotle 35; Rhetorical Triangle 35
artificial intelligence (AI) 194
Attempt, Accelerate, Arrive (AAA) Methodology 60, *61*, 144, 158
Attempt iteration 66

Balanced Scorecard 57
Base of Exploration 38
behavior management, full life cycle of 158, 166, 175; intervention stages *142*, 143, **167**, 170, 172, 178n3; planning stage 141, *142*, **167**, 172, 178n3; stability stage 142, *142*, **167**, 172; transition stage 142, *142*, **167**, 170, 172; warranty stage *142*, 142–143, **167**, 170, 172
behavior recidivism 141
Behavior Sustainability Plan 140–143
Berkshire Hathaway 8
Best-Fit Persona Template *113*
Bilbao Guggenheim, the Louis Vuitton Foundation, Paris 73
Bonaparte, Napoleon 192
Brin, Sergey 82
Broad Sustainable Building (BSB), China's 202
Brunelleschi, Filippo 77, 89
Burns, Robert 165
Business Process Leadership 97

Cadence 171
Change Curve *see* Emotional Journey
ChatGPT 111, 112, 193
Churchill, Winston 11, 179, 180, 191
cinematic visionography 19
clarifying or framing 32–33
Clarion Call 198
Clynes, M. E. 111
command-and-control model 77
commitment bias 166
compellingness 199
competitive positioning 66
continual improvement 185–186, *186*
continuous improvement 185–186, *186*
Corporate Strategy 43
Costco 82

COVID-19 22, 23
critical to quality (CTQ) metrics 187
cross-functional teams 81–82
Cybernetic Organization (CybOrg)
    69n11, 111, 206
Cybernetics 111
Cyborg Leader 122–125, 124, 130n7
CybOrg Mentoring Program 128–129
Cynefin Framework 29, 30, 30,
    56, 140

Damon, Matt 108
data-driven decision-making 82, 84
Decision-Driven Management (DDM)
    62, 63
Delta Force 93, 97
Deming, W. E.: PDCA (Plan, Do,
    Check, Act) cycle 187
Design Harmony, Alignment, and
    Reinforcement Modeling Approach
    (DHARMA) 73–74, 74, 79, 81,
    83–84, 86n8, 89, 101, 137
Digital Transformation 2
D-OCMIE Method 156, 156–160
Dome of Florence Cathedral 77

Edison, Thomas A. 88, 89, 206; "Black
    Maria" in West Orange, New Jersey
    88; "Boxing Cats" 88–89
egocentric design 72
egocentric organization 187
Eisenhower, Dwight D. 58
emanations 194
Emotional Journey 36–37, 37, 155,
    158, 168; Base of Exploration 40,
    41; Bridge of Denial 40, 40, 168;
    Gulf of Resistance 39, 40, 41,
    168–169; management of 40, 40,
    166; Pre-Denial stage 40, 40–41;
    Summit of Commitment 40
emotions 35–36; through
    transformational change 39–40
Employee Assistance Program (EAP)
    172
employees encouragement 91
engagements 173
Error Modes and Effects Analysis
    (EMEA) 146n3
Executive Mental Team (EMT) 155,
    172, 199; commitment to culture

46, 46–47, 47; Executive Coach 45,
    49n4; Licensed Psychotherapist 46;
    Trusted Advisor 45–46, 49n4
extravehicular mobility unit (EMU)
    123

Facebook 89–90
Failure Modes and Effects Analysis
    (FMEA) 146n3
Feedback Mechanism 57
folkways 188
Forest of Good Intentions 165

Gauntlet 1, 168–171, 169
Gehry, Frank 73
Generalized Anxiety Disorder (GAD)
    106
General Services Administration (GSA)
    65, 69n12
generative artificial intelligence
    (GenAI) 111, 123, 125
German National People's Party
    (DNVP) 36
Global Maximum 193, 193
Gmail 91
1849 Gold Rush 8
Google 89–90
Google Analytics 82
Google Hangouts 91
Googleplex 90, 100n3
Google X 91
go-to-market strategy 68n5
governance 136–138, 184
Gradient Ascent 194
Great Depression 195
Great Resignation Period 23, 105; quit
    rates over 13, 20
Guiding Light 56–57
Gulf of Resistance 38

Heffernan, M. 119
Heifetz, R. A. 136
high-performance leadership teams
    136–138
Hitler, Adolf 35, 36, 192
House of Commons 179–180
human-centered strategy 102
Human Resources (HR) 43
hybrid work environment 110
The Hyper-Growth Imperative 14

hyper-growth opportunity 18–19;
    precocious organizations 20;
    transformational 20

innovation 44; precocious
    organizations 44; value-based
    investments in 95–96
Innovation Center of Excellence 95,
    97, 110
Innovation Factory 91–93, 92, 94, 101
innovation space 93
Intel Corporation 28
Iteration Zero 3–4, 65

Jobs, Steve 90
Johnson & Johnson 8

Khan, Genghis 78
Kline, N. S. 111
Kotter, J. P. 149, 151, 152, 154, 155, 160
Krzyzewski, M. 107
Kübler-Ross, E. 37; model 49n2

leadership approach 32
Lean Sigma Black Belt 186, 194
local maxima 193
logic and emotions 45
Lovable Optimal Product (LOP) 64,
    65, 67, 157

management philosophy 79
Market Needs company 56
measures of success 32
MEDAL™ Model 41–42, 42, 199–201
Meta (Facebook) 7, 8, 8, 22
metamorphosis 149–151, 151
Microsoft 8, 31
Minimum Viable Product (MVP)
    strategy 51, 57, 59, 64, 65, 96, 118,
    126, 133, 199
Moore, G. A. 123; Technology
    Adoption Life Cycle 123
MSmc language 57, 63
Muir, William 119

Nvidia 8, 81, 89–90

Obsessive Restructuring Disorder
    (ORD) 70, 80, 112
One Winning Metric (OWM) 67

Operations 163–164
opportunities 32
organizational change management
    (OCM) 37, 133, 151–152; best
    practices for transitional change
    152–154
organizational change, types of 29;
    transactional changes 29, 29, 141,
    155; transformational changes 22,
    29–31, 29, 39–40, 44, 141, 148–
    151, 155; transitional changes 29,
    29, 141, 151, 155
organizational climate survey 121
Organizational Design and
    Development (OD&D) 71
organizational design (OD) 12,
    70–71, 89, 174, 186; contribution
    element of 76; culture element of
    75–76; culture-led 103; defense
    element of 75; image element of 75;
    information element of 75; power
    element of 76
Organizational GPT 57
Organizational Readiness Assessment
    167
organizational strategy 58

Page, Larry 82
Pareto Principle (80/20 rule) 62, 144
Patton, George S. 58
Pearl Harbor, Attack on 6
Planning 43
Poke-yoke 136
Positive Psychology 49n5
Post, Lever, and Balance (PLB) Method
    79, 80, 171
Potter, Jessie 181
precocious organizations 20; definition
    118; innovation 44; the "yips"
    121–122
precocious team 9–11
pre-frontal cortex (PFC) 45, 54, 158,
    198
probe–sense–respond approach 63
Products Offered company 56
Propelling Force 68n4
Prophet Center (Knowledge Base) 67,
    109, 112, 128, 184, 185, 206; see
    also Strategic Management System
psychological safety 23

Quick Reference Guide 183
Quiet Quitting 23, 25, 105

Rapid Application Development
    (RAD) 69n8
Remote Worker Diversity, Equity, and
    Inclusion (RW-DEI) 110
Renaissance Florence 77–78
Respectable Effective Product (REP)
    64, 101, 126, 133, 157
reverse mentoring 129
risk 140
Rock, D. 126
Roosevelt, Franklin D. (FDR) 191,
    195–197, **196**, 201
Roosevelt, Theodore 191

Santayana, George 181
SARS-CoV-2 *see* COVID-19
Saudi Aramco 8
Scaling Dilemma Statement 13–16,
    17n2, 199
SCARF® model 126
Schlesinger & Mayer Building 73
Semmelweis, Ignaz 192, 193
short-sighted myopic ignorance (SSMI)
    181, 182, 184
Silicon Graphics Inc. (SGI) 9, 18, 21,
    91
Silicon Valley 7–8, 14, 81–84, 89–90
Six Sigma 12, 136
Skunkworks Projects 82
Social Democratic Party of Germany
    (SDP) 36
Social Styles 4n1
Software Development Life Cycle
    (SDLC) methodologies 60, 163
stakeholders 32, 162n5
Stalin, Joseph 192
Steinbeck, John 165
strategic decision-making 62
strategic framework 54–55, 55

Strategic Guidance System 139–140
Strategic Leadership Team (SLT) 67,
    98, 158, 199
Strategic Management System 58, 188
strategic philosophy 27
strategic realignment 32
Strategic Technology Team (STT) 67
Strategy 51, 53–54; *see also* Adamant
    Triad
Streep, Meryl 168
Summit of Commitment 38, 44
sunk cost fallacy *see* commitment bias
Sun Microsystems 13–14
supply chain integration 82

Technology 56–57
Tesla **8**, 81
Thomas, George 179
top management, responsibilities of
    41–44
Total Quality Management (TQM)
    186
transformational change 154, 155;
    complexity of 147–149; insights
    from nature on **151**
transitional change 154, 155
Tregoe, B. B. 53

Uncertainty Matrix 6, 6

value drivers 71, 74, 84
vertical integration 83
vision of success 32

Walt Disney 73, 82
Weber, Max 12
Weiss, A. 53, 143
Welch, Jack 82

the "yips" 121–122, 126, 129, 130

Zero Iteration *see* Iteration Zero

For Product Safety Concerns and Information please contact our EU
representative GPSR@taylorandfrancis.com
Taylor & Francis Verlag GmbH, Kaufingerstraße 24, 80331 München, Germany